SACRED
INTENTIONS

*Daily Inspiration to Strengthen
the Spirit, Based on
Jewish Wisdom*

Rabbi Kerry M. Olitzky
&
Rabbi Lori Forman

JEWISH LIGHTS PUBLISHING

WOODSTOCK, VERMONT

Sacred Intentions:
Daily Inspiration to Strengthen the Spirit, Based on Jewish Wisdom

2008 Sixth Printing

For information regarding permission to reprint material from this book, please mail or fax your request in writing to Jewish Lights Publishing, Permissions Department, at the address / fax number listed below, or e-mail your request to permissions@jewishlights.com.

Library of Congress Cataloging-in-Publication Data
Sacred intentions : daily inspiration to strengthen the spirit, based on Jewish wisdom / [edited by] Kerry Olitzky and Lori Forman.
p.   cm.
Includes bibliographical references and index.
ISBN-13: 978-1-58023-061-2 (quality pbk.)
ISBN-10: 1-58023-061-X (quality pbk.)
1. Jewish devotional calendars. 2. Jewish meditations.
3. Spiritual life—Judaism. I. Olitzky, Kerry M. II. Forman, Lori.
BM724.S23   1999
296.7'2—dc21

99–36862
CIP

First Edition
10 9 8 7 6
Manufactured in the United States
Interior art: Cynthia Hackett
Cover design: Stacey Hood

Published by Jewish Lights Publishing
A Division of LongHill Partners, Inc.
Sunset Farm Offices, Route 4, P.O. Box 237
Woodstock, Vermont 05091
Tel: (802) 457-4000   Fax: (802) 457-4004
www.jewishlights.com

Featuring contributions to rekindle the spirit written by:

Judith Z. Abrams
Bradley Shavit Artson
Tsvi Blanchard
Lester Bronstein
Nina Beth Cardin
Michael M. Cohen
William Cutter
Amy Eilberg
Dov Peretz Elkins
Edward Feinstein
Mordecai Finley
Nancy Flam
Elyse Frishman
David Gelfand
Neil Gillman
James Stone Goodman
Leonard Gordon
Irving (Yitz) Greenberg
Joel Lurie Grishaver
Lawrence A. Hoffman
Abie Ingber
Elana Kanter

Irwin Kula
Lawrence Kushner
Lori Lefkovitz
Adina Lewittes
Arthur J. Magida
Vivian Mayer
Michael Paley
James Ponet
Bernard S. Raskas
Rachel T. Sabath
Jeffrey K. Salkin
Sandy Eisenberg Sasso
Amy Scheinerman
Harold Schulweis
Rami M. Shapiro
Mychal B. Springer
Ira Stone
Joseph Telushkin
Harlan J. Wechsler
Sharon L. Wechter
David Wolpe

For all those who support the work of
UJA-Federation of New York
with their time, spirit, and donations,
and for all the readers of *Sacred Intentions*.
LF

For Abigail and Leslie Wexner,
whose untiring vision for Jewish leadership
is an inspiration to all.
KO

For Susanna Zevi,
who inspired this book.

CONTENTS

ACKNOWLEDGMENTS

From its inception, this book immediately became a partnership between two rabbis who constantly seek to bring the inspiration of God's word into the daily lives of people with whom we work, as well as of those we have yet to meet. We have learned together and grown together.

I want to thank my colleagues at the Wexner Heritage Foundation who have welcomed me into their midst. From the day we started working together, I felt immediately at home. In particular, I acknowledge Rabbi Nathan Laufer, Rabbi Shoshana Gelfand, Lori Baron, and Howard Zack. I also thank my administrative assistant, Carolyn Levy Schrier, who quickly adjusted to the idiosyncratic nature—and pace—of my work and work style. The inspiring vision of Abigail and Leslie Wexner is apparent in everything that we do together in the community that we have formed and continue to build.

Even this book full of words is inadequate to thank my life's partner, Sheryl. Our souls met first in Paradise and have remained bound together ever since. I feel privileged for every day spent living in the Garden with her. To our boys, Avi and Jesse: The echoes of their voices resound in each word that I write. Torah takes on a greater dimension for me as I watch it take on new meaning in its reflection in their lives. Amid the daily challenges we face, we continue to grow as a family under the nurturing guidance of the Holy One of Blessing.

KO

I want to thank everyone at UJA-Federation of New York for their incredible support of the Jewish Thought of the Day program. Two years ago I began writing short thoughts for the staff, which they could find each morning when they opened their computers. The response was so positive that we began to distribute them to interested donors. It is truly rewarding to hear how these thoughts are forwarded to friends and family members around the country. That they have even touched one person's life is humbling. That they have touched the lives of many is incredible. A special thanks to Stephanie McFadden, my secretary, who contributed in many ways to the production of this book. Above all, I want to thank my husband, Simcha Jacobi, who enriches everything I do; and my parents, Phil and Elaine Forman, whose support has been with me throughout my life.   LF

Together we thank the entire Jewish Lights family, who constantly teach by example how Jewish publishing can extend our "work" in the world. In particular, our gratitude is expressed to our publishers, Stuart and Antoinette Matlins, who brought us together and constantly challenged us to stretch ourselves in order to reach out to those who hear the voice of God even when it seems to be hard to reach. We acknowledge with abiding thanks the careful eye of our editor, Arthur Magida, who probed each word, helping to make sure it clearly communicated exactly what we wanted to say. We appreciate the attention of Jennifer Goneau to every detail of the project as it moved from paper to production. And we want to thank Dr. Philip Miller, Director of the Klau

Library at Hebrew Union College–Jewish Institute of Religion in New York, and Annette Muffs Botnick, Rabbinical Assembly Research Librarian, for helping to track down elusive details concerning teachers and their texts.

Rabbi Kerry (Shia) Olitzky & Rabbi Lori Forman
New York City

HOW TO USE THIS BOOK

This book might be seen as a calendar companion. Just as you keep your calendar in your briefcase, in your purse, or on your desk, we invite you to keep this book handy. Consult it frequently throughout the day. Look at it in the morning. Check it over in the middle of the day. Begin your day or end it by reviewing the selection for that day. It will provide you with insight and inspiration as well as a prism through which you might review the day's events to gain understanding and perspective from them.

Just as we have learned that flexibility is an important value in life, so is the use of this calendar intended to be flexible. Choose a theme or idea that fits your mood as you flip through the pages. Or read it one day at a time, starting with today, regardless of the calendar date that has been assigned to it.

This volume follows the Gregorian calendar that most of us regularly use without much thought about its origin or rhythm. While we are conscious of measuring time with different calendars (tax years, fiscal years, academic years), it is that calendar that has become second nature to us living in the Western World.

INTRODUCTION

Most of us live our lives according to a schedule. There is a certain rhythm to our routine. To maintain this rhythm, we usually keep a daily planner or calendar on which we diligently mark appointments, meetings, and special days. Our lives also have a spiritual dimension, one that has no calendar or date book to guide it. However, what happens in the world around us does color our perspective. Holidays, seasons, and special times make their mark on the spiritual landscape of our lives. Rabbi Larry Hoffman sees it this way: "If your kitchen is like mine, you have two calendars: One for American dates, one for Jewish events. The two have very little in common. Fridays and Saturdays are usually empty on the first one, while on the second they are cluttered with times for candle lighting and titles of Torah portions. Similarly, one reads, 'October 13—National League Championship Game'; the other says, 'Tishrei 10—Yom Kippur.' American Jews learn to juggle the two, as if we inhabited a science fiction time warp spanning two alternative, overlapping and often contradictory zones."

While most of us think we would like to live a life of peak experiences, and some of us are even in constant search for them, most of us recognize that the majority of life is lived in the ordinary. And some days it is hard to face the challenges of the ordinary. Relationships are trying. Our marriages are difficult to maintain. Our children are hard to raise. Our parents make demands on us. Our jobs are stressful. Yet each morning we arise to face the day anew. This book is to help you face that day, to help you gain a perspective on life that is gently inspired and informed by the teachings of Jewish tradition. The challenge of our lives is to raise the ordinary to the extraordinary. In religious language, we sometimes say it is about making the sacred out of the profane.

This book is anchored in the calendar because the calendar is familiar. We direct our attention to calendars throughout the day. We keep them in our briefcases and purses. They sit on our desks. We hang them on walls. We may have hand-held electronic versions, as well as those installed in computers. We use them to plan our weeks and weekends. Calendars come in a variety of sizes and shapes, but they share one thing in common: They help us impose order on the perceived chaos of the world and of our lives.

Most calendars have blank spaces in which we can write. This calendar is already full, so you can't add any appointments to it. That is intentional. We want you to slow down rather than make your life more complicated.

This book has one simple goal: To lift the spirit.

JANUARY

An Attitude of Gratitude

1 JANUARY

*Praised are You, O God, Sovereign of the Universe,
who has sustained us, kept us alive, and helped
us to reach this day.*
LITURGY[1]

Although most Jewish people usher in the religious New Year at Rosh Hashanah in the synagogue—usually sometime in September or early October—January 1 in the secular calendar is also worthy of being called the beginning of a new year. This new year surrounds us: new calendars; new car models; new clothing styles. And living in North America, we really have no choice but to enjoy this new year, since everyone else designates it as such. So we too live our lives in its rhythm as well. Living in both cultures, as we do, is similar to "dancing at two weddings," as my grandfather used to say. As the new year surrounds us, we are swept up in the enthusiasm for resolutions to change. Some of us may celebrate the evening that precedes January 1 differently than do some of our neighbors, but it is nevertheless the beginning of a new year for us also, one in which we are committed to change, growth, and renewal.

But what is it about such blatant newness that is worth celebrating? To begin with, we have made it to this point in our lives. For many of us, doing so has been no simple task. Some of us may want to forget about the number of birthdays that have accumulated, but others just want to acknowledge that they are alive and to thank God for their life. This new year calls for a prayer of affirmation, or what our tradition refers to as a *Shehecheyanu*. With it, we thank God with all the strength that we can muster for sustaining us, keeping us alive, and helping us to reach this day. Think about it. Look at what it took to get us here. Many people supported us along the way—and continue to do so. We are grateful for their presence in our lives. With this day off from work, maybe we should take the time to thank a few of them. Then we can make their day as special for them as they have made the year for us.   KO

The Path Close By

2 JANUARY

Surely this teaching which I give you this day is not too baffling for you, nor is it beyond your reach. It is not in the heavens, that you should say, "Who among us can go up to the heavens and get it for us, that we may observe it?" Neither is it beyond the sea that you should say, "Who among us can cross the other side of this and get it for us and impart it to us, that we may observe it?" No, the thing is very close to you, in your mouth and in your heart to observe it.

DEUTERONOMY 30:11–14

Often we feel that spiritual growth is just too much for us to tackle. We may feel that we are unschooled or lack the necessary skills and vocabulary. All too often, unfamiliarity with Hebrew can distance us from Jewish traditional texts. Or perhaps our obstacle is a lack of time or focus. We all balance multiple responsibilities and interests, and adding spiritual growth to our daily routine just seems too daunting. Despite our interest in expanding our spiritual vocabulary and practice, doing so may seem like climbing a tortuous mountain path. So we put it aside.

Moses himself spelled out these words to the people of Israel as they were ending their forty-year journey in the desert and were about to cross over to the land of Canaan. He would not be able to join them as they were about to become a settled people. It was time for a new generation to assume the mantle of leadership. Although Moses' task as a leader is completed, he still has a final message to impart to the people. In it, he reminds them that their spiritual journey is not to end as they are entering a new stage. They will have new challenges and a new leader. He prods them to remember that God's teachings are forever close at hand though these may at times seem distant.

We too need to hear Moses' words today. We can easily deceive ourselves and think the spiritual path is distant when it is, in fact, as near to us as our mouths and hearts. Our spiritual journey can begin each and every day as we pay attention to the way we speak with others and the feelings that arise in our hearts. LF

Out from Hiding

3 JANUARY

And God said to Adam, "Ayekah? Where are you?"
GENESIS 3:9

Our tradition talks a great deal about the fact that human beings are hiders and concealers. We're always looking for getaways, whether through work or through leisure, in health or in sickness. There are appointments to be kept, and there are patients or clients or customers, and there are investments. There's jogging and there's dieting and there's bleaching and dying. There are mountains and seashores and cathedrals and museums to escape to. And there are committees to serve on. All these are ways for us to hide from the very first question posed in the Bible: *Ayekah?* Where are you?

We hide so cleverly that when we hear that question, we think it is a bank teller or sales clerk who is asking. So we produce our wallet and our Social Security number or our credit card to show who we are. We confuse identity with identification.

The ultimate question—the question of identity, of where and who we are—gets drowned in small talk, or in doubts, or in quarrels, or in drink, or in infidelity. Most commonly, people hide behind a complaint: "I am bored." People tell me that they are bored and I ask them how that can be since they have everything to live for. Nevertheless, they tell me, they are bored. What is it you want, I ask. And they tell me they do not know what they want: All they know is that they are bored.

Once in a while, in a crisis situation, when one has to face the gray walls of a hospital or a mortuary or a divorce court, the boredom ends, the strategies of evasion crumble, and the question comes out in the form of a scream: Where is the life I have lost while living?   RABBI HAROLD SCHULWEIS[2]

Shaping the Future

4 JANUARY

If you nurture resentments of the past,
you will destroy the future.
RABBI SHELDON ZIMMERMAN

The future has no shape or form. That is what is so intoxicating about it. The future is simply an unformed mass of experience brimming with potential. Worlds can be created in it. According to the book of Genesis, the world prior to creation was an unformed mass until God breathed order into it. Thus, each day—and particularly each new year—resembles the world at the point of creation, just before God breathed life into it. By calling on the Godlike qualities that reside in each of us, we have a similar opportunity to determine the future. Every decision we make, every action we take, contributes to the shaping of the landscape of the future. If we carry over resentments from the past year into the present one, then it cannot truly be a new year. Instead it will be the previous year relived, merely outfitted with new dates. The calendar may have changed, but we have not.

The past is the accumulation of isolated events, recorded and then understood through current experience and directed toward the future. This new year gives us the opportunity to shape the future through simple daily, routine acts that we elevate and make holy. The window of opportunity may be limited, so take advantage of it now. The potential to make sacred from profane rests in our hands.   KO

Act Now

5 JANUARY

*Act while you can: While you have the chance,
the means, and the strength.*

TALMUD[3]

This quote from the Talmud is the Jewish way of saying, "Don't put off until tomorrow what can be done today." Many of us are great at procrastinating. We put off the things that are difficult, time-consuming, or just plain boring. At some time in our lives—maybe too often, in fact—we all face tasks that have these qualities.

Yet even when we are not procrastinating, successful results do not occur every time we act. Simeon ben Elazar, in whose name the teaching above is passed on to us, suggests that prevailing action relies on proper timing, financial means, and inner strength. We are truly fortunate when all these factors line up. Yet in many situations, not all three elements may be in place. Perhaps the timing is to our advantage and we have the inner will yet we are lacking the financial resources. Do we stop? Or do we look for the financial means to make our dreams come true? What if the first two conditions are in place yet we lack the inner strength or conviction? What can we do to cultivate our inner resources to make them flow once again? Can we turn to prayer or meditation? Can we rely on a spiritual community to shore up our inner strength?

All in all, we are encouraged to evaluate the external and internal environments and then mindfully to take advantage of what is before us and act. For Judaism teaches that our actions do have power and effect.   LF

What Really Matters

6 JANUARY

Religion without science is blind;
science without religion is lame.
ALBERT EINSTEIN

A strong intellectual life matters deeply. Without reason, superstition prevails. Without a generation schooled in great literature and in humanities and math and science, our culture declines. Yet cultural literacy does not guarantee moral literacy. Some of the most culturally refined individuals a generation ago sent a people to death camps and crematoria. Intellectual excellence does not guarantee moral behavior. It is possible, as someone has said, "to get all A's and flunk life."

Sinai offers the character curriculum which ensures that we will not "flunk life" and makes us honorable and decent in a world of too much distrust and indecency. It is the covenant which teaches us to be thoughtful and compassionate even while others are indifferent and unkind.

Sometimes our institutions of higher learning fail us. And, sadly, at times our religious institutions fail us as well. But at their very best, our colleges and universities make us more literate men and women of discernment, seekers of truth. At their very best, our faith communities make us more human, men and women of character, seekers of meaning. We graduate from school; we are confirmed in meaning.

Rabbi Abraham Joshua Heschel, a great moral visionary of the twentieth century, taught that the world will not perish for "lack of information," but it might perish for "lack of appreciation." It is the joint task of the academy and our houses of worship to equip our young people with the tools necessary for nurturing the growth of mind and of spirit. So go out and give some young people you know the tools that they need for nourishing the growth of mind and spirit.

RABBI SANDY EISENBERG SASSO

Emerging Blessings

7 JANUARY

Blessings can come only from those things hidden from the eye.
TALMUD[4]

While some philosophers may deny the validity of what we experience in the physical world, we humans navigate the environment primarily with our five senses: hearing, feeling, touching, tasting, and smelling. Each new experience is added to those already stored in our memories. As we grow older, these experiences frame our perspective on the world. As they grow, so do we. And with each new encounter, we have the potential to change our perspective. But the important things in life, the things that really matter, those that can read just the way we frame the world, cannot be touched by the hand or seen by the eye. Nevertheless, what is most important is that we can gain blessing through them. Thus it is not in the context of things that are smelled or tasted that blessing emerges. Rather it is through the things that are felt in the heart or envisaged by the soul that blessing can come.

To encounter the world around you, your senses have to be constantly at the ready. This response is a natural one that requires little preparation on your part. But to feel love, your heart has to be open. And to be spiritually transformed, your spirit has to be open. As you go about your daily routine this day, open yourself up to the real world, the one that is hidden beneath the world of the senses.   KO

Real Strength

8 JANUARY

Who is the strongest of the strong? One who turns an enemy into the friend.
COMMENTARY ON THE MISHNAH[5]

How do we define strength in our day? Some might say strength is determined purely by our physical abilities and prowess. Others say strength is a quality of resoluteness that we carry within us. Still others suggest that strength is a spiritual quality which speaks to how we deal with life's uncertainties.

The text above clearly embraces the idea that strength is a spiritual quality. It goes a step further by stating that the specific act of turning an enemy into a friend is so difficult that one who succeeds is called "the strongest of the strong."

Most of us would be satisfied if we could just manage to keep our distance from our enemies. Who really wants to go out of their way to turn adversity into friendship? Doing this may mean putting aside deep hurts, betrayals, mistrust, and anger. It may require confronting how we create or sustain a contentious relationship. The desire to befriend an enemy takes an openness and a strength of spirit that is rare. While this may be a daunting challenge, it is well worth the effort.   LF

No Fear of Flying

9 January

*Adonai, open my lips that my mouth
may declare your glory.*
PSALM 51:17

One night a great rabbi, the Baal Shem Tov, the founder of Hasidism, returned home after a long day of helping others and lay down for a much needed rest. He fell deeply asleep and was suddenly awakened by an angel: "Baal Shem, wake up!" "What is it you want?" he asked. "Come with me." And suddenly they came upon a clearing and the Baal Shem saw a young man, about 16 years old, walking slowly on a narrow, dangerous path. The Baal Shem saw that to one side of the path was a raging sea of blood—a sea of hatred and violence, not unlike our world today or the wilderness Moses and the children of Israel crossed. And on the other side of the path was a deep abyss, the cold blackness of nothing; it was like our anxiety as we face the unknown future. The Baal Shem tried to call out to the young man, to warn him about where he walked, but the angel, or perhaps God, sealed the rabbi's lips so that he could not speak no matter how hard he tried.

Suddenly the scene was lit up by a blinding flash of lightning, and the eyes of the young man opened wide. He saw clearly for the first time the raging sea of blood on one side and the deep, unknown emptiness on the other, and his face twisted in horror. He began to totter back and forth and almost lost his balance, first almost falling into the sea and then into the emptiness. But then, using all the energy he could muster, the Baal Shem freed his lips and screamed out to the man, "Fly! You can fly!"

And God willing, you can! I know you can fly. Fly safely, with compassion in your hearts, righteous indignation in your words, and integrity and honesty in your actions. You *can* fly, my friends. And so, I pray, shall we all. O God, please let us fly!   RABBI DAVID GELFAND

Giving and Receiving

10 JANUARY

If you seize too much, you are left with nothing.
If you take less, you may retain it.
TALMUD[6]

This sounds like a script from a television game show. It is particularly sound advice during the month of January, which is known for clearance sales and deep discounts in stores. Everyone is preparing for the new inventory. But the source for the teaching above is not a newspaper supplement or magazine insert. Rather it is a piercing insight from a sacred text that is at the core of Jewish tradition. Here the Rabbis of the Talmud, known for their enigmatic guidance, offer us simple advice for daily living: If you try to grab too much, you won't be able to hold onto anything. We can hold only a certain amount in our hands. The more we juggle, the more something is bound to fall. However, if you are carefully selective in what you take, you may be capable of holding on to it.

The Rabbis believe that Torah, which is the wisdom of life, can be learned everywhere, even in the tasks of daily life. That is why the Talmud is full of stories of students following their teachers to the bathroom and the bedroom. A student of Torah is one who sees the potential for holiness in the mundane.

So don't take too much. Take just what you need. And save a little something for someone else. You'll be glad you did and so will your neighbor. KO

Be Righteous

11 JANUARY

As the fetus emerges into the world, it is made to take an oath. And what is that oath? "Be righteous."
TALMUD[7]

What an amazing statement! Of all the things that a new child could be made to promise when coming into this world, the Talmud relates that each child take the oath, "Be righteous." From our first breath, the sages seek to integrate into our very beings that our mission as Jews is to pursue justice and righteousness. How do we fulfill this oath? The paths are multiple. We can be mindful of our actions and how we treat others, from those closest to us to those we pass by and hardly acknowledge. We can seek involvement with local Jewish organizations and other communal organizations that seek to better our world. And we can make a conscious decision to give *tzedakah,* charity, regularly to organizations that pursue righteousness.

This oath, "Be righteous," is today a countercultural message. We don't find it on any bumper stickers. It is more likely that our contemporary culture would convey a message such as, "Be happy" or "You too can be a millionaire." One of Judaism's goals is to direct us outward toward the larger community and not solely toward fulfilling our own selfish needs. Today this worldview is out of favor. Yet the abiding wisdom of Judaism suggests that we balance our personal desires and the needs of the larger community and seek to walk the path of righteousness in all our actions—today and everyday.   LF

Healing

12 JANUARY

*Out of narrow straits I have called out to God,
God answered me with wide open spaces.*
PSALM 118:5

Our tradition believes in science. Unlike those faiths that either deny modern medicine or accept it suspiciously, Judaism sees the hand of God in every aspirin and x-ray. According to the Talmud, it is even forbidden to live in a town where no physicians reside. Proper doctors, moreover, should combine scientific know-how with humility before the divine web of scientific data they discover and interpret.

"The best of doctors," says the Talmud, "is fit for hell!" "The best" here means, as one interpretation advises, "doctors who think they are so good that they need no help from God" or even "doctors who are so high and mighty that they never even consult with each other." So find doctors who are medically superb but properly humble.

Do not be afraid to pray for healing. Many modern Jews are so thoroughly secularized that they cannot pray for themselves, let alone with and for patients whom they love, but they usually wish that they could. Do we really know all about the factors that go into healing? Or into just plain comforting, for that matter? How many times, while visiting the acutely ill, have you been unable to say anything except "How are you feeling today?"—as if you don't already know?

If the patient is willing to say a prayer with you, then try saying one. If you don't know one, make one up. If you can't say it out loud, hold the patient's hand and say it silently. You may cry, but with tears of love. And when the tears end, you will both feel better. You will return home knowing that for a brief moment you were a physician of the soul and in touch with the depths of human mystery.

Never give up hope, even as you necessarily prepare for the end. As Job well knew, it is not true that if we were only good enough, God would reward us with a cure. We therefore do not have the power, through either medicine or prayer, to bring healing everywhere and always.

The final lesson, then, if we see all efforts failing, is not to despair. Miracles do happen; they are cures that occur when physicians shrug their shoulders and words of prayer stick in their throats. So when all else fails, we are to do two things: We prepare ourselves and the patient for death, even while we hope for a miracle.

Medicine, prayer, and hope—these are Jewish mandates. I have pondered those certainties many times sitting in the hospital, watching generations come and go. But the cycle of birth, sickness, recovery—and yes, eventually death—does not change. Medicine, prayer, and hope are the Jewish way through illness.   RABBI LAWRENCE HOFFMAN

True Love

13 JANUARY

Love your neighbor as yourself.
LEVITICUS 19:18

The quote above seems like a rather straightforward statement from the book of Leviticus, whose core is called "holiness code," according to Jewish tradition. The observance of its long list of ordinances has the potential to elevate individual members of the Jewish community, as well as the community itself. But the move from thought to action, from word to deed, is not so easy. It takes more than a directive from the text, even if that text is in the Torah. Rabbi Hillel once said that this precept is the greatest principle in the entire Torah; the rest was merely commentary.

How indeed do we love our neighbors, especially when we don't even like or know some of the them? Some people say that to love our neighbors, we first have to love ourselves. That is probably true. And that means that the first step in the lifelong process of changing the world occurs only by changing ourselves. So why not begin today? KO

Riding the Waves

14 JANUARY

One who resists the wave is swept away,
but one who bends before it abides.
MIDRASH[8]

Think back to when you first learned how to "ride the waves" at the beach as a child. Our first tendency was to stand in front of the wave and let it roll over us. Soon we learned that this might not be the best method, since we were easily knocked down and pulled under by the water's force. Then perhaps someone took our hand and taught us how to dive under the wave. This technique may have taken some time to perfect, but once we mastered it we could ride any wave, big or small.

Here we are in midwinter and we're thinking about riding waves. Yet this is not only a summer sport. Life itself is made up of many waves. We can never be sure when a wave is beginning just over the horizon of our vision. At times we probably let an experience knock us down like a wave. Hopefully, we pick ourselves up and learn to dive into the very midst of the wave the next time it comes along. There is no way we can predict what waves we will ride during our life's journey. Sickness, unemployment, and divorce are just some of the difficulties that may face us. The spiritual challenge is to let ourselves know that each wave has a cycle—a beginning, a climax, and an ending—and that we can ride its crest and prevent ourselves from being towed away.   LF

No Action is Trivial

15 January

*If walking along the road, you chance upon a bird's nest, . . .
and the mother is sitting over the fledglings or on the eggs,
do not take the mother together with her young. Let the
mother go and take only the young, in order that you may
fare well and have a long life.*

Deuteronomy 22:6–7

The Talmud labels this mitzvah the "lightest"—the most insubstantial—of all the commandments, probably because it takes little effort to perform. Sending away the mother might well involve merely making a loud noise or just walking nearby.

Commentators in every generation have wondered why there is so extravagant a reward—a good, long life—for so seemingly trivial an act! Indeed, one talmudic commentator points out that the Torah specifies the same reward for honoring parents. Yet fulfilling the latter commandment takes a lifetime and often requires great money, emotion, and effort. He concludes that the equality of reward is the point. The "lightest" of commandments is rewarded as much as the "weightiest" in order to teach us to treasure and observe all commandments equally, since the reward of any mitzvah is incalculable.

Through this commandment, the Torah teaches that every act is of immense significance and no act is inherently trivial. When you eat, you can choose food and prepare it in such a way that you express reverence for life or for your commitment to being a Jew. When you speak, you can say a word of encouragement, truth, or love, or you can say a word of malicious gossip, falsehood, or degradation.

Maimonides, a renowned twelfth-century scholar, writes in his laws of repentance that every person should consider himself or herself as perfectly balanced between good and bad and the world as perfectly balanced between good and evil. The next action you do, however trivial, can tilt you and the whole world toward the side of good and life or toward the side of evil and death. Choose life!   RABBI IRVING GREENBERG[9]

Doing Time

16 JANUARY

The one who forces time is forced back by time, but the one who yields to time finds time standing at one's side.

TALMUD[10]

While we often take time for granted, it is probably the most precious commodity available to us. To "kill time," therefore, is particularly nefarious. Some of us naively refuse to acknowledge the passing of time, specifically when it comes to marking the years of our life as we get older. Others, however, thankful for those years and the life that has been granted to them, especially if they have survived serious illness or misfortune, enthusiastically welcome these birthdays.

The Jewish community uniquely recognizes the value of time. Take a look at your daily planner, which charts your day's activities. When you purchase it, it is usually blank, except perhaps for a few generally accepted holidays or special events. A Jewish calendar, however, is never empty when you purchase it. Holidays are identified, candle lighting times are listed, Torah readings are included. Often there is hardly any room for the addition of appointments. And many of those appointments pale in comparison to what is already written in for us. Jewish time is already full as we enter into it. Enjoy the day ahead and treasure each moment.   KO

Sincere Praise

17 JANUARY

You may tell part of a person's praises to him or her directly.
TALMUD[11]

Everyone thrives on receiving sincere praise. We see this happen when we encourage young children by applauding their smallest accomplishment. Yet how often do we tell an older child or adult just how much their words or actions have helped us? How often do we tell a co-worker how we value their input and contributions? Some of us may give compliments generously, while others may withhold praise out of a belief that it is not necessary or that it may inflate someone's ego. Yet praise is a great motivator. The next time someone goes out of their way to help you or impresses you in some way, let them know that you appreciate it. Don't keep these positive thoughts to yourself. Give them away freely.   LF

Your Love Lifts Me

18 JANUARY

Love and companionship go together.
TALMUD[12]

Love is always greater than our limited ability to anticipate, because it is part of something vastly greater than we can comprehend. In our petty presumption, we think we have mastered ourselves and our feelings, but we are made in God's image, and our ability to love is our reflection of God's great love.

Out of God's boundless love, God created a world of beauty and marvel. And God fashioned a creature in that world who could share the excitement and responsibility of creative love. We love each other as an expression of God's love. God loves through us, and we love God, in part, by loving each other.

Rather than seeing our ability to love creation and other people as somehow competing with our ability to love God, I'd rather see our love with God as the base upon which our other loves thrive. A child eventually grows to be a good spouse by learning to love his or her mother and father first, so that all loves are reenactments and permutations of that earliest love. We recycle and refashion that same old love throughout our lives.

That recycling means that all of our loves are connected to each other, and all are mutually reinforcing. Knowing that we can love and trust a spouse strengthens our love and trust in God—and vice versa. Learning to value and to cherish ourselves can permit us to recognize God's unconditional love for us as we are.

Learn to love more freely. By loving ourselves, our spouse, our children, our parents, our community, our people, our planet, we surprise ourselves by experiencing the transforming power of love beyond our fondest hopes. And all that love can connect us to the wondrous, surprising love of the One who gave us life: God. RABBI BRADLEY SHAVIT ARTSON

Knowledge Is More than Power

19 JANUARY

A person who has knowledge has everything.
TALMUD[13]

We have heard it said before. Knowledge is worth far more than anything money can buy. But this writer in the Talmud was probably not encouraging us to become a storehouse of information, the kind gained from amassing facts and figures. Instead, this sage was referring to the knowledge of God that we acquire by interacting with the world. In the nexus of that interaction, we come closer to God and see ourselves more clearly as well. Thus, real self-knowledge may be available to us only when it is filtered through a keen awareness of the ultimate Source of knowledge. As you learn something new today, this awareness can lead you to greater personal insight and understanding. Just remember: Don't hold it all to yourself. Learn to teach it to others. As you share what you have learned, your own knowledge increases. It is all part of the logic of the spirit. Go and learn. KO

Seeing the World

20 JANUARY

*In the future, people will have to give account
for everything that their eyes saw and that
they did not take time to appreciate.*

TALMUD[14]

Maintaining a grateful attitude is not an easy undertaking. Most of us are quite fortunate in not having to worry about the basics of life, such as shelter, clothing, and food. Others are fortunate in having engaging work, supportive friends, a loving family. We may also be blessed with good health. Yet we take all these blessings, and many others, for granted. We can choose which attitudes shape our lives. We can nourish an attitude of gratitude or walk around feeling deprived. In Judaism, we show our gratitude by saying blessings.

This talmudic text reminds us to slow down and appreciate what we have before us. In fact, it goes a step further by suggesting that we will be held accountable for all that we pass by without noting or appreciating. We think our eyes are open, but often they are not. How much do we appreciate about our family and friends? How much do we appreciate a beautiful sunset? It is so easy to take all our blessings for granted that we must make a concerted effort to appreciate what we have in this life. Thank You, God, for what we will see and do throughout today.   LF

Prayer as Paying Attention

21 January

Prayer is not a stratagem for occasional use, a refuge to resort to now and then. It is rather like an established residence for the innermost self. All things have a home: the bird has a nest, the fox has a hole, the bee has a hive. A soul without prayer is a soul without a home.

RABBI ABRAHAM JOSHUA HESCHEL[15]

Rabbi Abraham Joshua Heschel taught us that the act of praying is not about our paying attention to God. When we pray to God, we want God to pay attention to *us*, to know us and to know of our deepest concerns. This is how we escape our usual, natural, self-absorption: In prayer we become the *object* of God's concern; we try to register ourselves on God's radar screen, as it were. And our reward for our attempt to have God notice us is to feel God's attention turned toward us, to feel God's care envelop us.

To understand this, it might be helpful to think of a parent–child relationship. Children want their parents to notice them. Through that parental attention, care, and love, children develop inner strength, confidence, and the ability to contribute to the world around them. So it is with God and us. When we reach beyond ourselves spiritually in prayer, and when we feel God's attention turned toward us, we leave the prayer experience changed, stronger, more able to care for others and repair the world around us.

True prayer can change our lives. We usually don't think of prayer as having that kind of power, but it does. Its power, however, is solely in our hands. It is a challenge before us, a treasure to which we have access only if we put our heart into it.

Prayer is a challenge for all of us. I learned something from my father that helps me when I pray, and if you are looking for ways to enter the prayer experience, perhaps it can help you too. To turn my thoughts away from myself and toward God, I close my eyes during prayer. Doing this helps me focus on the work that I am trying to do within and helps me feel the power of the community as we reach toward God together. RABBI ELANA KANTER

Dreamers and Dreams

22 JANUARY

A person's every act
begins with a dream and ends with one.
THEODOR HERZL

Justice Louis Brandeis once remarked that while many people are able to dream, the extraordinary ability of the Jewish people is that it is uniquely able to realize its dreams. We have witnessed other dreamers in our day. The Reverend Martin Luther King, Jr., whose birthday is nationally commemorated on the third Monday of January, was one such dreamer. Many of us shared his vision and worked with him to make that dream real. We realized then, as we do now, that Dr. King's vision for the future transcended the boundaries of race and religion and included us all. The day that Dr. King was killed was one of those few days that remain forever etched in our memories. The dreamer was stopped, but his dream was not. In the spirit of his life, we have the obligation to keep our own dreams alive. KO

Gathering Nuts for the Winter

23 JANUARY

It is characteristic of a nut that no matter how much dirt or mud falls on it, once it is washed and cleansed, the inner fruit is edible.

MIDRASH[16]

You might be asking yourself, what do nuts have to do with Torah or daily spirituality? If we read this literally and say that this teaching refers only to actual nuts, then it would be more appropriate in a cookbook than in a collection of *midrashim,* or biblical interpretations. However, if we read this quote as a metaphor, then we understand that the Rabbis here are talking about much more than nuts. They are making an analogy with human nature. In essence, people are like nuts, whose soft insides are protected by a hard exterior. Moreover, the Rabbis use this analogy to teach a basic Jewish belief: While it is human to err, we can always return to our pure inner selves. And we get the chance to do so every time we greet a new morning feeling cleansed, restored, and renewed. Our external selves might get dirty and even banged up, but our inner core will always remain whole and holy. As we encounter difficult people, may their exterior—hard and crusty as they may be—not dissuade us from seeing the perfect purity of their inner core. LF

The Line Between Good and Evil

24 JANUARY

The paths of the Lord are straight—the righteous walk on them whereas the wicked stumble and fall on them.
HOSEA 14:10

Hosea expresses one of the great paradoxes of human life and behavior: Most often good and evil actions are often not polar opposites. The choice between good and evil is typically not a simple turn toward one direction or the other. As the Talmud puts it: "The line between Heaven and Hell is as wide as a hair's breadth."

In many aspects of life, it is not the action but how you do it that makes an act good or bad. For instance, parental love gives children the sense of worth that enables them to grow into mature human beings. But that same love can be overprotective and make the child dependent and fearful, destroying the child.

Giving criticism is a mitzvah, says the Torah. People can grow only if they are corrected. But criticism that is petty, corrosive, or dismissive is an assault on the other. The other person will not listen to it; it may even drive him or her deeper into sin and misbehavior. Is criticism, then, a mitzvah or a sin? It all depends on how you give it.

The line between prudence and irresponsible caution, between satire and cruelty, between being industrious and being a workaholic, between adventurousness and recklessness, between being open-minded and being opportunistic, between having faith and being a fanatic—all these are shifting, subtle, hard to define, subject to judgment and misjudgment. The line is often as thick as a hair's breadth; whether we overstep the line depends on whether we are driven by egotistic distortion or mature responsibility.

So how do we know when we do it right? The outcome depends on our maturity, our self-critical wariness, our sincerity. In the end, there is no guarantee that we will do what is right.

And also in the end, it is God's ways that are straight. The righteous will try hard to reach a moral and good outcome. The wicked will turn that same type of behavior into cruelty, excess and abuse. Sometimes they will convince themselves, and even others, that what they do is good. But God will know. RABBI IRVING GREENBERG[17]

Our Evolving Relationship with the Divine

25 JANUARY

The beginning of wisdom is reverence for God.
PSALM 111:10

Some people like to translate this verse in a different way. They substitute the word "fear" for "reverence." The Hebrew language allows for such freedom in translation, since the same Hebrew word is used to reflect both fear and reverence. I wonder if the early Hebraists had this text *and* their relationship to God in mind as they used this word. Or perhaps as their relationship with God evolved, so too did the meaning of the word. Certainly, our relationship with God includes both fear and reverence. Mine does. Often, one feeling causes the other. At other times, they are so closely related that I am unable to discern one from the other. This point is frequently driven home to me in the midst of one of the unrelenting northeastern winter storms that occur at this time of year, in which I feel completely helpless.

Others argue that our relationship with God should be more gentle and nurturing. They recoil from the very notion of fear of God. Even the idea of reverence brings up hierarchical ideas about kings and royalty. But relationships evolve and change. And regardless of how you translate the word, one thing remains clear: Wisdom is not possible without God. As we learn from our life experiences, we are frequently reminded as we encounter the world that the source of it all—the source of us all—is God.   KO

Handling Anger

26 JANUARY

A soft answer turns away anger.
PROVERBS 15:1

How do you respond to angry words? Most of us do not like confrontation, and a common response is to back down in the face of anger. Some of us may respond to anger with anger of our own. Anger feeds on itself. The Rabbis, using a wordplay, taught that one of the three ways you can know a person is to observe if one easily angers (*ka'aso*). The other two telling traits is the degree to which one is generous (*kiso*) and how much one drinks (*koso*).

An alternate way of responding to anger, however, is to use softness. Can you think of a time when your anger was dissipated by a kind word instead of being met with harshness? The next time you come up against anger, see if you can respond with a soft or gentle word to disarm its acceleration.

LF

Invisible Footsteps

27 January

I will put my spirit in you and you shall live.
EZEKIEL 37:14

Life can slip out from beneath us without our noticing. At times we work so hard and focus so intently that we do not realize what we are missing. Some people remind me of the coyote in the roadrunner cartoons, who is forever speeding off the cliff, finding himself suspended in midair. So long as his feet keep moving, he stays aloft. But the moment he looks down—the moment he realizes there is no foundation under his feet—he falls.

Perhaps we run so quickly because we are afraid of falling. Is there a foundation under our feet? Have we built one with the human bricks of love, learning, and wisdom? Or is the race so swift because the goal grows ever less certain? Much of contemporary life is designed to move us faster toward our goal. Often that is a blessing. But like most blessings, the blessing of speed comes at a cost.

Jewish life is a brake on our energies; it seeks deliberately to slow us down. On Shabbat we do not run. If we bless before and after meals, we cannot exactly eat "on the run."

For a little while, stop running. See what is under your feet. Find your support in this world. Then you can move forward again, this time with the certainty that you are get-ting somewhere. RABBI DAVID WOLPE

Personal Dignity

28 JANUARY

The dignity of a human being is extremely important.
TALMUD[18]

It seems odd that the Rabbis would be motivated to include such an obvious statement as this one in the sacred text of the Talmud—and that they would do so in such a straightforward, almost banal manner. No clever construction of language is evident. There are no cute wordplays. Human dignity is too important for the message to be hidden or lost behind rabbinic erudition. For the Rabbis, human dignity is clearly one of the most important values to uphold. It is at the heart of much of Jewish tradition, especially in the many *mitzvot*— God's commandments—that govern the relationships among human beings. That point seems to go without saying. But maybe it doesn't. Maybe the Rabbis feel the need to simply state the idea—and not overstate it—so that we might take it to heart in our daily activities.

Consider a routine day in your life. Are you conscious of how you treat the people you encounter? Start with your family and friends, but also pay attention to the people you encounter on the street and in the marketplace, even the nameless people whom you bump into on a commuter train or in a busy shopping mall. What you say and what you do when this happens can transform a person's day. And in watching your behavior toward others, you can also change the world. KO

God's Presence in Diversity

29 JANUARY

If one sees a great crowd, one should thank God for not having made them all of one mind. For just as each person's face is different from another, so is each person's mind different from any other mind.

TALMUD[19]

Here is a talmudic statement that speaks directly to what we today often call "diversity." The Rabbis were aware of the human tendency to seek homogeneity. They knew that we commonly choose friends on the basis of similar likes and dislikes and a shared world perspective rather than seek out friends whose lifestyle differs significantly from our own. The Rabbis also recognized the inherent difficulty in accepting our innate differences, since, as we all have experienced, differences can cause tension and unease. So instead of ignoring the diversity among us, we are taught to be thankful each time we realize humanity's full spectrum.

What would it be like to stop and marvel at the complex nature of humanity, to contemplate everything from the varying contours of our outer appearances to the inner workings of our minds? The next time you encounter someone who thinks differently than you, pause for a moment and express wonder at the uniqueness of this person's mind and their way of looking at the world.   LF

On Our Choices

30 JANUARY

Make yourself a new heart and a new spirit.
EZEKIEL 18:31A

When we are lucky, we are aware of the choices we have made. When we are blessed, we are able to reflect on what we want our lives to mean. When asked what choices they regret most, many people reveal how profound the smallest choices have become over the course of a lifetime.

The regrets sound something like this:

I would have written more.
I would have traveled more.
I would have given more attention to my mother
or my father.
I would have loved being Jewish more.
I would have become a lawyer.
I would have finished that degree.
I would have made more time for myself.
I would have loved myself more.
I would have loved others more.
I would have thrown away my old bills and saved
the love letters.

That's the past. What of the future? Are we compelled to relive the past? Or, if we become familiar with what lies fluttering in our hearts, can we reinvent ourselves?

RABBI RACHEL SABATH

Walking the Talk

31 January

*What does God require of you? Only to do justice,
love mercy, and walk humbly with your God.*
MICAH 6:8

It is often difficult to know how to act in this world. There
are so many competing demands on our spirit and psyche.
Many roles that were once clear to us no longer seem so self-
evident. Social mores are changing drastically, and we are
often expected to affirm them whether or not we really feel
comfortable with them. And as society's structures continue
to change, this state of *hefker* (ownerlessness), as the Rabbis
sometimes label it, threatens to grow to the point of overwhelming us. We want to stand firm, but it is not always so
easy to do so. So what are we to do? The answer is quite simple. Just follow the advice of the prophet Micah: Do justice,
love mercy, and walk humbly with God. This is all that is
necessary to live a good life. The prophet's words provide us
with an action plan for living, and all we have to do is *try* to
follow it. When we do, we are in sync with the One Who
provides the rhythm for the world.   KO

FEBRUARY

Flexible Growth

1 FEBRUARY

*A person should always be flexible like a reed
and not rigid like a cedar.*
TALMUD[1]

The Rabbis often take their cues from the world around them. Doing so helps them elevate the mundane to the sacred. There is much to learn from the order of nature, even when it is not clearly visible to us. This is particularly true this month, when we celebrate trees and nature on the holiday of Tu BiShevat, which marks the time when the sap begins to flow deep inside the trees.

As we think about trees, especially those of us who live in northern climes, where rivers and lakes are frozen during winter, it may be easier to reflect on the strength of the mighty cedar than to perceive the subtle resilience of the reed struggling for survival. The cedar stands its ground, pitting brute strength against the forces that might try to uproot it. The reed, gentle and pliant, responds to these forces by bowing before them. That is its genius.

There are times when it is important for us to be like the cedar and stubbornly stand our ground when we are threatened. Wisdom comes with learning when to do so. Often the wisdom comes after we have chosen the wrong posture and learned from that mistake. But when you stand your ground, growth is not possible. You're stuck in one place. To move forward and succeed, we must be flexible. This flexibility helps us grow beyond that place.   KO

The Newness of Each Day

2 FEBRUARY

The Architect of the world never does the same thing twice. Every day is an entirely new creation. Take as much as you can from what each new day has to offer.

RABBI NACHMAN OF BRESLOV[2]

It is easy to perceive our days as flowing into one another, seemingly all the same. This perception is not surprising, since most of us arise each morning to face another day at work and then return home to spend time with our families or friends. When someone asks, "What's up?" we may often respond "Not much" or "Same old, same old." These responses signal a certain malaise about the sameness of life. However, most of our lives are indeed made up of numerous tasks which we will have to do time and again, whether making a meal, chairing a meeting, or negotiating a contract. Although we might have new and exciting experiences from time to time, they do not make up the warp and woof of our life's fabric. An important spiritual lesson is to learn how to approach these everyday tasks with a renewed and open spirit. Each day, the rising and setting of the sun gives us an opportunity to relate anew to our lives. As Rabbi Nachman's teaching suggests, God also approaches everything anew as if experiencing it for the first time.   LF

Living to Create a Legacy

3 FEBRUARY

*None may enter the Academy who is not inwardly
as he or she is outwardly.*
TALMUD[3]

Given the pace of our lives these days, it shouldn't surprise us how easy it is to lose sight of what we want our lives to be about. That kind of reflection is often reserved for the dying or the gravely ill. Trauma sends us into that more internal part of ourselves, away from the details of our everyday lives. Yet it's in our everyday lives that we determine what our lives are and what they mean.

Every day we must focus on our core purpose. We must be intensely aware of the legacy we are leaving by how we live our lives. Keep your heart and mind open to what counts. If you know what counts, live as though that is what really matters. Devote yourself to it, immerse yourself in it. But whatever you do, don't do it alone. Focus on your core values. And do it with such joy that others will want to join you.

RABBI RACHEL SABATH

Real Wealth

4 FEBRUARY

*The one who loves money [absolutely] will never have his
[or her] fill of money.*
ECCLESIASTES 5:9

Money can buy luxury. There is no doubt about it. And Judaism encourages us to enjoy the pleasures of this world while occasionally also reminding us that these are fleeting and impermanent. The Hebrew language does not even have a way to express extended ownership. It can only suggest a kind of time-limited possession. Bartering served us well in our early history, but money is what we now use in commerce. It is what our employers use to measure our worth, and it is often how we measure our own worth. We use it in exchange for goods and services. We buy education with it. Whether we have a lot of it or only a little, as long as we see money only as a tool for living, we can retain mastery over it. But as soon as it becomes a prism through which we see the world, it begins to control us. With such a love of money—even if we have a lot of it—we can never be truly wealthy. With such a love of money, we will always remain poor.

Real wealth comes not from the count of one's money. Instead, it comes when money no longer counts.　　　　KO

Taking Count

5 February

Treat no one lightly and think nothing is useless, for everyone has a moment and everything has a place.
Mishnah[4]

Here's an exercise for today: Count how many people you speak with from the time you wake up until the time you go to sleep. Don't count anyone twice. Some of these people will be family or friends whom we love or colleagues whom we respect. Some will only briefly cross our paths, and we may never see them again. How do we treat all these people? With whom do we share a smile? With whom do we speak hastily and then brush off? With whom do we give a loving comment?

Reflect for a moment on those whom we don't know well even though we might buy coffee from them or ride the elevator every day with them in silence. All of them—from those we know well to those we only briefly encounter—are made in God's image. It is too easy in our service-oriented society to forget that those who help us get through our day—our secretaries, our child-care providers, the people who serve us in restaurants—have lives full of joys and worries of their own. Let us never denigrate anyone no matter what role they play in our lives. Let us share with them a kind word and a warm smile.   LF

The Appearance of the Divine

6 FEBRUARY

On this eighth day . . . God will appear.

LEVITICUS 9:1–4

Our most famous medieval commentator, Rashi, cautions us against expecting to find God only in the extraordinary. God's presence is most evident, he insists, precisely on the eighth day because it is then that God appears "in the world of our hands." This is to say, God appears in the trivia of everyday life, in the chores we mistakenly push off as unimportant, in the business as usual.

Judaism glories in this business as usual, and we affirm the world so we can delight in its small things: taking the children shopping, finishing a project, planning a dinner, or cleaning a closet. When we say *L'chayim* (To life!), we acknowledge that we accept life as it really is: The ordinary life on the eighth day when the whole new week lies before us.

Reality is more than screaming headlines in tabloid news-papers. It includes follow-up stories of "the day after." On the day after the Temple was destroyed, say the Rabbis, God went into exile with us, and ever after God has accompanied us to our desks, to our schools, to parents' sickbeds, to our children's pediatrician, and to all the other ordinary places where life goes on because Elijah and the messiah have not quite managed to show up.

So when the eighth day dawns, resist disappointment. God might be sitting next to you in the waiting room or even at the breakfast table. The eighth day may be the day when God appears. RABBI LAWRENCE HOFFMAN

Spiritual Longing

7 FEBRUARY

Oh God, You are my God; early will I seek You, my soul thirsts for You; my flesh longs for You in a dry land, and it is faint without water.
PSALM 63:2

Spirituality is not possible without a relationship with God. Our ancestors knew that. Our grandparents knew that. The entire Torah documents the journey of faith and the struggle of our forebears in the context of that relationship. Yet when it comes to the here and now, conversations about spirituality seem to focus more on the self in relationship to the self and less on the self in relationship to the Other. Some people are simply afraid to speak the language of our past; they are afraid to use the "God" word. But it is clear to me that my spiritual life emerges out of my relationship with God.

It hasn't always been that way. Nor is it always that way even now. Faith may be a struggle, but it is the yearning for God that I feel deep within me that motivates all that I do. The rituals that I practice and the prayers that I speak all help me further that very relationship which sustains my faith. Thus I look for new opportunities to encounter God as I encounter the world. You might want to do the same.   KO

Extending Ourselves to Others

8 FEBRUARY

Do not stand idly by the blood of your neighbor.
LEVITICUS 19:16

How many of us will go out of our way to help someone in need? Our answer probably depends on how well we know the person, the nature of our relationship with the person, and what we are being asked to do for them. Many of us probably help our friends and family in big and small ways. Yet how many of us will help a neighbor whom we do not know? How many people do you know who live on your street or in your apartment building? Unfortunately, many of us may live in the shadow of the anonymity that characterizes our modern culture. Our challenge is to break down these barriers that isolate us from each other so we can rebuild the social cement which creates bonds between people. A strong community is one that creates webs of interconnection between its members.

We are commanded by the Torah not to stand idly by when someone is in trouble. We can interpret this mitzvah broadly and think about it when we are asked to donate blood or to have our bone marrow tested for compatibility with someone we do not know, or when we dedicate our-

selves to eradicate physical or verbal violence in our neigh-
borhoods. Especially in today's world, it is a constant challenge to maintain our connection to others and not allow
apathy and cynicism to erode our concern for them.   LF

Faith in Our Lives

9 FEBRUARY

*Faith is experienced not . . . as something which has been
brought into existence by man's creative cultural gesture,
but rather something which was given to man when the
latter was overpowered by God. Indeed, faith is born of the
intrusion of eternity upon temporality.*

RABBI JOSEPH B. SOLOVEITCHIK[5]

Judaism, through story, deed and law, teaches us that what
really matters are not necessarily the questions we ask, and
sometimes not even the answers, but the attitude of the person who is asking the questions. What matters is an orienta-
tion of faithfulness, which in Hebrew is called *emunah*. How
does that faithfulness help us through a terrible night of sorrow or sickness or loneliness? Is Judaism a source of comfort
at such times?

In my own life I have known such moments. And I will tell
you one thing that my Judaism didn't do, and that I didn't
ask of it: The questions I posed to God were not meant as
real questions. I was not operating in the mode of thought
and analysis. That came later. My questions were really pleas,
hopes, terror, and rage, all masquerading as dialogue. While I
may have been using words, what I was seeking was beyond
words. I was seeking belonging, rootedness, and connection.

Judaism provided that. In my deepest terror, I never felt alone. Even in my fear, I could sense the nurturing love of my community, the connection of the Jewish people, our rootedness in the *mitzvot*, and the love and concern of God. I didn't have answers, but I had *emunah*, the ability to trust in faithfulness.

Faithfulness feels to me exactly like going limp in the ocean or trusting myself to the rocking of an earthquake. The Hebrew meaning of *emunah* isn't assent. It means "to trust." To have faith is to be able to trust in something beyond ourselves, to trust that we have the strength and commitment to get through whatever comes, to trust that we are never alone.

To be able to retain a sense of belonging in something transcendent and eternal, to know that we are a people in covenant with God and linked across generations, is a great source of strength and courage. The ability to turn over to God our need to control and to manipulate, even while doing all we can to assist God in bringing about a positive outcome, is the very core of Jewish faith. We can practice faith by saying the words of Rabbi Eliezer: "Do Your will, O God, in heaven above, and bestow tranquillity of spirit on those who revere You below. And what is good in Your sight, do."

RABBI BRADLEY SHAVIT ARTSON

The Force of a Regular Routine

10 FEBRUARY

Humans are grounded by the deeds they do habitually, and ideas are influenced by the work of their hands whether good or bad.
BIBLE COMMENTARY[6]

When daily routine is raised to a sacred level, we call it ritual. Now that we are in the middle of winter, rituals can help us make it through until spring arrives.

Rituals are more than just habits. They anchor our lives and provide us with stability. They offer us depth and meaning and purpose. They become familiar friends as we repeat them regularly, and they help us to measure our days, weeks, months, and years. They provide us with memories to hold and to share. And when we accidentally or even intentionally skip them, we may find ourselves bereft of our compass which helps us locate our bearings as we go through life.

Rituals are not designed to serve the self. They help put into concrete terms the religious narratives that shape our lives, the same narratives and beliefs that our ancestors carried as they made their way through the desert. But the ideas that are inherent in them extend beyond the limits of time and exceed the few moments that we may dedicate to them every day or every week. Their meaning carries over into our daily lives. They fuel our acts and our activities. They become the foundation on which we build our lives.   KO

Learning from the Animal World

11 FEBRUARY

If the Torah had not been given to Israel, we could have learned modesty from the cat, intimacy from the dove, respect from the rooster, and integrity from the ant.
TALMUD[7]

In this extraordinary comment the Rabbis suggest that there are certain basic qualities that we could learn from God's creation. This is an exceptional statement because, for the Rabbis, Torah was the source of all knowledge and wisdom, yet here they state that we can learn lessons even from observing animal life.

How do we learn modesty, intimacy, respect, and integrity from the cat, dove, rooster, and ant? Through attentiveness and study. And then by abstracting from the behaviors we observed, looking at consequences, and drawing conclusions. How do we learn these same qualities from Torah study? The same way. For modesty, intimacy, respect, and integrity are not necessarily in the words. We learn these traits from engaging with others, by listening to others' interpretations of Torah, and through give-and-take discussions with teachers.

Reflect for a moment about where you learn these attributes. From whom did you learn modesty? Where did you learn respect? Who taught you intimacy or embodied integrity for you? All of us can model these traits for others. So today try to conduct yourself with modesty and integrity and be respectful to everyone and intimate with those you love.   LF

Trees in Our Lives

12 FEBRUARY

Trees were created for the companionship of humans.
MIDRASH[8]

As the seasons change, some of us find ourselves staring at the woods, whether they are leafy and green or bare and gray-brown. Observing the changes in nature can inspire a profound prayer of gratefulness. At the full moon of midwinter our people have always stopped to stare at the trees. We have thought all kinds of thoughts, from the mystical to the prosaically practical. If you know some Hebrew, you may see "the tree of life, the *etz chayim* that shaded and nurtured the Garden of Eden, or you may see "the tree of splendor," the *etz hadar,* whose lemony fruit became the essential ingredient in the sacred celebration of Sukkot, the fall harvest festival.

Or you may see the "tree of knowledge," the *etz da'at,* which carried the formula for synthesizing those two incompatible realities, goodness and truth.

Of all these mythic trees, we perhaps think most about the "tree of knowledge" which stood in the center of the Garden of Eden and which Adam and Eve were prohibited from touching. What does this prohibition tell us? Perhaps it suggests that by embracing the truth of our wrongdoing, we can find our way back to that garden. That if we reenter the garden with full awareness of where we've gone wrong, we can feel a goodness more powerful than anything we could have imagined. Becoming responsible for the garden is our most sacred truth.

We are the sacred priests of planet Earth. When the midwinter moon is full, look outside. Even if the trees are bare, connect to their power and strength. Plant a tree and recommit yourself to being responsible for our Earth.

RABBI LESTER BRONSTEIN

The Power of Memory

13 FEBRUARY

Forgetfulness leads to exile while remembrance is the secret of redemption.
BAAL SHEM TOV

Often our memories are triggered by such annual events as festivals and celebrations or by certain pictures or music or films. But most people also have their own inner calendars; others cannot enter these private worlds uninvited. These special, private days are set aside for personal recognition. Some are just flashes that require a moment of attention and then are put aside. Others are so permanently sealed into our psyches that we carry them throughout our lives. Some have the power to influence all that we do.

Sometimes we don't fully understand the power of memory until we forget to acknowledge a particular day, when the routine of our lives eclipses even its own rhythm. This is especially true when we fail to remember a birthday or a wedding anniversary or even a *yahrzeit,* the anniversary of the death of someone close to us. Often little things jog our memories in remarkably powerful ways. It may be the flash of recognition in the face of a stranger who reminds us of a person whom we loved and lost or who remains distant from us. Maybe a certain fragrance of flowers. Perhaps a fleeting image that surfaces in our memory. Any of these can elicit tears or exhilaration; all contribute to the tapestry of life that we share with others.

But what is the value of memory? What is its real purpose? For some people memory is an important reminder that we all survive bodily death; the memories of acts of people who are now dead provide them with eternal life. For other people memories remind them about something others taught them.

Remembering is more than just not forgetting. It is an act of faith and of profound belief. For as we remember, we are motivated to help shape the future. And we expect of others no less than what we expect of ourselves: Remember the deeds of our lives and the kindnesses of others. KO

Watching Our Hearts

14 FEBRUARY

Above all that you hold dear, watch over your heart,
for from it comes life.
PROVERBS 4:23

The heart is our most important organ—physiologically and emotionally. It is our most powerful muscle and it is also commonly thought to be the seat of our emotions and feelings. Describing others as having an "open heart" suggests they are personable and warm. A "closed heart" means that they are distant and detached. In many ways an open or closed heart characterizes the degree to which we share the most important part of ourselves with others. While we know this trait has nothing to do with physiology, these metaphors are both vivid and powerful. So let us take care of our hearts in all ways—by exercising, eating properly, and connecting with others so that we can fully rejuvenate both our physical *and* spiritual selves.   LF

Giving with No Limits

15 FEBRUARY

There are actions for which there is no minimum set in the
Torah. These are: Leaving the corner of the field for the
poor; bringing the first fruits to the priest; appearing before
God on Passover, Sukkot and Shavuot; and performing
loving acts of kindness.
MISHNAH[9]

These are actions of enormous consequence for which, given their importance, there is no fixed measure in Torah.

Offering the first fruits expresses gratitude. What is the minimum expression of gratitude? There is none.

Similarly, what is the minimum amount of effort that will help the poor to help themselves? The answer: Any amount of help will suffice.

In the third action, appearing before God, we seek inspiration and a profound religious experience so we feel that we are in the presence of God. How much time must you be there? How often must you be in the presence of God to be inspired and changed by the experience? The answer: One second, one minute, one day, or an entire year may be enough. A whole lifetime can be transformed by one experience.

In the last action, performing loving acts of kindness, there is no minimum. A hug, a statement of support to a person on the brink of collapse, a smile—all these cost no effort and have infinite value.

This lesson of the Mishnah is fundamental: There is no act that is trivial, and no good act is wasted. Every deed that we do can have enormous impact for good and bad. Keep that in mind when you act next.   RABBI IRVING GREENBERG[10]

Learning from Others

16 FEBRUARY

If you have learned much Torah, do not
take credit for it yourself.
MISHNAH[11]

When I tell people the name of the person from whom I learned something, I can tell that they often don't understand why I would bother to give credit to someone else. After all, we learn many things from many people during our lives. But while there are many things that we learn for ourselves, there are also many people who are responsible for bringing us to this point in time who have offered us indispensable insight about life when we needed it most, or who simply gave us direction and then pushed us forward. All of them deserve our thanks. Moreover, they need to be recognized for their contribution to who we are and what we have become.

Doing this is a simple process. As you go through your day, consider who taught you whatever it is you are doing at any given moment. And when you are sharing what you have learned with others, remember to tell them the name of your "teacher." Then they can do the same for you.   KO

Lifting Us from Despair

17 FEBRUARY

*May it be your will, O God, to place us in an illumined corner and not to place us in a darkened corner.
Let not our heart be sick nor our eyes darkened.*
TALMUD[12]

In the Talmud the Rabbis record many blessings that reflect their own spontaneous prayers. Many of the prayers we say today were adopted from these. In the prayer above, for instance, which is ascribed to Rabbi Alexandri, he asks to sit in the light. Perhaps he composed these words when feeling despair or depression. Such feelings can be overwhelming and debilitating if we don't reach out. It is particularly difficult to extend ourselves at those moments. Yet we all desire to leave the dark corners of our lives and have the weight of melancholy and isolation lifted. At such moments we can turn to God and pour out our heart in our own words.

What prayer could you spontaneously address to God at this very moment? While the above prayer asks for relief, our own prayers can express gratitude, praise, or a sense of longing. May we allow ourselves time each day to turn to God and speak openly about the places in our hearts that are content and those places where despair lurks.   LF

Hands of God

18 FEBRUARY

God does not punish with both hands.
YIDDISH SAYING

This expression, one that my family taught me in Yiddish, *"Gott shtruft nisht mit beide hendt,"* has stayed with me for a long time. What does it mean that God doesn't punish with both hands? That good must always be found even in the harshest tragedy or the most severe heartbreak? This idea seems difficult to accept at a moment of tragedy. But often the passage of time and the healing of reflection allows us to see redemption and not just the pain, to see joy and love and not just the loss.

At the moment of death of someone we love, we reflect on the loss of any physical future encounter. But the pain and the intensity of loss is an accurate reflection on the love of the life that was. It would not be better never to have lived and never to have loved. It should never be.

A child or adult suffering through illness is a challenge to any family. It is also often a challenge to faith. And yet, many times families and friends come together and find hidden strength to bear the burden.

Ours is an imperfect world. God has left it to us to perfect it. For the privilege of birth, we gamble on life, and inevitably we face death. For the privilege of love, we gamble our hearts, and inevitably face loss. But if one hand strikes, the other comforts. If one hand falters, the other embraces. That is the way of this world and that is our blessing. To be held in the hand of God is to live life to its fullest.   RABBI ABIE INGBER

Emulating Leadership

19 FEBRUARY

The acts of the leader are the acts of the nation.
ZOHAR[13]

The logic of this statement from the Zohar, Judaism's primary mystical text, appears rather straightforward. It is rather obvious that we have to bear the consequences of decisions made by our leaders. Perhaps the author of the Zohar had something else in mind. Maybe he sees causation running in a direction opposite from what we would expect. The Zohar reads the situation this way: The actions of leaders are shaped by the actions of the citizens of their nation. Thus everything that we do impacts directly on the decisions taken by our leaders, no matter what community or nation we live in. Therefore, rather than simply responding to our leaders' decisions, we *can* take control of our own destiny. Jewish tradition likes to put this another way: A leader can lead only where a community wants to follow. Where do you want to go today?   KO

Removing Barriers

20 FEBRUARY

Do not curse the deaf or place a stumbling block before the blind.
LEVITICUS 19:14

In the book of Leviticus we read the above verse in the section called The Holiness Code. This includes a series of laws that are ritual, communal, and interpersonal and which we are commanded to fulfill in an attempt to emulate God's holiness. This verse, if read narrowly, seems to suggest that we should not create obstacles for someone who is handicapped; such behavior would certainly demonstrate a mean spirit. The Rabbis, however, took the liberty of interpreting this verse more expansively. They suggest that this verse applies to all of us since, in one way or another, we are all blind and deaf. How is this so? While we may strive to be aware of all that is going on around us, it is only natural that we cannot absorb it all or even be aware of all of it. At those moments, we hope that others will not take advantage of us but rather will remove unseen barriers from our path.
LF

Spiritual Energy in Our Homes

21 FEBRUARY

Blessed be you when you come in, and blessed be you when you go out.
DEUTERONOMY 28:6

Often we prevent ourselves from entering our own promised land of fulfillment because we are afraid. Judaism may be intimidating for many of us. You may not want to get on a lot of synagogue committees. You might be concerned about having to attend services morning, afternoon, and night. You don't want to feel compelled to give donations when you really don't want to. And you may not want to go on some spiritual quest which will disrupt your life as it is presently configured.

You don't want to change, yet at the same time you don't want to stay the same. So how does Judaism suggest you begin changing without toppling the construct of your existence? Change one tiny thing at a time. Don't run out and buy an entire Jewish library or six sets of dishes so you can keep kosher every day, on special occasions, and during Pesach. If I were to start with one mitzvah, I would put *mezuzot* on my doors. And if I weren't comfortable putting them on my outside doors, then I'd put them on the bedroom doors of my children and myself. Why start there? First, because it is an easy mitzvah to perform. You buy some *mezuzot,* say a blessing *(Barukh Atah Adonai Eloheinu Melekh HaOlam, asher kidshanu b'mitzvotav v'tzivanu likbo'ah mezuzah),* and put the *mezuzah* on the doorpost.

But this is just the beginning. Now that you have these *mezuzot* up, you can, in the privacy of your home, experiment with kissing the *mezuzot* as you walk through the door. These *mezuzot* fulfill the commandment in the *Shema* to "write them on the doorposts of your house and on your gates" (Deuteronomy 6:9). What they also do is change the energy flow in your house.

Perhaps that last sentence made you a bit uncomfortable. You probably wouldn't feel uneasy if a decorator said that people need to be able to move through your house in an organized flow that is directed by architecture and furniture. But spiritual energy flow in a house? If we were talking about the Chinese art of *feng shui,* of spiritually directing energy through a space, you might think, "How fascinating!" So why not allow Jewish teachings about space, holiness, and energy to shape the way your house and the relationships in it work? That's why I suggest starting with *mezuzot.* It's something you have to do only once. It's a central precept of Judaism. It can be done in total privacy. It's not expensive, certainly less expensive than a decorator. And it works—spiritually. What do you have to lose?   RABBI JUDITH ABRAMS

Following Our Own Feet

22 FEBRUARY

One is led only in the direction he or she chooses to follow.
TALMUD[14]

While some say that we suffer from a dearth of leadership, somehow leaders emerge in our work, at school, and in our communities. These are not the men and women who are elected or appointed to positions of authority. Rather these are the few among us who assume these positions because they are driven to lead. Some will even claim that they are called to lead. But what is actually going on? Are *we* doing the following or is it the *leader* who is really leading?

The Rabbis of the Talmud think that the answer to this question is rather simple and straightforward: We follow only where we want to be led. There is no one pushing us in one direction or pulling us in another. Thus, wherever we go, we are freely making the choice to go there.

What choices are you prepared to make today? Where will you be going and who will be leading you? And how will you be leading yourself?   KO

Seeing Beyond the Exteriors

23 FEBRUARY

*Don't look at the jug. Rather, look at what is within it.
You can have a new bottle full of old wine, and an old
bottle which does not even have new wine in it.*

MISHNAH[15]

How often do we judge others by first glances or by appearances? Most of us are guilty of this at one time or another. It is all too easy to be impressed with surface appearances rather than with the true quality of someone's character. For in truth, it takes time to get to know someone and fairly evaluate their strengths and gifts along with their deficiencies. In most situations, these characteristics may have nothing to do with how they appear at first.

In fact, many of us may spend more time on our appearance than we do on our internal states. What would it be like if we spent as much time developing our "insides" as we do our "outsides?"

Searching below the surface and seeing others for their full selves is a spiritual challenge. Let us be swayed not by elaborate exteriors but rather by the content of what and who we meet in our lives.   LF

The Plague of Darkness,
The Blessing of Light

24 FEBRUARY

God, may it be Your will to place us on the side of light.

TALMUD[16]

The last of the Ten Plagues that God visited on Pharaoh and his people, the slaughter of the firstborn, may well have been the most terrifying. But it is the ninth, the Plague of Darkness, that is the most mystifying.

We can understand that all of the other plagues were properly "plaguelike": They all created pain for their victims. But what is particularly painful about living in darkness for three days?

The Bible says this darkness was so thick that it had physical substance and could be "touched." People could not see one another nor get up from their place for the three days. Even if this description is not hyperbole, this plague is still qualitatively different from a bloody Nile, or locusts, pestilence and inflammatory boils, and certainly from the slaughter of the firstborn.

But, we are told, "all the Israelites enjoyed light in their dwelling." This strange quality of the Plague of Darkness convinces me that it was not, strictly speaking, a plague that God visited on the Egyptians, but rather a description of the state of Egyptian society as it existed at that time.

Certainly any society that permits the oppression of an entire community is living in profound darkness. In fact, it was a society in which people could not see the other's face, the other's oppression and despair. This was a society in which not only the king, but *everyone* suffered from a hardening of the heart. This was a plague because a society that lives in this kind of darkness is self-destructive. And it was a plague that the Egyptians brought upon themselves. By contrast, the Israelites had learned very painfully that in the society that they were destined to create, people had to be able to see one another, to recognize the face of another person as being fully human and deserving the utmost honor and respect.

This theme speaks directly to our society today. More and more, we are threatening to become a society that lives in thick darkness, a society where the face of the oppressed—particularly of our poor, our elderly and our children—is not being seen. And the startling contrast between the darkness that reigned among the Egyptians and the light that shone among the Israelites suggests that we above all have the responsibility to protect our society by not allowing the darkness to become a self-imposed and self-destructive plague.

That responsibility is conveyed in another metaphorical use of light: Isaiah's charge that we are to be an *or lagoyim,* a light unto the nations. But before we can become that, we have to make sure that in our own community, light continues to shine and we retain the ability to see the faces of our own "others."   RABBI NEIL GILLMAN

Lifting the Eyes

25 FEBRUARY

I lift my eyes to the heavens. From where will my help come?
PSALM 121:1

This line from the Psalms is the first line of what I like to call a "psalm of strength." While we find it in various places in liturgical context, I often find myself repeating the words as I walk down the street on my way to work. As I repeat it over and over, in the morning it helps me steel myself each day for the problems I may encounter. At other times I sing the verses to myself as a lilting chant. Reciting it helps me get centered and focused for whatever the day—and the world—may have in store for me.

In the Torah, whenever a character "raises their eyes," say to behold a mountain, the reader knows that a significant event is about to occur. Perhaps when we recognize that our help comes from God (which is when we truly "raise our eyes"), then we are able to transform what follows into an event of significance.

See what you can do to change your ordinary day and turn it toward the mountain. You will be pleasantly surprised to find "from whence your help comes." It comes from the Maker of heaven and earth.   KO

The Path of Learning

26 FEBRUARY

Inspire us to understand and discern, to perceive,
to learn, and to teach, to observe, do and fulfill gladly
all the teachings of your Torah.
LITURGY[17]

Learning a new subject or task never takes a direct path. How much more so personal spiritual journeys, which will be full of unknown curves and surprises. Whenever we embark upon a new learning venture or spiritual task, there are many skills we call upon. These include understanding, discerning, perceiving, teaching, observing, and integrating. We could even think of these as a step-by-step blueprint to acquire new knowledge. First we have to apply our cognitive skills, then we find applications for this new information. At times we can do this by trying to explain the subject to another person.

In all situations, we have to find a way to integrate it into our lives.

This path is especially applicable when we seek to integrate any spiritual teaching. We can listen to the wisdom of others, but at some time we have to make it come alive for ourselves. This path itself is not necessarily a straight line. It is common to go back and forth between the cognitive and the experiential. No matter where we are on our spiritual journey, there can never be a final destination, since our journey continues to unfold as we mature and move through life.   LF

Study As Prayer; Prayer As Study

27 FEBRUARY

When I pray, I speak to God; when I study,
God speaks to me.
RABBI LOUIS FINKELSTEIN[18]

Speaking and listening are both endangered activities in our culture. There is so much information exchanged each day and each hour that it is hard to pay attention to our speech: Are we saying what we really need to say? Are we speaking from the heart? Do we know when not to speak? As for listening, who can hear anything at all amid the noise around us these days? There is such a flood of messages coming in, how can we discern which are important, or even holy?

In prayer, we can speak from the heart. It does not matter if we are not sure "Who" is listening, if we don't understand how prayer is supposed to work, if we're not certain we believe in prayer at all. For moments at a time we can set our questions aside and just say what we need to say. What a relief to be able to speak, as loudly as we want or as softly, without worrying about being understood, without anticipating the other's response. Prayer is speech in its purest form. It is our heart speaking in its own way, in its own voice, just as it needs to.

In the study of Torah, we listen for God's voice. When we open a sacred book, we instantly tune in to our people's ancient, eternal dialogue with God. We hear the voices of our ancestors speaking to one another across the generations. They argue with each other, they learn from each other, and we hear it all. But then, if we let the cacophony of voices settle, if we listen quietly, we can hear the timeless call of truth, of justice, of compassion, of meaning. In the pages of Torah we are back at Sinai, listening again for the voice of the Divine. We needn't do anything but listen, and the voice will speak to us.

Jewish practice gives us rich ways to speak and listen. When we need to speak to God, when we are too filled with joy or rage or despair to hear anything but what is in our heart, it is time to pray. When we need to hear the voice of Spirit, we can open any sacred text and hear God's voice speaking to us. And, with God's help, we have a whole lifetime to learn how to listen to God.   RABBI AMY EILBERG

The Birth of Freedom

28 FEBRUARY

With the Torah, freedom came into the world.
MIDRASH[19]

Any student of history knows that freedom came for different people at different times in history. We say that for the African American it came with the Emancipation Proclamation, but it actually did not come until the civil rights movement in the 1960s. And if we want to be honest, there is still a struggle for it. Although this decade has seen an unprecedented number of countries burst into democracy, many people still have not tasted the sweet taste of freedom, even in those lands that call themselves free. In the selection from the Midrash that is quoted above, the Rabbis are suggesting that the Torah is a reflection of the idea of freedom. Perhaps that is the problem: not enough people know Torah. When you apply its principles, though, the only conclusion you can draw is that freedom is the right of all people.

But there is a second level to the idea of freedom that is contained in the text and that is even more persuasive. It is the kind of freedom that lives in the soul, the kind that even a totalitarian state cannot squelch. No matter what happened to our people during its history, even in the worst of times, they remained free in their hearts. In Egyptian slavery, according to one midrash, God chose to redeem the Israelites at that specific time because they had resigned themselves to being slaves. In subsequent history we learned the lessons of Egypt.

And it is the Torah—and its study—that keeps you free to live and free to be you. KO

MARCH

Raising Standards of Achievement

1 MARCH

Lead me to a rock that is too high for me.
PSALM 61:3

If we begin our day prepared for challenges, we are better suited to rise above them. Too often we get into the familiar routine of daily living and allow ourselves to get into a comfortable rut. Without even realizing it, our energy wanes, we become less productive, and everything is predictable.

Yet during significant moments in our lives we may take stock, often in an effort to raise ourselves above the routine. This is a helpful way for us to redirect our lives. When it is not possible to stop and examine our lives, our sense of routine may grow to crisis proportions. For many, this oppressive routine does not hit us until midlife. Then we might make rash judgments just to break free of those things that we perceive are fettering us. How do we ready ourselves so we don't do this?

There are no overnight solutions. There is no one process that will prepare us for those moments that have taken a lifetime to evolve. For many people Shabbat offers a weekly opportunity to reflect on the past, to set our sights on the future, and to find spiritual renewal in the process. Shabbat is unique in that, by capturing time, it makes time irrelevant. The past and future become merged and the days of Eden are brought together with the future of potential paradise. The weekly ritual of Shabbat helps us understand the untapped sacred power that is inherent in routine. Shabbat occurs weekly, but we can bring Shabbat moments at various times into our week, for Shabbat prepares us to begin the day with the statement of the Psalmist echoing in our ears: "Lead me to a rock that is too high for me."   KO

Taking on Responsibility

2 MARCH

It is not your obligation to finish the work and neither are you free to refrain from it.
MISHNAH[1]

This teaching speaks to our responsibility to become involved, to participate in the work before us even though we are not required to see it through to its completion. Some among us may question this advice, arguing that serious involvement requires staying the course. Certainly such an attitude is needed for short-term endeavors. However, for long-term enterprises such a perspective provides a ready excuse for many people not to get involved. But this teaching doesn't let us justify remaining on the sidelines. It correctly recognizes that our efforts are valuable even though others will succeed us and add their own contribution to what we have already done. It wisely reminds us that some undertakings require the participation of many individuals who will contribute as the tasks unfold. Think of how many worthy projects have been started by one group and continued by others. In fact, we should feel pleased when others continue our work, for their activity speaks to the power and worthiness of our vision. LF

Bodies, Selves

3 MARCH

*You will be for me a community of priests
and a holy nation.*
EXODUS 19:6

Judaism extols the body that has been given to us like priestly garb, "for glory and for beauty." It does not have the made-up beauty of the marketplace, but beauty shaped by labor and by love.

Our bodies are a genuine expression of who we really are. A worker's gnarled knuckles can be beautiful; wrinkles are not ugly; hair that is thinned or streaked with gray is no disgrace. These are the badges of aging. They speak to us of the ordinary heroism of ordinary people who show up for life each day, who help a neighbor, who do an honest job, who spend a quiet evening at home.

The Rabbis so revered the real body of real people that they imbued it with the sanctity that typified priestly vestments. They prohibited tattoos, for instance, and banned self-laceration. They forbade autopsies, teaching that even a corpse should be treated with dignity, washed clean and laid gently to its eternal earthly rest.

We follow all these rules because bodies are the priestly garb for all of us, since we are made in God's image. Our bodies are given "for glory and for beauty"—not the glory of eternal youth or the beauty of the sexy look, but the genuine luster that tells the tale of our lives, our work, our joys, and our struggles, and which becomes more beautiful with every passing day.　　　　　　RABBI LAWRENCE HOFFMAN

Speaking with Silence

4 MARCH

The less you speak, the less you err.
SOLOMON IBN GABIROL[2]

Many of us feel that we always have to have a ready answer to a question, the right solution to a problem. Perhaps this has come about because of the way we were raised. We sought and received answers from our parents and feel that we have to do the same for our children. Perhaps it is the influence of the information age. We naively believe that the answer to every question is available electronically on the computer. When we don't have the answers, we feel we have failed. We think that our children will be disappointed or our teachers or our colleagues will be displeased or let down. Some of us cover up by trying to talk our way through things. We think that if we *seem* to know what we are talking about, then maybe others will believe that we, in fact, do.

Take the opportunity today to try a different approach. Wait for others to talk. Let someone else attempt to solve a problem. Reflect before you speak. You may be surprised at what you hear. Remember, God was heard in the silence at Sinai and not in the noise that surrounded the mountain. KO

The Connection Between Study and Action

5 MARCH

One who devotes oneself to the study of the Torah but neglects the service of God is like a bookcase filled with good books. The bookcase stands by itself and the books stand by themselves, entirely without connection. A zealous reader is required.

RABBI SIMCHA BUNEM[3]

To what degree do we make connections between what we study and learn and how we act? Today we can gain access to tremendous amounts of information electronically, but how often do we make connections between all this information and the world we live in? Jewish teachings stress the need to take our learning out into the world. We need to anchor all that we learn in action that will contribute toward mending our world. It is never enough to keep our learning and knowledge to ourselves and not manifest it in good deeds. How easy for us to create superficial distinctions between book knowledge and actions. We have all known people who are learned but don't treat others kindly or use their gifts to create a more whole, loving world. Let us dedicate ourselves today to being active readers who search for ways to translate knowledge into *mitzvot*.   LF

Physical Safety and
Spiritual Wholeness

6 MARCH

*When I have gathered the house of Israel from the peoples
among which they have been dispersed . . . they shall settle
on their own soil . . . and they shall dwell on it in security.
They shall build houses and plant vineyards . . . and they
shall know that I* Adonai *am their God.*
EZEKIEL 28:25–26

The prophet Ezekiel describes the vision of the gathering of
the exiles following the Babylonian destruction of Jerusalem
as a two-stage process. First the people of Israel will experience physical redemption: They will "settle on their own soil
. . . in security . . . [and] build houses and vineyards."
Second, they will experience spiritual redemption: They will
"know that I *Adonai* am their God."

This two-stage process is also found in the story of the
Exodus, which we know from Passover. Then God said, "I
will free you from the labors of the Egyptians and deliver you
from the house of bondage . . . and I will take you to be My
people and I will be your God" (Exodus 6:6–7). Here physical safety preceded spiritual understanding and fulfillment,
and bodily and economic well-being were critical prerequisites to spiritual wholeness.

Our tradition recognizes the powerful need for human
beings to achieve physical dignity and self-esteem before they
can stand upright and complete before God. God does not
desire a weak and vulnerable people, but a strong and independent people who recognize the inherent sacredness of the
resources with which they have been blessed, and who will

use those resources to help build a world that reflects the presence and perfection of God.

As Abraham Joshua Heschel once said, "In our relation to the immediate, we touch upon the most distant. Even the satisfaction of physical needs can be a sacred act. Perhaps the most essential message of Judaism is that in doing the finite we may perceive the infinite."　　　RABBI ADINA LEWITTES[4]

Honest Speech

7 MARCH

*Do not speak one thing with the mouth
and another with the heart.*
TALMUD[5]

Some people say that we are what we eat. Judaism spins this idea a little differently. To the Rabbis, we are what we say. And what we say is very important. Words are among our most powerful tools. According to the Torah, the world was created with words spoken by God, the Holy One of Blessing. We all know the powerful effect that words can have on us, whether they be kind words or harsh words. Reading the Torah's discussion on leprosy, the Rabbis suggest that leprosy is really an acronym in Hebrew for evil speech and that speaking disparagingly about others and engaging in gossip is like leprosy.

In the quote above from the Talmud, we are being offered some simple advice: Say what you mean and mean what you say. This is the best way to secure a relationship between others and with yourself.　　　KO

Our Teachers

8 MARCH

A roving commission of rabbis was sent to encourage education and to establish schools. They came to a town where there was no school or teacher. They asked the residents of the town to produce the town's guardians. The heads of the municipality appeared. "These are not the guardians of the city," the rabbis exclaimed. "Who are they then?" the citizens asked. "The guardians of the town are the teachers."

TALMUD[6]

Unfortunately, society today does not value teachers. Once parents were proud if their sons or daughters entered the teaching profession. Today, instead of respecting those who dedicate themselves to opening the minds of our children, we often criticize them and put more and more responsibility on their already overburdened shoulders. Shame on us.

Judaism views teachers as essential to the vitality of a community. Without teachers, how would the future be guaranteed? How would Judaism be transmitted? As parents, we need teachers to be our partners in raising competent, curious, responsible adults. Neither parents nor teachers can do this alone. If you have children in school, show your appreciation for their teachers. They need to know their efforts are appreciated.   LF

Dealing with Fear on the Journey

9 MARCH

There is no hope unmingled with fear, and no fear unmingled with hope.

BARUCH SPINOZA[7]

Dealing with fear, not acquisition of knowledge, is the first step toward becoming a Jewishly knowledgeable soul. Our holy texts have much to say about fear and how it prevents us from entering any Promised Land toward which we journey. The Torah (in Numbers 13:1–33) tells the story of the twelve scouts sent ahead to assess the Promised Land for the Israelites still in the wilderness. Two scouts reported that the land was a place of great bounty and that the Hebrew people could easily vanquish the hostile people who lived there. But the other ten spies said, "The enemies there looked like giants and we looked like grasshoppers to them and to ourselves" (Numbers 13:33). They let their fear overcome their hope.

This story may be understood metaphorically. Each of us has a Promised Land: A state of being characterized by fulfillment, generosity, piety, and enlightenment. Too often, however, we fail to reach this state because we feel inadequate. In short, we are afraid. "Someone else is smarter," we say. Or "Someone else is prettier, or stronger, and I can't do this thing that fills me with holy joy because everyone else thinks success means X when my soul tells me that for me 'success' will stem from Y and I can't do something so unusual." We will not enter our own Promised Land until we stop seeing ourselves as inadequate. Seeing ourselves as important, as being made in God's image, means honoring the image of God that resides in us and in all human beings. Today let us commit ourselves to seeing ourselves as the giants we can become.

RABBI JUDITH ABRAMS

Timeliness

10 MARCH

Who ignores the time walks in darkness, and who explores it is illumined by a great light.

MOSES IBN EZRA[8]

About this time of year I find myself wanting time to move more quickly. There is not a lot to celebrate in either the secular calendar or the Jewish calendar right about now. So we especially look forward to Purim and all its silliness. It feels like winter is almost over but spring has not quite begun. There are no flowers yet, just the beginning of the bulbs poking their way through the defrosting earth. And just when we think that winter had ended, snow flurries might remind us that there are still a few weeks left.

But we can't push time forward. Nor should we. For when we do, we are pushed back—in a reminder that we are not in charge, that the passage of time brings us closer to our own mortality. So instead of waiting for time to pass us by or even trying to push it forward, we instead can take cognizance of these moments and let them carry their blessings with us along the way.

KO

Wise Charitable Giving

11 MARCH

Rabbi Yonah said: The verse doesn't say "Happy are those who give to the poor," but rather, "Happy are the ones who use their insight when giving to the poor" (Psalm 41:2). This means that one should use all their faculties when considering how to do the mitzvah of tzedakah.

TALMUD[9]

Many of us return home each day to a pile of mail containing appeals for *tzedakah* contributions. These pleas for donations most likely come from many kinds of organizations. Hospitals, synagogues, educational institutions, *tzedakah* collectives, social service agencies, and cultural institutions all depend on our generosity. How do we make wise decisions regarding where to send our contributions? If we take the obligation of giving *tzedakah* seriously, then we need to learn about what needs our donations will alleviate. In some situations we can creatively combine our resources with those of friends and family to fund a project that would have been beyond our means.

These mail solicitations are also an opportunity to help our children learn about *tzedakah* and become informed donors. Each month we can have them choose one organization's materials to read and we can engage them in a discussion about these organizations' goals. Then, as a family, we can decide where to give our *tzedakah* contributions.

Be thoughtful, curious, and creative when you make your *tzedakah* contributions. Do give and be generous. The Rabbis teach that ten percent of our earnings is an adequate amount to donate. For some of us, that may be a significant amount of money. So, let us commit ourselves to giving a *tzedakah* of ten percent each year—and giving in an informed way.   LF

Overcoming Alienation through Our Story

12 MARCH

There is no one today who is not alienated, or who does not contain within himself some small fraction of alienation.
FRANZ ROSENZWEIG

In an age when Jews are concerned about "continuity," what is striking is that our story begins with discontinuity. To fulfill God's command, Abraham must break with his father's house. Continuity represents our concern for the future, but the role model for many of us is Abraham. For some of us, our Jewishness too began by a breaking with our past, with our parents' homes. We too felt summoned by God to set out for a new land which God would in time show us.

Philosopher/theologian Franz Rosenzweig is another, more recent model for many of us because, like Abraham, he too had to break with his past to become a committed Jew. He was on the threshold of conversion to Christianity when he discovered Judaism. Rosenzweig emphasizes that this sense of alienation between continuity and discontinuity should not be disparaged, for not only can we never totally break with our past, but we shouldn't even want to. Continuity is important, but in telling our personal Jewish stories, we should remember that these stories must cover the totality of our life experience, including the experiences of alienation. They too make us who we are.   RABBI NEIL GILLMAN

Ordering the Universe

13 MARCH

*A person should first put one's house together,
then one's town, then the world.*
RABBI ISRAEL SALANTER

In the mid-1880s in Lithuania, Rabbi Salanter was the founder of the *musar* movement, a school of thought that focused on personal piety and ethical behavior, on the behavior of the individual as a lens on the larger world. He knew that if we concerned ourselves with our own behavior, then we would not have to worry so much about the rest of the world. This philosophy may seem counterintuitive to the passionate idealism of youth that once set out to conquer the world. But that is the profound insight of spiritual logic: It persuades us in ways we least expect.

What does it take to "put one's house together"? Kind words, unconditional love, nurturing guidance. These are certainly a start. But Rabbi Salanter expects more from us. He wants us to start by working on our own flaws, focusing on our own shortcomings, and constantly striving to improve our essential selves. We don't have to wait until Yom Kippur, the traditional day when we focus on repentance and address our misdeeds, to start the process. It is far too important to tarry. Make a conscious effort today, to change one thing. The rest will follow—and so will others around you.   KO

No Knowledge

14 MARCH

*What is the greatness of a great person? That person is not
ashamed to say "I don't know."*
TALMUD[10]

Today this might seem like a truism. We hear it in professional training sessions and teach our children that it is okay
to say, "I don't know." In this ancient Jewish source, which
dates approximately from the fourth century, it is taught not
as a communication technique but as a religious principle.
Being able to admit that at times we just don't know speaks
to a person's character. No one knows everything, especially
in this age of information overload. Even so, admitting so is
not easy. We often stumble on this simple truth. Too often we
think we must know it all and feel embarrassed if we do not.
However, when we are able to see the limitations of our
knowledge, then we can see ourselves in a clear way. For only
God, the Source of All, can truly know all. We can only grasp
at partial refractions of knowledge and wisdom and do our
best to represent what we know and what we don't. When
we are at a loss, that lack does not expose us, but rather
reminds us of our humanity. Let us not try to "know it all"
but rather have the humility to acknowledge that at times we
must say, "I don't know." LF

Love Is Blind

15 MARCH

*I remember for you the devotion of your youth,
your love as a bride; how you followed me in the
wilderness, in a land not sown.*
JEREMIAH 2:2

There is a popular saying: "Love is blind." What do people mean by that?

Some people might mean by it that those who are in love often ignore their lover's faults, not in a kind and generous way, but naively. For example, love might lead someone to overlook the fact that a lover exploits or manipulates him or her, or has a terrible and abusive temper, or engages in morally questionable behavior. Someone's love for a partner makes the person blind to these serious character flaws.

But others use the expression far more lightly, indeed in a good-hearted and kind manner. For example, love might lead us to overlook a physical condition of our partner. Tall or short, large or thin, love often blinds us to these matters in favor of the deeper spiritual connection between two people.

Or a relationship may be fraught with obstacles and challenges: geographical distance, conflicting religious or lifestyle priorities, financial hardships, and others. Many partners might think twice about whether the relationship is worth pursuing. Others, however, may have such a deep love for each other that they cannot perceive any issue as a challenge: They refuse to conceive of the possibility of failure.

It is this last use of the phrase "Love is blind" that I think the prophet Jeremiah had in mind when he spoke these words of God to the people of Israel: "I remember for you the devotion of your youth, your love as a bride; how you followed me in the wilderness, in a land not sown."

Israel's love for God was blinded to the real uncertainties and dangers that lay before them. They had trust and confidence in God. This is true of any love that is unconditionally offered, love that can withstand pain and suffering, love that reveals the *tzelem Elohim,* the image of God, that is inherent in each partner.

This is the love we strive for with both the Creator and with all of creation.   RABBI ADINA LEWITTES[11]

The Greening of North America

16 MARCH

It is forbidden to live in a town that does not have a green garden.
TALMUD[12]

This sounds like something that could have been written by any city dweller who longs to be surrounded by the beauty of nature. But what were the Rabbis getting at? Maybe they were joking. Or maybe they had been cooped up in their academies for too long. Perhaps the Talmud was harkening back to the agricultural period of our people, remnants of which we frequently find in the Jewish calendar.

I see it this way: Nature is one means by which we can readily experience God's handiwork in the world. In a garden we can watch the cycle of nature. We can see plants reemerge after a dormant winter. We nurture seeds and watch them grow and flower. We are inspired by nature and awed by its Creator. Each time we see a bulb breaking through the soil, struggling against the remainder of winter, pushing its roots deeply into the soil and reaching out to bless the world with its beauty, we must remember its Source and our own.   KO

Eating As Contemplation

17 MARCH

The most important discipline of Judaism involves the blessing. When a blessing is recited before eating, the act itself becomes a spiritual undertaking. Through the blessing, the act of eating becomes a contemplative exercise.

RABBI ARYEH KAPLAN[13]

Our culture has perfected the eat-and-run meal. We spend little time chewing and tasting our food; we eat hurriedly in order to move on to the next meeting or the next task. What would it be like to slow down and eat an entire meal as a contemplative exercise? First we would offer a blessing of thanksgiving to express our gratitude for having food. We often take for granted the food we eat. But think of how many people are involved in getting food to our tables. First the food is grown, harvested, packaged, distributed, and then cooked. There are so many steps along the way that we do not think about the complexity of the process. We are removed from it and seldom do we reflect on our privilege. So many millions of hungry people around the world spend much of their days in the pursuit of food. By offering a blessing we remind ourselves not to be inured to the gift of food.

By pausing before eating and reciting a blessing (whether we say the traditional Hebrew blessing, *Barukh atah Adonai Eloheinu Melekh Haolom hamotzei lechem min ha-aretz,*

"Praised are You, Adonai, our God, Sovereign of the Universe, for bringing bread from the earth," or an alternative prayer), we can quiet our mind and pay attention to the act of eating itself. As we eat, we don't read, talk, or watch television. We just eat and pay attention to the smell and texture and taste of the food.

Try eating once a day in this contemplative manner and see the results.

LF

Moving Forward, Leaving Behind

18 MARCH

God buried him (Moses) in the valley of the land of Moab, opposite Bet Peor and no one knows the site of his burial place until this day.
DEUTERONOMY 34:6

In our yearly cycle of reading the Torah, a week after it tells us that Moses has died, Purim is celebrated. Esther, the heroine of the story, we read at this time, at first hides her Jewish identity. In fact, her name actually means "hidden." In addition, God is not mentioned at all in this *megillah*, the Book of Esther we read on Purim. Finally, on Purim, we hide our faces by wearing masks. Similarly, Moses is never mentioned in the Haggadah, the story of our liberation, nor is his burial place known. Esther hides. Moses is hidden. And at times we hide ourselves. We need to ask ourselves: What is going on here?

One of the most profound messages of Judaism is that life is more than what it appears to be. We need to go deeper to uncover that which is hidden, to participate, as Rabbi Arthur Green has taught, in the drama of the hidden and the revealed. This dance between the hidden and the revealed is part of the ongoing cycles of the world and the entire universe.

If Purim is about putting our masks on and hiding, then Passover, our redemption from exile and from each other, is about when we take off our masks and reveal ourselves to ourselves and to the world around us. The search for *chametz,* leavened products which we don't eat during Passover, has begun. It might be hidden in the corners of our closets, underneath our tables, in our pockets, in our hearts. Clinging to the corners of our soul, it waits to be revealed and released. The lesson is that only when we take off our masks and get rid of the *chametz* will we be able to stop hiding from each other and truly be able to see each another.

This dance of the hidden and the revealed comes together when the *afikoman* is hidden at the beginning of the seder. It is found only near the end of the seder. Then, at the second seder, we begin the countdown to Shavuot, a time when we celebrate receiving the Torah from God. For God's exile to end, for Revelation to take place, we have to stop hiding from one another.   RABBI MICHAEL M. COHEN

Finding the Essential Self

19 MARCH

If there is any miracle in the world, any mystery,
it is individuality.
RABBI LEO BAECK[14]

Rare is the person who discovers their essential self during childhood or adolescence and carries that sense of self into adulthood. Most of us spend a good part of our formative years trying to discover our unique gifts and gain confidence in them, and then apply those skills to our chosen field of work. Some of us discover our special skills in volunteer work or the way we relate to others in more informal settings. We may change majors in college, or select several different career choices, or even change careers—often to the chagrin of our family—in the middle of what appears to be a successful career.

I often think about what Rabbi Baeck taught as I have sought to discover what I have to offer my community. What amazes me is not that God has been able to create me uniquely. Rather it is that God has created all of us that way. That is what remains a mystery to me. And perhaps to all of us. KO

Strengthening Connections

20 MARCH

The opposite of love is not hate but indifference;
the opposite of life is not death but insensitivity.
ELIE WIESEL[15]

Unfortunately, we don't have to look far to find insensitivity in our world. Common courtesy, what our tradition calls *derekh eretz,* is lacking. Some people seem to act out of meanness and spite. Others have just developed bad social habits, which seem to have seeped into North American culture. All too often we even think such behavior is funny and assume a standoffish attitude. Note at how many successful television sit-coms have characters with uncaring, indifferent attitudes toward other people. Yet as Jews, we are taught to care, to take a stand, and to fight the apathy of indifference. We are also taught to act out of compassion and to guard against the hardness of heart which leads to insensitivity.

Each of us can turn the tide if we embrace love and life and rebuke those who choose indifference and insensitivity as acceptable values. For in truth, the latter lead to inner emptiness and social disconnection. Instead, let us strengthen our connection with ourselves and with others. Stand up and speak out against indifference and insensitivity. You'll be glad you did.   LF

Being Partners with God

21 MARCH

A person does with one's hands: The Holy One blesses the work of one's hands.
MIDRASH[16]

Rabbi Abraham Joshua Heschel once wrote a book called *God in Search of Man.* The title itself speaks volumes about the dance of relationship between the Divine and the human person.

Surely this is a relationship of imbalance and inequality. God is all powerful, all knowing, infinite, awesome. And we humans are flawed yet endowed with a spark of the divine, finite yet overflowing with potential. We long to experience holiness and connection but must make do with occasional glimmers of spiritual encounter, for this God is invisible. As Heschel and the mystics would have it, God also aches for partnership but cannot consummate the partnership, for God has no body. We need God and God needs us; we yearn for each other.

What are You to do if You are the Creator, the Supreme Power, the Source of Life, the Wellspring of Compassion? How does an invisible, incorporeal Divinity work in the world? In some awesome and mysterious way, God can do the "big stuff" without having a body: God somehow "speaks" and performs grand acts of creation and revelation. But what about the day-to-day acts of creation and redemption? How does God bring joy to a lonely person, offer comfort to someone in pain, build loving relationships, inspire healing and reconciliation, create community? For such acts as these, a body is needed: human hands to create, arms to embrace, a human voice that can be unmistakably heard. For the ongoing work of perfecting the world, God needs us.

Perhaps God blesses us both before and after our Godlike actions in the world, just as we recite a blessing before and after eating, or before and after reading Torah. Before we act, God opens our eyes to see what needs to be done, awakens in us the desire to act, inspires us with courage, fills us with strength, so that we will be moved to do divine work in the world, as surely as if God had whispered in our ear or written our instructions in the sky. In some mysterious way, we receive the blessing, and we act. And then God blesses us again—with well-being and satisfaction, with gratitude and fullness, readying us for our next task of acting as God's partner on earth.

We have to "listen" very carefully to hear and feel these blessings. But they are "recited" every day that we do God's work in the world. RABBI AMY EILBERG

Cleaning Off the Mud

22 MARCH

If you want to help pull a friend out of the mud,
don't hesitate to get a little dirty.
BAAL SHEM TOV

Like so many of the baby boomer generation, I have become enamored by the spiritual insight of the Hasidic rebbes. The Baal Shem Tov, the founder of Hasidim, sought to understand the world through the simplicity of everyday living. He saw clearly as a young teacher what many of us have struggled a lifetime to learn: We have to reach beyond the self in order to touch another. Only if we are willing to do so—and willing to risk getting dirty in the process—can we really help someone in need. In doing so, we also help ourselves. That's the baffling part of the way the spiritual method works.

While we sometimes write off the ancient priests and their peculiar sacrificial system, they understood the process fully. As they went about their work in the ancient Temple in Jerusalem, the only way to help another person get rid of his or her ritual impurity was to become one with them and take on that impurity himself. That ancient process brought cleansing to the other and to the self.

So don't be afraid to get mud on yourself. You can always wash it off.   KO

Inspiring Friends

23 MARCH

*What is a person like? Like someone who goes into
a perfume maker's shop. Even though they did
not take anything or give anything; nevertheless
they took out with them a wonderful scent.
So, too, anyone who walks with the righteous—
takes with them some of their good ways and deeds.*

MIDRASH[17]

We often tell our children to choose their friends wisely, since we know that they are greatly influenced by their friends and easily pick up ways of speaking and acting and thinking from them. Therefore, we steer them to pick friends who share our values.

We can also apply this advice to ourselves. Who are *our* friends? How do they influence us? Are our friends critical or supportive? Are they available when we need them? At times we may have to limit our relationships with others who have a negative influence on us. Especially if we are trying to rid ourselves of an addiction such as drinking or smoking, we may have to separate ourselves from those who pull us back to these destructive patterns. Doing this is never easy. Yet we can find friends and mentors who inspire us with their integrity and wisdom. In this way we can acquire new ways to think and respond to life's events. Which of your friends inspire you today?   LF

The Merit of Women

24 MARCH

*It is because of the merit of the women that
God freed us from bondage.*

TALMUD[18]

The time between Purim and Passover is anticipatory, designed in various ways to heighten expectation. When I was
growing up, conversation about Passover food shopping and
cleaning began at Purim. My grandmother, until her last
days, *schlepped* cartons of Pesach dishes up from the base-
ment and assigned us all our Passover duties.

The seder is, of course, the main event. But often it is the
behind-the-scenes work which we are likely to take for
granted that makes the event feel important. The cliché tells
us that God is in the details. At no season is that more apparent than in the spring, and Passover is the holiday of the
spring. All of which is to say that God and grandmothers have
a good deal in common. Their work is often done so reliably
that unless we pause to take notice we might forget to appreciate the greatness in the details. If we have been lucky in our
lives, we have found comfort in an infinity of detailed loving
attentions, from mittens to hot lunches, blessings that are
blessings precisely because they were given naturally and
unconditionally.

I like to think of the weeks between Purim and Passover as
the time of Miriam, who was Moses' sister. Behind the central
liberation myth of our people is the story of the bravery of a
slave mother and her daughter, and an Egyptian princess who
was moved by the sight of a slave baby in a basket. At an even
earlier moment, we are told that although the Pharaoh
ordered midwives to ensure that there would be no male

babies, Shifra and Puah, the Hebrew midwives, defied these orders and bravely did their work.

In these small ways the Passover story recognizes the significance of women's work and courage. By saying that it is because of the merit of women that our people were freed, our tradition suggests the great value of the work behind the scenes and the importance of details in Jewish life and community. Passover especially invites us to take notice of every crumb. Such attention makes us mindful of—and grateful for—not only the grand miracles of liberation, but also the small miracles of our everyday lives. LORI LEFKOVITZ[19]

The Price of Pain

25 MARCH

If you want life, expect pain.
MIDRASH[20]

To avoid pain, many of us avoid taking risks. We are afraid of rejection. We are worried about failure. And we dread losing public face. When we are afraid of rejection, for example, we may be hesitant to express love to another. So we retreat into the comfortable rhythm of our daily lives. We hide behind the masks we create so that others will see only the parts of us that we choose to reveal. It is a natural human tendency to act this way. But if we follow that path, life gets stale—and so do we. Sometimes our complacency grows to crisis proportions without our even realizing it. But we are obligated to take the risk, even when there seems to be no need to do so. Those of us in loving relationships understand this point. Those who invest in business also understand it. The bigger the risk—financial or emotional—the greater the potential reward. Death of the spirit is the ultimate price we pay for not taking the risk.

So what do we do? Simply put, we go out and take hold of the world around us. It is the only choice worth living for.

KO

What is Asked of Us?

26 March

This is what the Holy One said to Israel: "My children, have I deprived you in any way? What do I want from you? I only ask that you should love each other and treat one another with dignity and stand in awe of each other."

Midrash[21]

It seems that no matter how long we live, this teaching will always be necessary. Just why is it so hard to love others, to treat others with dignity, to be in awe of another human being? Perhaps because we live in a highly competitive economy where respecting others does not always enhance profits. Perhaps because we live in a fast-paced society where we rush from one appointment to the next and the simple pleasantries of human interaction seem too time consuming. The Rabbis have a long discussion in the Talmud in which they struggle with how to formulate the 613 *mitzvot* succinctly. In other words, how can the essence of the Torah be simply stated? In their discussion, the Rabbis refer to this famous verse from the book of Micah: "God has told you what is good and what God requires of you: Only do justice, love goodness and walk modestly with your God."

The Rabbis teach, in many ways, that we are to treat others lovingly, that we should treat them as we ourselves would want to be treated. Not only is this precept a central teaching of Judaism, but a most difficult one to do consistently and well, since we are all complex beings with different traits, gifts, and approaches to life. Let us be in awe of the richness inherent in each person as we go about our work today and interact with colleagues, friends, and family members.   LF

The Spiritual Power of Charitable Giving

27 MARCH

Tzedakah *delivers from death.*
PROVERBS 10:2

How many of us believe this literally? Judaism does believe that giving charity works to help not only those in need, but also those who give on a spiritual level. The reason, I suggest, is that we can control the energy that comes to us by putting out the sort of energy we would like to receive. In rabbinic literature, this concept is called *midah k'neged midah,* literally, "measure for measure." If you would like positive, generous energy to come back to you, send out positive, charitable energy through giving *tzedakah* and caring for others. In essence, by giving *tzedakah,* we extend ourselves beyond our own fear of mortality and affirm life by helping those who need our help.

This concept is best seen in a story about the Israelites' exodus from Egypt. The Israelites stood before the Red Sea, whining, while the Egyptians were rapidly closing in on them from behind. Finally, a man named Nachshon ben Amminadav jumped into the sea. It was only then that the sea parted (Babylonian Talmud, *Sotah* 37a). God wants a mature relationship with each individual. That means that God will not participate in infantilizing behavior. Like Nachshon, we must do what we can do to show God that we will put out energy;

that we are not afraid. Then God will become our partner in all that we do. And having God as a partner is a wonderful thing! I do not advocate that we abandon fear altogether. Fear can be a source of strength, but if we allow it to control our every move and emotion, it will destroy us and those around us. Just as a broken bone grows back stronger where the injury occurred, so pain and fear can give us strength once we survive the acute phase of trauma.

In Rabbi Adin Steinsaltz's summary of Jewish mysticism, he outlines the way we can progress from fear to strength. How can we do this? By seeing that we are on an upwardly spiral staircase and must focus only on the step just above us. If we look at the length of the journey yet to go, we'll give up and tumble back to the bottom of the staircase. One step at a time. One mitzvah at a time. One act of *tzedakah* at a time. This is how we can elevate ourselves.

The sea is before us—whether it be Nachshon's Red Sea or the sea of our uncharted hopes and dreams. But perhaps the threat in the water is a mirage that we have created. Perhaps, when you dip your foot in, you will find dry land and a smooth path toward dreams that once seemed terribly distant. May we all reach our own Promised Land!

RABBI JUDITH ABRAMS

The Still Small Voice Within

28 MARCH

Quietness and confidence shall be your strength.
ISAIAH 30:15

Usually we think of strong persons as those who go out with brute strength to conquer the challenges they face. Even if they have already faced defeat, they still raise themselves up to meet new challenges. Sometimes doing so means reaching inside themselves to find the strength necessary to face the burdens of daily living. But we too readily overlook other people: the quiet ones, the ones from whom we hear little or, if we hear anything, we hear it softly or tentatively. These people seem to go about their lives in more mysterious ways. Perhaps it is mysterious because it is different from the way some of the rest of us operate in the world. Yet these people are somehow able to exude a certain quiet confidence, the kind that comes with little fanfare or recognition. I am convinced that they are really the strongest among us. The prophet Isaiah understood this truth and acknowledged it. Somehow we must do the same.

Ecclesiastes said it another way. He wrote, "The race is not to the swift nor the battle to the strong" (Ecclesiastes 9:11).

KO

Knowledge and Understanding

29 March

Without understanding, there is no knowledge;
without knowledge, there is no understanding.
MISHNAH[22]

This *mishnah* teaches that understanding and knowledge go hand in hand. In Hebrew, the word for understanding is *binah* and the word for knowledge is *da'at*. In some Kabbalistic systems these qualities are included among the upper *sefirot,* the Divine emanations. *Da'at* refers to intellectual knowledge, while *binah* refers to the awareness we acquire through personal experience.

Each of us has a preferred way of acquiring mastery of a subject. Some of us may spend hours reading and researching it; others may throw themselves into a new situation so they can directly experience it. A good example is someone who has a new-found interest in learning about Judaism. One may read book after book and never set foot into a synagogue. Another may go to services regularly but never open a book. Both of these ways are deficient. To gain a full picture, we must join together intellectual exploration with firsthand experience. Then and only then can we truly integrate new learning. Keeping qualities in balance is an ongoing spiritual dilemma.   LF

The Sounds of Silence

30 MARCH

If speech is silver, silence is gold.
MOSES IBN EZRA

We encounter Elijah several times throughout the Jewish year: At the end of each Sabbath, at Passover, at ritual circumcisions. But who was Elijah? Queen Jezebel decreed that Elijah would die because he had destroyed the prophets of Baal. So he fled into the wilderness and hid in a cave. When God asked Elijah, "Why are you here?" he responded plaintively, "I alone am left, and they are out to take my life."

God then passes by Elijah. What follows is one of the most celebrated of biblical texts. First Elijah experienced a mighty wind—but God was not in the wind. He then experienced an earthquake, and then a fire—but God was in neither of these. Finally Elijah heard what is usually translated as "a still, small voice." With this, Elijah emerged from the cave, and God ordered him to return to where he came from.

What did Elijah hear? Undoubtedly a sound—clearly not a very loud sound, but a sound nevertheless. What did the sound/voice say? Nothing that we are told about; there were no words to the sound. God's command that Elijah return to society followed the sound but was not identical with it.

Elijah may have heard what we, in the words of a popular song, might call "the sounds of silence." God was in the silence. We hear silence all the time, and in many instances that silence is as important as the sounds. In music, for example, the gaps between the notes are intrinsic to the melody. Every composer knows how to structure the silences so as to contribute to the cumulative effect of the score.

We are uncomfortable with silence. I experience feeling this all the time in my teaching when I make a particularly controversial point, or pose an unexpected question, and I am greeted with a wall of silence from the class. I have learned to accept that silence and let it be. It generates tension within me, and I feel the urge to fill the silence with words. But I work hard to resist that impulse. Silence and tension can be enormously creative.

We experience God's presence in many different ways and at many different moments. Sometimes God is closest to us in our moments of silent contemplation. Let us let them in.

RABBI NEIL GILLMAN

Blessing Others through the Self

31 MARCH

First become a blessing to yourself so that you may become a blessing to others.

RABBI SAMSON RAPHAEL HIRSCH

What do we do if we want to follow Rabbi Hirsch's suggestion but don't know how? The answer seems to be contained in the question itself. Too often, the "I" of self gets in the way. That's what Jacob was trying to teach us when, according to the book of Genesis, he dreamed one night of angels going up and down on a ladder. He arose, awed by the experience, and proclaimed, "God was in this place and I, I did not know." Jacob's "I" was occupying his life to such an extent that he could not be cognizant of the presence of God.

Most of us look forward to such peak experiences and are disappointed when they do not come. What seems to get in the way of these is the self. Jacob discovered that it got in his way also. We might even say that it is what prevents a routine experience from potentially being transformed and raising us heavenward.

How do we make sure that we don't get in our own way? There are no easy answers, but here is one to think about. Consider how you might go about providing blessing for another person. What might you do? What would you say? Bearing that in mind, do the same thing for yourself. KO

APRIL

Foolish Acts

1 April

To the wise person, a hint. To the fool, a fist.
MIDRASH[1]

According to the way most people in North America reckon their calendar, this first day of the month is April Fool's Day. It is a day dedicated to making jokes at the expense of others. Given the sensitivity of the times, it's hard to believe that April Fool's Day has stayed on the calendar and remained part of our culture. What would motivate a person to wittingly do others harm, even under the guise of fun? Perhaps it is insecurity, the kind that lurks in everyone's soul. Perhaps it is what the Rabbis call the *yetzer hara,* the evil inclination, the dark side of our personality generally held in check by our goodness and decency. It might even be the remnant of adolescence that lies inside all of us. Maybe we just deceive ourselves into thinking that when someone else looks bad, the rest of us look better. This is not the way to succeed or to live.

Some would argue that the fool is the one who lets tricks be played on him or her. To me, what really makes any person a fool is the inability or unwillingness to see experience through a lens of faith. We think that we are in control of our lives, making all the decisions that direct our destiny. But we are mistaken. The author of Proverbs, whom Jewish tradition says was King Solomon, says that "fools hate knowledge" (Proverbs 1:22) and would prefer to make their way through the world in ignorance. For the author of Proverbs, knowledge is more than the accumulation of facts and figure. It is a basic understanding of the way the world functions. This basic principle is summed up by Rabbi Lawrence Kushner. In his wonderful book *Invisible Lines of Connection,* he teaches us that there are no coincidences in life. Things are connected to one another and thereby are meant to teach us a lesson.

What lesson can you learn today? Maybe the most important one is that none of us gains by harming another person. Anyone who believes otherwise is the true fool.   KO

Lessons for Living

2 APRIL

We derive lessons for conduct of life from men and women whose paths greatly intersect our own, glorified only by their rectitude and purity. If now we find such gems, we dare not let them lie in the dust of ages.

HENRIETTA SZOLD[2]

Who in your life have you most admired and from whom have you drawn inspiration? Perhaps their words, their actions, or the way they dealt with difficult situations gave you hope and courage. These individuals need not be famous; in fact, they rarely are. Fame, fortune, or charisma may or may not be part of a role model's persona. Yet their greatness touches us in a profound way. They provide us with a light to follow as our life unfolds. Have you ever said to yourself, "I want to be like so-and-so"? What are the qualities that drew you to this individual? Have you been able to integrate these into your life?

Remember those who were your role models and how they shaped you. We often forget these important people and their influence. Don't let their impact and contribution to your development be lost with the passage of time.   LF

The Divine Light Within

3 APRIL

A person is the candle of the Holy One.
MIDRASH[3]

Think about the last time you watched a candle—*really* watched a candle. The silent, flickering candle has enormous power. It draws us in, invites our full attention, beckons us to be still.

The candle is endlessly fascinating, constantly changing, yet somehow absolutely constant. Its flame is fragile and it can be easily extinguished. Yet it is also awesomely powerful. It can bring light and warmth. It can also unleash enormous destruction.

The midrash above says that we are God's candle. We too are endlessly fascinating, ever-changing, exquisitely vulnerable, and enormously powerful. We embody a hint of God's power and radiance, yet we can be extinguished in a moment. We can create light and hope and joy, and we can unleash rage and hate. We change moment by moment, and yet some part of us—the divine part—is eternal.

Sometimes it is easy to look into the eyes of another person and see the reflection of the Divine. We can see the light in the eyes of a lover, brimming with passion and tenderness. We can see the twinkle in the eyes of a laughing child. We can see the light go on as a child learns to read or as an adult discovers new possibilities. We can see the inner glow as a friend speaks the truth with deep genuineness. We are warmed by the light as an older person radiates vitality and wisdom.

The midrash invites us to look deeply for the divine light in others and to honor the light within ourselves. If we could see each person as a divine candle—exquisitely beautiful, vulnerable yet powerful, changing yet eternal—perhaps we would treat other people and ourselves with more respect and greater care. Perhaps we would more readily see them as a treasure, a gift, a wonder. Perhaps if we saw each other in this way, we would bring more light to the world.

RABBI AMY EILBERG

A Sacred Routine

4 APRIL

Follow the middle course again and again, until it involves little effort and by repetition becomes a fixed habit.
MOSES MAIMONIDES[4]

Everyone's life is made up of rituals. From the time we rise in the morning, we have a routine that we repeat almost every day. For some of us, the routine is punctuated by religious acts. For others, the force of family obligation shapes our morning routine: We might be the last one in the shower, or we make breakfast for the kids, or we car-pool to work or school. We could even say that daily living is a tapestry of rituals: Generally, we do the same things in nearly the same way most days of our lives.

Rituals provide us with stability. We are reluctant to change them except when we are forced to. They bring us comfort and familiarity; they provide us with dependable mooring in a rocky world. When we are able to incorporate the sacred into our rituals by instilling them with essential religious teachings, then mere routine has the potential to become religious ritual.

At this time of year, Jewish people are getting ready for Passover: We begin preparing the seder, we order special foods, we clean the house. Instead of the quick middle-of-the-night departure that was forced on our ancestors when they left Egypt, our preparation for Passover includes a complex, elaborate set of rituals. Each family has its own way of preparing them. The challenge is to find what level of preparation works for you.

As we prepare to celebrate our Exodus from Egypt, we can also prepare to be transformed by it. For philosophers like Moses Maimonides, the repetition of Passover activity year after year is what turns it into the routine of ritual that relives the Exodus experience. Maimonides argues that the safest and most desirable place for living out that repetition is in the middle, not at the extremes. It is here that moral standards and virtue emerge.

Is the "middle" where you live with your rituals? Or do you live your life on the extreme, where even in the routine of ritual you cannot find anchor? The lesson for this day is clear: Find your mooring with the routine ritual of our people. There you will find stability and strength.   KO

How We Perceive Ourselves

5 APRIL

In my judgment, it is better to be wicked who knows one is wicked, than righteous who knows one is righteous. Worst of all is to be wicked and think one is righteous.

MENACHEM HACOHEN[5]

How do we perceive ourselves, and in what ways do we deny those aspects of ourselves that make us feel uncomfortable? Sometimes we need to ask someone to help us take a reality check about ourselves. Do we think too much of ourselves and err toward grandiosity? Or do we think too little about ourselves and err toward low self-esteem? Spiritual pursuit is about seeing who we really are so we do not hide the good or the bad from ourselves. It is not about denigrating our personal strengths or pretending we have certain qualities.

In the quote above by Menachem Hacohen, a former member of Israel's Knesset, we learn that acknowledging our errors makes us open to change. If we think of ourselves as righteous, we may lose any sense of being humble and deny that we have any deficiencies. Doing this blocks the path of repentance, *teshuvah*. If we are open to acknowledging all the parts of ourselves, then through study, prayer, and loving acts of kindness we can serve our communities and God without any false pretenses.   LF

Rejoice in Righteousness

6 APRIL

When you do rightly—rejoice. But do not proclaim yourself righteous. This was but one moment; in the next you may do differently. When you do wrong—reflect. But do not call yourself evil. This was but one moment; in the next you can do differently.

AFTER ECCLESIASTES 7:13–14[6]

People love to debate whether humans are essentially good or essentially evil. I find those alternatives unacceptable. People are capable of doing both good and evil, so why assume that one is more essential than the other? What difference does this assumption make? If good people can do evil and evil people can do good, I have to be on my toes with other people regardless of what their essential nature is.

Making assumptions about human nature can be dangerous. You must know at least one nasty person who is convinced that people, especially that person in particular, are basically good. I can think of half a dozen people who are convinced that they are righteous and that, by definition, whatever they do is righteous. These are people who preface hurtful statements with "I have to be honest. . . ." Why do you have to be honest? Maybe silence is the better choice here.

When you do good, feel good. When you do bad, feel bad. But don't make the mistake of identifying with either.

RABBI RAMI SHAPIRO

Empirical Truth

7 APRIL

Experience is more forceful than logic.
ISAAC ABRAVANEL[7]

Sometimes I think that it would be easier to have unflagging faith if I had lived at the time of the Exodus from Egypt. After all, according to the Torah and Jewish tradition, the Jewish people frequently experienced the presence of God as they wandered through the desert. I often try to imagine what it must have been like to be released from slavery, cross the Red Sea, and then receive Torah at Sinai. The people felt a palpable, ongoing relationship with God. The ancient Israelites did not have to work at their relationship with God as hard as I feel like I have to. Sometimes I think that it is even beyond my ability to comprehend such an intimate relationship. But during the Passover holiday season, all my apprehension is put to rest. Suddenly it is 1250 B.C.E.—the time of the Exodus—and I am in Egypt with my ancestors.

The Hebrew calendar helps me with a "countdown to revelation," called *sefirat haomer*. Day by day, we count the seven weeks between Passover and the holiday of Shavuot, which celebrates our receiving the Torah on Mount Sinai. In biblical times we counted a measure of the barley harvest each day; this was a method farmers used to determine the proper dates to harvest their spring crop—and then to bring a grain offering to the Temple. This practice may even be the origin of the concept of daylight savings time. Over the years, other aspects of the Jewish experience were superimposed on *sefirat haomer*. By far the most significant to me is the anticipation of receiving the Torah—so I count my way toward it.

With the approach of the holiday of Shavuot in late spring, I am able to renew my relationship with God. And that is indeed worth waiting for.   KO

Keeping Ourselves Open

8 April

Why was the Torah given in the desert? To teach you that if you do not hold yourself as unpossessed as the desert, you do not become worthy of the words of the Torah; and so, as the desert has no end, similarly with the words of Torah; there is no end.

MIDRASH[8]

The Torah was given in the middle of the desert, not in Egypt, the land of our servitude, or in Israel, the land promised to us. No, the Torah was given to us in the expansive desert, a place with no boundaries, only open skies and endless sand as far as the eye could see. Anyone who has ever spent any time in the Sinai desert knows that its geography is both beautiful and overwhelming. It was here, in a place that did not belong to anyone exclusively, that the Torah was given. There were no territorial disputes in this desert. By giving the Torah on this land that had no owner, God was making Torah's wisdom available to all of us, whether or not we were Jewish.

We are also taught to keep ourselves open, just as the desert was open. By making more and more space within ourselves and expanding our preconceived notions of what is possible, we are reminded that we, like the Torah and the desert, have no preset boundaries. Just as Torah's wisdom is bound by neither time nor space, so too can we keep ourselves open to receive new wisdom as it comes to us. If we keep ourselves open to new interpretation and meaning, our lives will be Torah in the making.   LF

The Voice of the Prophet

9 APRIL

Deborah, wife of Lappidot, was a prophet; she led Israel at that time. She used to sit under the Palm of Deborah . . . and the Israelites would come to her for decisions.

JUDGES 4:4–5

Deborah is the only woman we know who functioned as a judge for the early Israelite community. But why, if she was a judge, was she referred to as a prophet? Rabbi David Kimchi, a biblical commentator who lived in Spain in the 1200s, replies that she was called a prophet because she was inspired to grapple with the great questions of the time.

When you think about Kimchi's idea, it makes wonderful sense. Anyone who is engaged in rectifying the troubles and injustices of the present in effect sets the tone for the future. Anyone dedicated to eradicating poverty and oppression is in effect declaring that the direction of life should move toward equality and democracy.

In his book *Halakhic Man,* Rabbi Joseph B. Soloveitchik reflected upon the creative personality of the prophet and deemed it to be the personality human beings must strive to emulate. He wrote, "The power stored up within man is exceedingly great, that is all-encompassing, but all too often it slumbers within and does not bestir itself from its deep sleep. . . . Awake ye slumberers from your sleep. Realize, actualize yourselves, your own potentialities, and go forth to meet your God."

Just as a classical prophet with his or her voice declared the future of communities, so must we, with our commitments and our actions, declare the perfection of the world.

RABBI ADINA LEWITTES[9]

Sharing Experiences

10 APRIL

In every generation a person is obligated to look upon the self as if he or she had been personally delivered from Egypt.

PASSOVER HAGGADAH

This directive comes from the Mishnah, the primary text in Judaism's tradition of oral law. Because it was placed in the Haggadah by the Rabbis, many people are familiar with this verse. It is the core notion of the Passover holiday and provides us with the educational impetus to celebrate the festival. The text teaches a truth that I personally relearn each year as I observe the festival with family and friends: Sharing transcendent experiences brings us closer together.

This idea of reliving any experience each year helps form part of the Jewish community's culture code. Its understanding helps nurture Jewish cultural literacy. Like the beginning of the baseball season for the sports-minded American, which occurs around this same time every year, it is a phenomenon with which the entire community can resonate.

We may not be able to recreate the Passover experience of former generations, but we can create our own.   KO

Enriching Our Lives

11 APRIL

We have a tradition that one is not poor unless they lack knowledge.
TALMUD[10]

When we hear that someone is poor, we most likely think it refers to one's financial status. However, poverty can affect many aspects of our lives, regardless of the state of our wealth. Think of all the areas of life in which you could become impoverished. We can be impoverished socially, culturally, intellectually, emotionally, spiritually, and physically. Without friends, we are poor. Without books and music and art, we are poor. Without intellectual stimulation, we are poor. Without prayer and sacred song, we are poor. It is our responsibility to pay attention to all aspects of our being and not, solely, to our financial state. In this way, we ensure that no aspect of ourselves is diminished.

The talmudic sage Abaye, in whose name the above teaching is recorded, suggests that knowledge is the paramount value. Without it, we are truly poor. To gain knowledge, we must sharpen our curiosity, our skills of exploration, our sense of self-discipline. We must hone our abilities to observe and listen. With knowledge, we can approach our material and spiritual problems from many perspectives so we can find creative solutions to them.

In what area of your life do you feel impoverished? How can you best address this "poverty? Would acquiring more knowledge help? LF

Winning and Losing

12 APRIL

*Measure the loss of the mitzvah against reward,
and the reward of a sin against its loss.*

MISHNAH[11]

Here is a famous teaching from *Pirke Avot.* Do you see anything strange about its structure? As my teacher Rabbi Simon Greenberg once pointed out to me, the structure is not what one would expect: The first phrase about mitzvah mentions the loss first, and the second phrase about sin mentions the reward first. Why?

His answer is that every mitzvah begins with a loss: say a loss of money or of time. And every sin begins with a gain. If this were not so, why would we even commit the sin? So in deciding what action to perform, we must reckon the immediate consequence of gain or loss against the eventual consequence of loss or gain.

Successful living depends in part on the maturity to take the long view. What thrills us now may be a temporary gain weighed against a deeper loss. What feels to be a painful loss might, with the settled perspective of time, be seen to be a marvelous gain. We cannot know for sure, but we should decide by recognizing that each decision changes, even if slightly, the balance of our lives. "Who is wise?" asks another saying in *Pirke Avot.* The answer is: One who foresees the consequences of one's actions. RABBI DAVID WOLPE

Holiness and Morality

13 APRIL

Holiness is the essence of moral perfection.
RABBI KAUFMANN KOHLER[12]

In our age, imperfection seems to be considered a virtue. On talk shows and in autobiographies and newspaper gossip, just about everyone is willing to talk to anyone about anything. I find this is especially true with strangers on airplanes who share intimate stories, disembark at their destination, and usually never see their fellow passenger again.

Unfortunately, while sharing these stories, we may make intimate contact with one another but we do not find a place to make the *teshuvah*, the repentance, that will make things right. Perhaps the social limits have been blurred in the marketplace by so many outrageous best-sellers. Maybe in our efforts to be inclusive and politically correct, we have diluted our moral standards. Behaviors are now acceptable that only a short time ago were not even discussed. It does not have to be this way. Through holiness, any moral standard can be perfected and holiness can become the standard by which morality is measured.

Here is the test that I use: Before I act, I try to ask myself one simple question: Can a blessing be said on taking this action? Only when I am satisfied that I can answer affirmatively do I know that the action I am about to take may be considered holy.

Jewish tradition views the possibility of holiness from three perspectives: In relationship to self, in relationship with others, and in relationship to God. These three are equally important. Why? Because all of us reflect the image of the Divine. As we act, we should be mindful of that Divine reflection so our acts can shine more brightly in the world and make it a holier place in which to live.   KO

Listening

14 April

Each person was given two ears and one tongue so that one may listen more than speak.

HASDAI IBN CRESCAS[13]

Today we realize that listening skills are paramount. Contrary to common lore, listening is important for everyone, not only for those in the "helping" professions. Entrepreneurs must listen to their clients to know what the marketplace will bear, just as doctors must listen to their patients to make a correct diagnosis.

How well do you listen? Can you give someone your full attention without being distracted? Or does your mind easily wander? One exercise we can do to sharpen our listening skills is to listen to someone with a focused mind and without interrupting. Then, we can try to summarize what we have heard and ask for feedback.

Obviously, there are times to talk and times to listen. As Hasdai ibn Crescas suggests, we should listen more than talk. This is an ancient principle which we need to learn and relearn—especially today when talking is so highly valued. The next time you find yourself speaking nonstop, take a break and listen.   LF

On Rebuilding Trust

15 April

God is the Healer of Shattered Hearts

PSALMS 147:3

When trust is shattered, not only is the relationship broken, but the hearts of the individuals involved are shattered. How do we heal? How can we heal?

Many people put their trust in you: partners, children, parents, colleagues. In which of these relationships is trust strong? In which is it weak?

What might you do to strengthen it? Trust does not emerge on its own; it has to be built and rebuilt. As the Psalms teach, "God is the healer of broken hearts." God allows for a shattered world and for a people who are broken and scared. But God also insists on our going forward, continuing with what is whole as well as with what is broken.

We learn this from the incident in the Bible where Moses breaks the first set of tablets that he brings down to the Israelites. These shattered tablets were not discarded. Rather, both the new tablets and the shattered ones were placed in the ark.

Let us hold gently those broken parts of ourselves and others so that healing and renewed trust can be established.

RABBI RACHEL SABATH

The Strength of Self

16 APRIL

Drink waters out of your own cistern and running waters out of your own well.

PROVERBS 5:15

This adage is the kind of thing that you probably learned at some time and forgot as the years crept up on you. Perhaps the teaching was framed in a different metaphor, since we don't think much about collecting waters in cisterns anymore. We simply turn on the tap and water flows. But it was not always so. We once had to dig our own wells and draw water from them ourselves. In the Torah, Isaac learned that he had to redig the well that his father, Abraham, had once dug—it had become plugged up—before he could dig his own. For some reason, water that emerges from our own well tastes the sweetest of all. We may try to approximate the taste today by drinking bottled spring water. Although perhaps fashionable, this just isn't the same.

It is easy to look at the wells that others have dug and be envious. But there is more to this text than simply "be happy with your lot" or "the grass always looks greener on the other side." Rather, this text from Proverbs suggests that we can drink and be satisfied only when we drink from the waters of our own well. No other well will satisfy us.   KO

Finding our Soulmates

17 APRIL

What has God been doing since creation?
Making matches of loved ones, for making matches
is as difficult as dividing the Red Sea.
MIDRASH[14]

As we know from contemporary literature, finding our life mate can be an arduous experience. We hear that men and women come from "different planets," and volumes have been written about our problems in communicating with one another. Judaism believes that everyone has a soulmate, someone with whom to share a life and build a home. In Yiddish, the phrase that expresses the search for one's life partner is "to find one's *beshert*." The Rabbis recognized that finding our mate is so extraordinary that it is a divine task. It is also a time-consuming task that has occupied God since liberating us from slavery! If we have yet to find our life mate and are still searching, the above metaphor can help us be easier on ourselves, for God, it seems, has as much difficulty doing this as we do.

In one sense, we know that our relationships require attention and work. If our communication with our partner falters, our relationship could be at risk. On the other hand, there is something miraculous about these relationships, and the connection between two people can supersede words and definitions. At such moments, we can feel so understood and so loved that we glimpse God's presence in the eyes of those we love and those who love us.   LF

Divine Strength

18 APRIL

God gives strength to the weary.
ISAIAH 40:29

Every morning as we are refreshed from sleep, the prayer-book, quoting Isaiah, reminds us that the Holy One gives strength to the weary. We are reminded that sleep need not be an inert suspension of active life. According to the Mishnah: "In sleep our souls leave behind the wearying boundaries of joy and find their way to the limitless realm of the Divine." As a metaphor, the daily blessing celebrates the renewed strength we may feel as we return from this world of new visions. We may leave behind our cynical weariness and awake ready to see possibilities beyond our restricted vision of the day before.

Isaiah knew that people grow weary. He saw an Israel exhausted by defeat and exile, humbled and humiliated to the edge of despair. If the Holy One of Israel did not care, after all, why should the people of Israel? He perceived that such despair could easily become a paralyzing cynicism, blocking all vision of return, renewal, and repair. And he opened himself to the power of the presence of the Divine word to free the exiled people Israel from their situation.

The Divine world in Isaiah links us to a power whose depths can never be fathomed. It reminds us of the divine force that joins with us when we face the seemingly insurmountable difficulties of transforming the real world into an ideal one. In Isaiah, and in our lives, the Divine voice calls upon us to transcend the cynical alibis and excuses we use to avoid our moral and spiritual responsibilities.

RABBI TSVI BLANCHARD[15]

Wholly Truth

19 April

A half truth is a whole lie.
YIDDISH FOLK SAYING

It seems odd, but apparently there are different perspectives on the truth. You would think that the truth is the truth and that would be the end of it. But that just isn't so in our society. Think about it. Even educators are taught to answer only questions that children ask—and nothing more. We're told that when children want additional information, they will then ask additional questions, since they can focus on only certain amounts of information at a time. But it is the adult in us that wants to tell children what they may not yet be prepared to know. The *whole* truth is for those who, like the youngest child sitting at the Passover seder, "does not know how to ask."

Some people would have us believe that truth is not so simple, that there are many of us who possess truth, and that none of us is the sole purveyor of it. So we are constantly looking for loopholes in life, ways to massage the truth to fit our own perspective on reality. That's where the above Yiddish quote comes in. Like the forthright culture that this language represents, this folk saying is quite clear. So too is the moral message that stands squarely behind it: When we are asked a question, by children or adults, we need to respond fully and *truthfully*. That is our only option. Consider this as a paving stone on the path to the Ultimate Truth, where real knowledge can be found. KO

The Spiritual Path and Our Personal Traits

20 APRIL

If you want to be able to observe the commandments perfectly, you must first sanctify yourself by perfecting your personality; eliminating such traits as pride, jealousy, hatred, and anger. The more you perfect your personality, the higher degree of perfection you will have to be able to have in your observance.

RABBI ELIMELEKH OF LIZENSK[16]

How many of us see our personality traits and our emotions as essentially religious or spiritual? I suspect not many of us do. Before Freud and the rise of psychology, some people used their personality in their spiritual development. People went to rabbis for advice on how to rid themselves of troublesome traits. This practice was especially prominent in the Hasidic world, where disciples would approach their *rebbe* with a written note called a *k'vittel* on which they had scribbled their problem. The *rebbe* in turn would offer spiritual prescriptions to help his followers excise certain qualities from their personalities.

Today many of us recognize the psychological roots of our emotional lives. However, we can also view them through a spiritual lens. For example, we cannot strive to get close to God and still throw temper tantrums. Excessive anger has always been an obstacle to a spiritual life. If we are constantly angry, it is impossible to feel our vulnerability, for we are always on the defense. So too with pride. A swollen ego blocks our ability to be humble and to turn to God in earnest prayer. While we cannot completely rid ourselves of these very human traits, we can become aware when they block our spiritual work and needlessly rule our lives.   LF

Paying Attention to Moments of Transition

21 APRIL

We are touched at night. . . . There are night thoughts and night imaginings. There are certainties of the night that can be shaken by nothing except the coming of the dawn. Fear is a night child. So is faith.
RABBI DAVID WOLPE[17]

The night is a time of transition: The retreating light of day turns into the darkness of the night sky, the alertness of being awake turns to comforting rest and sleep. Each evening we go through this transition, surrendering our watchfulness and inquisitiveness for quiet, vulnerability, and inwardness.

As we let go of one mode of living and embrace another, there is always the possibility that we will fall through the cracks in between. That's why rituals tend to congregate at transitions—at the doorposts of our houses, at the day that ends the week, at the moment before sleep.

Any parent can report that children feel most anxious at night. That is why they develop elaborate bedtime rituals. Without the right stuffed animals in bed, the window opened or shut just so, the right words and songs, many children refuse to sleep. Adults aren't that different. They may lie awake for hours reviewing the day's events or planning for the next day. Few of us can claim never to have experienced anxiety or fear during these hours.

Judaism provides a lovely and simple ritual to ease the soul into sleep. It provides for some structure and repetition while also reminding us that no Jew is ever alone, that we are connected to a web of other Jewish souls across the globe and throughout time, and that we sleep under God's watchful care.

That ritual is the recitation of the *Shema* just prior to sleep. What a lovely way for parents to ease their children's fear before sleep. What a lovely opportunity to assist them in learning to pray to God: By asking God to remember loved ones and friends, or by thanking God for the highlights of the day that just ended.

What a lovely way for adults, too, to end each day reminding ourselves of God's love and the privilege of being Jews.

This prayer is the perfect vehicle to take us to a restful night, to teach our children that they are not alone, to remind us of who we really are. Won't you try reciting the *Shema* tonight: *Shema Yisrael Adonai Eloheinu, Adonai Echad,* Hear O Israel, the Eternal is Our God, the Eternal is One.

RABBI BRADLEY SHAVIT ARTSON

Neighborly Knowledge

22 April

A person does not know what is in his neighbor's heart.
TALMUD[18]

The Talmud teaches us that we can never really know what lives inside another person's heart. I imagine that the Rabbis felt that we have enough trouble discovering what goes on inside our own soul, let alone the soul of another. On the other hand, the Rabbis would certainly agree that true friendship demands a profound level of empathy. One rabbi is even reported to have chided his followers for claiming to love their friends without trying to discover their pain. So we get caught in the middle. We want to understand the anguish of others so that we can provide them with support and comfort, but we recognize that we can never fully understand them. Our only option is to reach inside of ourselves and touch the pain that lies buried in our own souls. Only then might we be able to reach out and touch another.

There is a collective aspect to this teaching as well. On Pesach we are taught to imagine ourselves as slaves, just as our ancestors were. Then—and only then—might we be able to appreciate the freedom that is ours to enjoy. Freedom never tasted so sweet. KO

Renewing Judaism

23 APRIL

There are no important moments in the life of a Jew for
which there are no blessings. God is present at all times;
it is up to us to notice God, to feel God's presence. . . .
Sometimes we are remembering, uncovering, discovering—
exploring Torah with new eyes, different questions.
But failing that, we invent.

RABBI LAURA GELLER[19]

The classical rabbis taught us the importance of saying blessings. The traditional prayerbook has blessings to recite upon seeing a rainbow, meeting a long lost friend, eating a fruit for the first time each year. In many ways blessings use a simple formula to capture both the small and the grand events. Yet there are moments of our lives for which we have no traditional blessing. Judaism has always been reinvigorated by each generation's expressing its deepest longings and needs in the idiom of religious language. Medieval poets poured out their passions in religious poetry called *piyutim*. Today we join this tradition by creating new blessings which speak to us. In particular, women have realized over the last three decades that many moments of their lives were not sanctified by a blessing. In response, we have seen the writing of new blessings to mark moments such as the birth of a child, the onset of menstruation, and the celebration of an anniversary. Writing these blessings allows us to capture and sanctify moments when we feel truly blessed by God. What would you write as a blessing for today?   LF

Climbing Staircase

24 APRIL

*Jacob came upon a certain place and stopped there for the
night, for the sun had set. Taking one of the stones of that
place, he put it under his head and lay down in that place.
He had a dream. . . . [God said to him:] "I will not leave
you until I have done what I promised you."*
GENESIS 28:11–12A; 15C

When the Bible describes a night in the life of Jacob that
was filled with heavenly visions, it begins by telling us
that Jacob rested his head on a pillow of stones. He had left
his family the day before, and he was carrying with him enormous—and justifiable—reasons for guilt. He had tricked his
father into giving him a blessing destined for his brother,
Esau, and he was running away partly to escape his brother's
revenge. On nights like that, a person's head rests on rocks.
That is how comfortable he felt, and all of us feel, in many of
the guilt-filled nightmares of our lives.

But Jacob then saw heavenly visions. He saw angels going
up and down a ladder (Genesis 28:12). Step by step, rung by
rung. That, he realized, is the way to reach upward to heaven.

Hucksters come along every day and offer quick and easy
remedies for every human ill. Such remedies are often prof-
fered for guilt. But spiritual ascents are made on a ladder, not
a high-speed express elevator—a ladder that requires climbing rung by rung.   RABBI HARLAN J. WECHSLER[20]

The Wholeness of Brokenness

25 APRIL

The broken tablets were put with the new ones into the ark.
TALMUD[21]

When we think about the Ark of the covenant which the ancient Israelites carried on their shoulders throughout their wanderings in the desert, we usually think of the Torah that is housed in the ark of the modern synagogue. Often nestled in a beautiful mantle and adorned with silver crowns, it bespeaks beauty and elegance. The Rabbis remind us, however, that Moses received *two* sets of tablets. Upon descending the mountain for the first time, he saw the golden calf, fumed with anger, and smashed the tablets. He acted the way many of us do when we are angry. God chastised the people and now, through our ritual lives, we try to make up for the sin of our ancestors.

Once again Moses ascended the mountain. This time he chiseled out the tablets himself. These tablets were very heavy, so the tradition teaches that as long as Moses carried the law in his heart, the tablets lifted him as he made his way down the mountain. According to the Torah, the tablets were eventually housed in the Ark that the Israelites carried with them through the wilderness and into Israel. But the Rabbis add an insight that is not mentioned in the text of the written Torah. Wondering what happened to the tablets that Moses shattered, they teach us that the fragments were gathered up by the people and placed in the Ark along with the whole tablets. In our journey through life, as in the journey of our ancestors, they remind us to embrace the broken parts of ourselves.

We make mistakes. That is part of being human. And once we get beyond specific challenges, we are anxious to just move on beyond the past. But the text above teaches us a different lesson. It tells us to collect the broken shards of our past even as we work to create wholeness in our lives. The wholeness (*shalom* in Hebrew) can be accomplished only after we embrace the brokenness as well.   KO

The Wheel of Life

26 APRIL

There is an ever-rotating wheel in this world. One who is rich today may not be so tomorrow, and one who is poor today may not be so in the future.

MIDRASH[22]

No matter how hard we try to lead secure, stable lives, life is still precarious. We save for the future, buy insurance, pray for our health and the well-being of those we love. At any time, though, what appear to be certainties in our lives can change without notice. We can try to safeguard our material possessions, but they can be lost as readily as they have been gained. Change is a given, though we never know which direction it will take. Either the fluidity of life can make us anxious—or we can be grateful for what we have at this very moment. As difficult as it might be, being able to adjust ourselves to the contingencies we face every day is a spiritual skill. Some of us do this by developing a deep relationship with God and reaching out to the Holy One when the going gets rough. Some of us nourish long-term friendships which bolster us at difficult times. No matter where we are in the cycle of life today, we can be grateful for the fullness of our lives.

As you read this, think about what you are grateful for. Be grateful for what you have in your life today by appreciating the loving relationships that you have with your family and friends, by telling them of your love, and by becoming involved in the life of your community. For you cannot be sure what tomorrow will bring.   LF

Waking Up

27 APRIL

I will awake the dawn.
PSALM 108:3

Sometimes we resist waking up and instead stumble through our days as if in a dream. For we human beings are given to drifting with the tide, heedless of our destination. It may take an outside force to stun us, to scare us out of our fears, to push us out of our daily idolatry wherein, like sleepers, we have eyes that do not see, ears that do not hear, noses that do not smell, hands that do not feel. God created Jews in order to keep newness in the world; it is the responsibility of the Jew to awaken the dawn. And it is the task of the soul to waken the self.   RABBI JAMES PONET[23]

True Happiness

28 APRIL

When you eat the labor of your hands, you shall be happy.
PSALM 128:2

The above passage is found in the book of Psalms, which the tradition ascribes to King David. Even those who question his authorship suggest that he was somehow involved with this book. Perhaps these were poems that he sang to himself and to others. To me, the Psalms do not read as if they were written by a king. Instead they speak the simple truths that are learned by living life. They are the kind of truths that are written by ordinary people like you and me.

How can we find happiness? The Psalmist is offering his (or her) answer to this question. And in doing so, the Psalmist is offering us guidance for our lives: Work hard. This is the first lesson. It continues not "enjoy the fruits of your labor," as others might read it. Rather, the only way to enjoy it is by eating the fruits of your labor (and not the labor of others). KO

Finding Freedom

29 APRIL

We are not born free and equal, but are born to become free and equal. It is the goal of all social endeavor to bring about equality in the inequality into which people are born. It is the goal of spiritual endeavor to make humanity free.
RABBI MORDECHAI M. KAPLAN[24]

One of the central experiences of us as a people is the journey from slavery to freedom. We recall this core event each Passover when we retell the story of our Exodus from Egypt. In the retelling, Judaism elevates economic, social, and psychological freedom to a religious principle. Freedom is an ongoing endeavor As individuals, we need continually to reflect on the ways we get stuck—in other words, how we live imprisoned lives through which we are diminished.

How can we free ourselves from the inner demons, fears, and limitations which constrict our spirits? How can we help others tear down barriers which limit their freedom? Though we have never experienced slavery firsthand, it is such a pivotal event in our history as a people that it is never far from the surface. In the daily morning prayer is a blessing that says, "Praised are you, *Adonai,* our God, Sovereign of the Universe, for not making me a slave." This has sometimes been rephrased to read, "Praised are you, *Adonai,* our God, Sovereign of the Universe, for making me free." May we be ever mindful of the freedom in which we live, and may we extend its blessings to those who still live under external and internal oppression.   LF

Love is Service

30 APRIL

Love is the voice of God. Love is the rule of Heaven.
GRACE AGUILAR[25]

Service is love in action. When we love or serve others, we cause their inner resources to surface. We find pleasure in giving. Our love expresses itself in opening our hearts and sharing. By our doing so, the other person grows with us. When we serve others, we enlarge our vision for the future, release positive feelings, stimulate creativity, increase self-confidence, have a greater interest in life. We tap our highest energies and evoke a joyous sense of independence in others. We find great release and expansion through loving service. When we serve others, both the one served and the self find their path to heaven is paved.   RABBI DOV PERETZ ELKINS[26]

MAY

Surviving the Past and Securing the Future

1 M AY

The community is Israel's rampart.
TALMUD[1]

So many themes mark this time of year in the Jewish calendar. On the surface these themes seem to contradict one another and pull us in a variety of directions, yanking on our emotions, tugging at our spirits: Yom Hashoah (Holocaust Remembrance Day), Yom Hazikaron (Israel's Memorial Day), Yom Ha'atzmaut (Israel Independence Day), Yom Yerushalayim (Jerusalem Day). This month speaks to what can be called the prime prism for the Jewish people during the twentieth century: Physical survival. Since the founding of the modern state of Israel, the survival of the Jewish people has been guaranteed by the technical sophistication and success of the Israel Defense Forces. We are reminded about that strength constantly, and it has taught us a great deal about personal strength and its relationship to Jewish identity. I recall in particular the euphoria over Israel's triumph of the

Six Day War in 1967. Eleven years later, in October 1973, this euphoria was shattered when Israel was taken by surprise by several Arab armies. Suffering many losses, Israel emerged victorious one month later. In triumph and in defeat, we call to mind this teaching of our sages: The community is Israel's rampart.

In the local communities where we live it is the same way. We depend on one another. This mutual dependence unites us and gives us strength. We are there when a brother or sister is in need. We are there because our togetherness makes it possible for us to stand and be strong.   KO

Welcoming the Holy Spirit

2 MAY

*The one who undertakes to fulfill one precept faithfully
is worthy of the Holy Spirit.*

MIDRASH[2]

This seems like the spiritual version of a "get rich quick" scheme, the kind for which many people are searching. Too many people want to find spiritual ecstasy immediately—and regularly—without investing much time or energy. This may be why so many Jewish people shy away from the required discipline of Jewish religious life. But the rabbis who are quoted in the text above are dangling the reward of the "Holy Spirit," of an intimate relationship with the Divine. This is an extraordinary spiritual goal, yet how can the Rabbis suggest that it can be attained merely by fulfilling one religious precept?

The key to this notion and to our spiritual work lies in the word "faithfully." When we earnestly fulfill a religious precept, when we work hard to get it right, when we do something with the fullness of self, it is then that the potential for the Holy Spirit is greatest. That posture provides us with the foundation necessary for the religious life.   LF

Jumping Toward Life

3 May

The righteous person, even when brought to death, has hope.

PROVERBS 14:32

It was a dark, cold night at the Janowska Road labor camp in Lvov, Ukraine. Suddenly a shout pierced the air: "You are all to evacuate the barracks immediately and report to the field. Anyone remaining inside will be shot on the spot!"

Pandemonium broke out. People pushed their way to the doors while screaming the names of friends and relatives. They finally reached the field. In the middle were two large pits. Suddenly the inmates realized to what they had been rushing.

Again the voice roared: "Each of you dogs who values his miserable life and wants to cling to it must jump over one of the pits and land on the other side. Those who miss will get what they deserve: Ra-ta-ta-ta."

It was clear to the inmates that it was impossible to jump over the pits. The prisoners were all but skeletons, feverish from disease and starvation. To the S.S. and the Ukrainian guards, this was just another devilish game.

Among the thousands of Jews was Rabbi Israel Spira. He was standing with a friend, a skeptical young man about 16 years old.

"Spira," said the youth, "everyone's efforts to jump over the pits will be in vain. We only entertain the Germans. Let's sit down in the pits and wait for the bullets to end our wretched existence."

"My friend," said the rabbi, "we must obey the will of God. If it is decreed from heaven that pits be dug and we be commanded to jump, then jump we must. And if, God forbid, we fail and fall into the pits, we will reach the World of Truth a second after our attempt. So, my friend, we must jump."

The rabbi and his friend were nearing the edge of the pits, which were rapidly filling up with bodies. The rabbi glanced down at his swollen feet. He looked at his young friend, a skeleton with burning eyes.

As they reached the pit, the rabbi closed his eyes and commanded in a powerful whisper, "We are jumping!" When they opened their eyes, they found themselves miraculously on the other side of the pit.

"Spira, we are here. We are here! We are alive!" the teen repeated over and over again, while tears streamed from his eyes. "Spira, I am alive. Indeed, there must be a God in heaven. Tell me, Rebbe, how did you do it?"

"I was holding on to my heritage and my faith. I was holding on to the coattails of my father, and my grandfather and my great grandfather, of blessed memory. Tell me, my friend, how did *you* reach the other side of the pit?"

"I was holding on to you," replied the rabbi's young friend.

And so it is for us. No matter what life puts before us, no matter where our journeys lead us, no matter how dark the night or how deep the pits, no matter how intimidating or scary the unknown, let us hold onto one another! And for dear life, let us jump! RABBI DAVID GELFAND[3]

Hearing *the* Voice Around the World

4 MAY

*When the Holy One gave the Torah to Israel, God's voice
was heard from one end of the world to the other.*
TALMUD[4]

Rabbi Stephen S. Wise once attended a meeting that celebrated the legacy of those Americans who could trace their lineage back to the *Mayflower.* One woman boasted to Wise that her ancestors had been on the *Mayflower* and asked the rabbi about his own ancestors, knowing full well that his ancestors were recent immigrants from Europe. The rabbi, never to be outdone, replied, "I can trace mine to Sinai."

We are very aware of Sinai at this time of year, because we have spent many days counting from Pesach to the holiday of Shavuot, which celebrates the giving of the Torah. This process of counting, which is called *sefirat haomer,* reminds us of our connections to the land and to our lineage. We long to hear the voice of God once again, as we did so long ago on Sinai. No matter where you come from, no matter how far back you can trace your ancestors, if you open your heart, then you can hear the voice of God and the message of Sinai. KO

The Longevity of the Jewish People

5 MAY

*All things are mortal but the Jew; all other forces pass, but
he remains. What is the secret of his immortality?*
MARK TWAIN[5]

The Jewish people have been around since time immemorial. While we cannot be exact with dates, it is possible to say that our people are close to 3,500 years old. We have survived exile, persecutions, and anti-Semitism. Today we number approximately 13 million around the world.

There is probably no one answer to Twain's question, "What is the secret of our longevity?" For many of us, it is our constant concern with interpreting our sacred story found in the Torah. These five books—Genesis, Exodus, Leviticus, Numbers, and Deuteronomy—have been read and reread by Jews wherever they lived. Whether in Morocco, Yemen, Poland, America, or Israel, we all read and interpret the holy words our people call Torah.

This joint venture, and the meaning these words have for our lives today, creates a common endeavor which binds us one to another. We may not all speak the same language, or live in the same country, or look alike, yet when we open Genesis or Exodus or any of the other books of the Torah, we know that many others have preceded us in reading these words and that they are now sustaining fellow Jews around the globe just as they are sustaining us.

In the words of Ahad HaAm, an early Zionist thinker, "Learning, learning, learning: that is the secret of our survival." Make a note to yourself to learn one new thing today that will give you new insights into yourself and the world.　　LF

More or Less

6 MAY

The more you have the more you are hounded.
The more you have, the more you have to defend;
and you will have, no time for appreciation and joy.
AFTER ECCLESIASTES 5:9–11[6]

We imagine that things bring us joy. And that is often true. There are pieces of art in my office, for instance, that touch my soul every time I gaze upon them: A set of ceramic rabbis deep in mystical discussion triggers my imagination every time I drop in on their conversation.

Would you want to live in a world without beautiful things? Of course not. So let's not pretend that things are bad. Ecclesiastes is not making a moral judgment on things, but simply noting a practical fact: I worry that I may lose what I have, and it is that worry rather than the things themselves that is the problem.

"The more you have, the more you have to defend." This is true not only of things. It is true also of emotions, feelings, opinions, ideas. The more invested we are in what we have, the more defensive we have to be. And being defensive makes us nervous, anxious, fearful. We are always looking over our shoulder to make sure we are safe. But we don't really mean "we." We mean "our stuff." We can usually tell whether or not we are in danger simply by taking note of where we are. We really don't worry about that. It is our *stuff* that causes the worrying.

The solution? Not to get rid of stuff. Doing that would lead us to worry about divestiture, which is no less troublesome than our concerns about owning. No. The solution is to retract the energy we put into things and ideas. Yes, the ceramic rabbis are beautiful and pleasant to look upon. And that is all. If they break, if they are stolen, I'll survive. This is true of ceramics. It is true of ideas. It is true of relationships. Enjoy them while they are there. Move on when they are not.

RABBI RAMI SHAPIRO

Directing Destiny

7 MAY

*All appointments are from heaven, even that
of a synagogue sexton.*
JEWISH FOLK SAYING

We are still in the classic mode of counting the *omer* which began after Pesach and continues to Shavuot. As the weather changes and spring fever hits, we are counting other things as well: The days to summer vacation, to going to the beach or the mountains, or just lying around and doing nothing. These are the simple pleasures that make the hard work we do all the more worthwhile. So now begins the planning: What should we do this summer? Where should we go?

We often deceive ourselves into believing that we are in control of our lives. It is true that we chart our work day, make career decisions, plan our leisure time, and set a course for the general direction of our life. But so many things happen that are out of our control and impact directly on what we do each day.

We may also think we determine the direction of our communities as well. We vote leaders into office, take a role in politics, make our voice heard. But the saying above is trying to teach us something. Some people will simply read it as fatalistic and deterministic and say it negates the idea of free choice and free will. But I think it is saying something more than that. God is not just at work in what appears to be the important decisions in our lives. God is also involved in less significant decisions as well. How will we know this? We must listen for the voice of God in each decision that we make. If we try to listen to the hearts of others, we may be able to hear our own. In doing so, we may hear God speaking to us as well.   KO

Hope in the Face of Destruction

8 May

O Lord, my God, I pray that these things never end:
The sand and the sea, the whispering of the waters, the
thundering of the heavens, the prayer of the heart.

HANNAH SENESH[7]

This prayer was written by Hannah Senesh, a young para-trooper from Israel, who was captured and tortured by the Nazi collaborators in Hungary during World War II. During her captivity, Hannah wrote letters to her mother in Palestine documenting her state of mind and the torture she suffered. She refused to reveal any information to her captors and was eventually killed. Hannah didn't despair. She voiced hope for the future of the world and humanity.

It takes an incredible act of faith to express hope in the face of evil. Often overwhelmed, we respond by backing down. How do you respond? Do you stand up and act courageously, as Hannah did when she parachuted behind enemy lines? Do you fight, in whatever way possible, to keep hope alive? Judaism teaches that evil is an inherent part of the world and we cannot ignore it. We must face it and conquer it, wherever and whenever it appears. Do not lose hope. When hope is lost, the world will surely perish.   LF

It Is Up to You

9 May

Encouraging words are as honey, sweet to the soul
and health to the being.

PROVERBS 16:24

All day long we have the opportunity to increase our well-being. It is so simple. One word of praise can make all the difference in the world. A teacher's word can make or break a student. A parent's praise can lift or drop a child. An employer's judgment can be given gently or caustically. These feelings are real and very important. All of them come out of a choice and a faith. Faith in one's self and faith in others, choosing a way of being that celebrates life—these make happy and productive human beings.

We must constantly emphasize the positive and eliminate the negative. Negative feelings frustrate, deny, and destroy. Positive expressions help the individual to realize himself or herself and affirm the meaning of life.

RABBI BERNARD S. RASKAS[8]

Expanding Ourselves

10 MAY

I exist not to be loved and admired, but to love and act. It is not the duty of those around me to love me. Rather it is my duty to be concerned about the world, about humanity.

JANUSZ KORCZAK[9]

Janusz Korczak was a renowned Polish-Jewish pediatrician who ran an orphanage in Warsaw during World War II. Instead of accepting international help to save his own life, he chose to perish along with the children in his care. His selflessness is a model for those of us who are too frequently caught up in our own self-centered concerns.

Often our gestures of love and concern are intertwined with our desire to receive love, admiration, and, at times, power and social status. But it is challenging to put aside our own needs and extend love to others, with no expectations. Though we may strive for unconditional love, we have to admit that much of our love is clouded with conditions.

Janusz Korczak was able to extend his love to hundreds of orphans even while living in the desperate conditions of the Warsaw Ghetto, which fell on this day over 50 years ago. With the true spirit of a righteous person, a *tzaddik,* he reached out to others in the midst of abject circumstances.

In the spirit of his teaching, let us try to give love each and every day to those closest to us without concern about what we receive in return. Then let us try to give love freely even to those we do not know. KO

The Values We Hold Dear

11 MAY

The pursuit of knowledge for its own sake, an almost fanatical love of justice, and the desire for personal independence—these are the features of Jewish tradition which make me thank my stars that I belong to it.

ALBERT EINSTEIN[10]

Einstein identified the aspects of Judaism—knowledge, justice, and independence—that made him proud to be Jewish. The pursuit of knowledge is a fundamental Jewish value that is transmitted in many ways. This passion for study is best captured in the teaching, "The study of Torah is equal to all other commandments"(Mishnah *Peah* 1:1). Some of us might think this is hyperbolic, for as Jews we also believe that people must balance their study with action. However, we can understand this statement to mean that study deepens our religious and social commitments. Our passionate commitment to pursuing knowledge has allowed us to excel in many fields. What area of study excites you?

Justice is the second Jewish value noted by Einstein. *Tzedek,* the Hebrew word for "justice," stands at the center of how we work to right the inequities in our society. As Jews, we have often been the victims of injustice. Today we can champion justice for those who are mistreated and lack avenues of redress. Where do you see injustice and what can you do to address it?

Lastly, Einstein mentions the value of personal independence. This is a modern concept unknown to Jews in earlier ages. Jews always sought to expand their freedom of movement and freedom of trade, since we experienced many restrictions in these areas throughout the centuries. Today we can be thankful for the personal independence we enjoy in a modern society. What other areas of freedom do you appreciate?

We all know that other values in Judaism move us. Not all of us are moved by the same values to an equal extent. Take a moment to reflect on those aspects of Judaism that make you grateful to be part of the Jewish people.   LF

Breakthrough Faith

12 MAY

In every generation there are those who rise up against us seeking to destroy us, but the Holy One of Blessing delivers us from their hands.

PASSOVER HAGGADAH

The Exodus from Egypt was a Divine turning point in history which decisively altered our concepts of God, humans, and society. God intervened in the events of history and redeemed the Children of Israel from slavery. They were liberated from the spiritual bondage of idolatry and paganism; they were also liberated physically from persecution and oppression. The Exodus from Egypt is not simply a past event, but is a living encounter with the Divine Presence. It commits us to struggle against idolatry, injustice, and oppression in every generation. Time and again, when it would appear that we are at the brink of oblivion, we emerged defiant, victorious through our own effort and the will of God.

Faith gives us the substance of our values and ideals and sustains us with the belief that they will be realized.

RABBI BERNARD S. RASKAS[11]

Speaking the Truth

13 MAY

Open your mouth and let your words be clear.
TALMUD[12]

I believe in speaking the truth and enjoy my reputation as a "truth-teller." Sometimes this trait gets me into trouble, because people do not always want to hear words spoken with such candor. They prefer to live behind partial truths or even the deceptive and seductive bliss of ignorance. Of course, we have to be careful to preserve feelings. That goes without saying. Nonetheless, whether in the form of compliments or criticism, many people would rather have words "sanitized" before they reach their ears. But hearing these revisions would force us to dig deeply to try to figure out what is really being said.

The ancient Hebrew prophets had a completely different idea, one that is echoed in the rabbinic notion cited above. They spoke the truth. They saw no other option for themselves or for the people of Israel. As spokespersons for God, they had only one choice. And their words were generally not pleasant to hear. They were often words of rebuke or what is called *tokhachah* in Hebrew. Out of their love for the Jewish

people, they felt the obligation to do this. Maybe we should
do the same. Or as Jewish folk culture puts it, "Better the bite
of a friend than the kiss of an enemy."   KO

Holy Living

14 MAY

A holy people must be a living people.
MIKHA YOSEF BERDYCZEWSKY[13]

Only in the past fifty years have we, the Jewish people, had
a sovereign state to call our homeland. For thousands of
years we wandered from east to west and from west to east;
more often than not, we experienced oppression, hatred, and
inequity. Despite the painful aspects of our history, we maintained a sense of holiness and vitality. Through literature,
drama, music, and religious study, we created and recreated
our culture time and time again. We prayed with fervor and
passion. At times, when nothing made sense, we accused God
of abandoning us.

Today with the State of Israel over fifty years old, our existence as a people is much more secure. We are a living people. Mikha Yosef Berdyczewsky, a Hebrew writer and
thinker, wrote today's text in 1899 when the very survival of
the Jewish people was in question. He spoke about the need
for a national homeland to ensure the survival of the Jewish
people. In essence he was asking, "What good is it if we are
holy if our existence is at stake?"

Today we need to rephrase his statement and say: A living
people must be a holy people. We can be alive, but is that
enough? No. Our covenant with God is to be holy. As we
read in Leviticus, "You will be holy." We must strive for holiness in our own lives and in the life of our people. Let us
begin today.   LF

Belief in the Human Spirit

15 May

Laugh, yes, laugh at all my dreaming,
This do I the dreamer say:
Laugh at my belief in people
For I still believe in you.
SAUL TCHERNICHOWSKY[14]

For Jews, the Holocaust is our family story—the darkest chapter in a long, proud history of faith and achievement. It is the *zevach olah*, the "total burning" of over one-third of our people, not because of their beliefs, their politics, or their military or social threat, but simply because of who or what others imagined them to be. Other people had demonized them beyond the brink of human rationality.

For all of us, even those who are not Jewish, the Holocaust is *our* story. All of us are capable of extending our prejudices to the point of intolerance, and from intolerance to hatred and domination, and then to wanton murder. All of us need to remember this most horrible of cautionary tales, lest we allow ourselves or others to devolve into the demons whose names we fear.

Let our tears fall, for then we realize that we are still human, that we still care, that there is still much hope for each human being and for the great human family. Our tears tell us that we still believe in the human spirit, in the dream of tolerance and trust. RABBI LESTER BRONSTEIN

Discovering Knowledge

16 MAY

Wonder rather than doubt is the root of knowledge.
RABBI ABRAHAM JOSHUA HESCHEL[15]

Most people believe that you can experience something for the first time only once. Our tradition understands things a little differently. Jewish law may require a short time period between the experiences. For example, we are not permitted to eat matzah during the thirty days before the first night of Pesach, so that the taste of matzah will be "fresh" during the seder. And each season presents us with the opportunity to taste seasonal fruits again for the first time. Our tradition even has a blessing for these experiences. Using the traditional form of blessing, "*Barukh ata Adonai Eloheinu Melekh Ha-olam,* Praised are You, O God, Sovereign of the Universe"— which brings us into a relationship with the Divine—the blessing continues, "Who has kept us alive, sustained us, and helped us to reach this day."

Reciting this helps us maintain a sense of wonder throughout our lives. Often we lose this sense of wonder as we journey from childhood into adulthood. Rabbi Heschel is urging us above to maintain it, since it is the foundation stone of knowledge. So leave your doubt at the door and open yourself instead to the many wonders of the world. KO

Creation

17 MAY

*Though whether I shall ever "create" is something I can't
really tell. But I do believe that it is possible to create,
even without ever writing a word or painting a picture,
by simply molding one's inner life. And that too is a deed.*

ETTY HILLESUM[16]

When we create music, or art, or drama, we might say, "We
just produced a new piece." Since we live in a society that is
so product driven, it is no wonder that we have adopted this
language to describe the fruits of our creativity. What language do we use, though, when our creativity is not external
but internal? What if we are engaged in knowing the contours and depths of our own inner life? Would we call this
deep, reflective work "a creation"? Or would we discount it
because there is nothing tangible to show others?

Today's inspirational text was written by Etty Hillesum, a
young 27-year-old woman who lived in Amsterdam during
World War II and perished in Auschwitz. Even in the face of
death, she spoke of taking refuge in the inner life and exploring its many realms.

Our spiritual work often involves stepping back and not
clinging to any specific goal or product that we may, or may
not, desire. We, who are so goal oriented, must give up pre-
cise results. We can act according to our conscience, but we
have no control over the outcome of our actions. In spiritual
work, there are no products. There is just an ever-deepening
knowing and unfolding of our selves. LF

God's Prayer

18 MAY

What is God's prayer? Rabbi Zutra says, "May it be My
will that My mercy overcome My anger, and My loving
qualities override My strict traits, that I treat My children
with My quality of mother's love and that I always deal
with them beyond the letter of the law."

TALMUD[17]

Most of us associate prayer with being weak or in need.
When we are in trouble, we turn to God naturally. As the popular saying goes, "There are no atheists in foxholes." Con-
versely, when we are feeling strong or triumphant, we rarely
pray. If we are fully in control, why should we defer to God?

The Talmud teaches us otherwise. The Holy One, the
Blessed, does not want humans to be weak so they will turn
to God. God—as much or more—wants our service when we
are strong and wants us to perfect the world with our compe-
tence. Then we should pray, out of strength, that we use our
strength properly.

We should learn from God and imitate God. God, the all
powerful, prays: May my good qualities dominate My lesser
qualities.

So should the doctor pray: May my judgment be accurate
and not distorted by too much knowledge or egotistic consid-
erations. May my quality of caring and listening overcome
my technological approach to the patient.

The celebrity should pray: May my integrity and creativity
override my desire for fame and fortune.

The person in business should pray: May my drive for success and wealth be guided by my ethics and my concern for
people.

The parent should pray: May my authority over my child be directed by selfless love, not by the need to control or show off my child.

We all need to pray: May we use our freedom constructively, not destructively. May our generosity overcome our self-centeredness. May our care for others override our need for conspicuous consumption. RABBI IRVING GREENBERG[18]

The Wonder of Silence

19 MAY

Silence is good during prayers.
A SIGN FOUND ON THE WALL OF MANY SYNAGOGUES

Many of us have the mistaken notion that silence is empty. We are therefore moved to fill the void with noise. This is not our fault. We were socialized that way. No matter where we go today, we are assaulted with noise. Elevators, stores, cars, banks, and airports are all filled with sound. We can't escape it. And now, thanks to sophisticated computers, appliances talk to us. So it is not surprising that our children do their work with a stereo blaring in the background. Or that as soon as we come home to an empty home, we turn on the television—after we have listened to our voice mail or answering machine. Some of us even have radios in our bathroom showers or "white noise" machines that help us sleep. Maybe we do this to stay connected with the world, maybe it's a form of companionship. Or maybe we're just afraid of being alone with ourselves.

But silence can be much richer than even the most celebrated of music. Silence allows us to appreciate the sounds of self, to hear the breath of life passing through our lungs. It provides us with the opportunity to gain an appreciation for the natural sounds of the world.

Most important, it allows us to hear God speaking to us. So during study and during prayers, the only thing I want to hear is silence. It speaks the loudest to me when I am at prayer.   KO

Profound Belief

20 MAY

I believe. I believe in the sun even when it is not shining.
I believe in love even when feeling it not.
I believe in God even when God is silent.

ANONYMOUS

This poem was found on the wall of a cellar in Cologne, Germany, where Jews hid from the Nazis. We marvel at the hope and faith that was displayed in the darkest of times. What does it mean to hold onto belief when everything around us is crumbling and our life is at risk? It takes inner fortitude and a belief that life extends beyond the narrow limits of our personal existence. Whoever wrote these words was not afraid of death. He or she knew death was imminent. Yet this poet also believed that love, goodness, and God would persist after his or her own life ended.

For most of us, the thought of mortality is a frightful one. Not only are we afraid of the actual experience of death, we also dread parting from our family, friends, and our entire existence as we know it. Yet, can we project hope and faith beyond our own finite existence? It is one of life's greatest challenges to know there are qualities that are eternal, that love, sunshine, and God will continue to exist after we die.

May the faith of those who needlessly perished inspire us to live our lives fully both in moments of doubt and in moments of belief.   LF

God's Messengers

21 May

A messenger from God appeared to me. The messenger looked like an angel of God, very frightening.
JUDGES 13:6

Some people can't tell an angel when they see one. Such people were Manoah and his spouse (whom the Torah does not name). They were Samson's parents. They didn't understand the significance of the visitor's refusal to eat. They even managed to learn that the messenger's name is unknowable, without sensing what was happening.

Confronted with flames and fire that leap toward the sky, Manoah finally realizes that their visitor is a Divine being. But Manoah is overwhelmed. He panics, fearing that no one can survive so intense a confrontation with the Divine. His wife, clearly the wiser of the two, has to calm him down.

And yet we can understand why Manoah does not get it. Meeting a force so awesome that it seems divine has a way of making us forget where we are. We lose track of others and even of ourselves. Without a sense of boundaries, we may be intimidated by the nearness of the Divine Presence. Divine power threatens to engulf and consume us or fill us until we explode. Made clumsy and inept by his astonishing experience, Manoah comes off as a bumbling fool.

But Manoah's wife is more discerning. She will bear Samson, whose uncut hair embodies his awesome powers, but who is not to drink wine or any other intoxicant so that he will not lose his sense of internal boundaries. Manoah's wife senses that the messenger she meets is frightening, but she has the calmer nature necessary for meeting the Divine without being overwhelmed. Somehow she feels the secure boundaries she needs in order to stand in the face of the "divine" visitor and the task he brings.

How do we keep our boundaries and take on tasks that seem overwhelming? While we might be visited by a Divine messenger, are there other ways we receive messages about the responsibilities that lie before us?

RABBI TSVI BLANCHARD[19]

Saving the Sabbath

22 MAY

More than Israel has kept the Sabbath,
the Sabbath has kept Israel.

AHAD HAAM[20]

These words from a formidable Zionist thinker read like an advertisement for synagogue participation. But Ahad HaAm (the pen name of Asher Ginsberg) was not talking about synagogue attendance. Nor was he suggesting that Shabbat observance protected Israel from harm. Instead he wanted to suggest that the Jewish people's adherence to its unique principles, such as Shabbat, protected it from becoming like other nations. Week in and week out the Jewish people celebrated Shabbat, even when they were threatened. Once a week the Jewish people rested, and from that rest they gained renewed strength. The observance of Shabbat fortified them.

So when Friday night rolls around, instead of rushing out to the theater or taking in a movie, put your feet up and relax. Light the candles that usher in the light that allows us to glimpse the messianic future. Sit with your family around the dinner table. Take a walk to your synagogue. You'll be glad you did.   KO

Our Task

23 MAY

The task of organizing human happiness needs the active cooperation of man and woman: it cannot be relegated to one half of the world. And active cooperation for such noble ends cannot be secured unless men and women really work together.

LILLIAN WALD[21]

In the midst of the season of university and high school graduations, it is important to remember what Lillian Wald taught us. Over eighty years have passed since Wald, community activist and founder of the Henry Street Settlement in New York, addressed these words to students at Vassar University. Much has changed over the past eight decades; stereotypes and gender roles are more fluid. Yet it is always wise to pause and reflect to what degree we actively cooperate with both men and women. Too often, life still breaks down along gender lines. Men tend to spend their leisure time with one another; women do the same. We may work together in the workplace, but do men and women share a common vision, the same goals and objectives?

How can we work more cooperatively to speak of a shared vision, and become fuller partners in addressing the problems of our generation? One pressing challenge is to figure out how to balance career and work so that all of us have time for one another, our families, our communities. Our spirits crumble under the weight of all we try to accomplish. Let us speak together to find ways to slow down our pace of life and build personal and work relationships that will nourish, sustain, and inspire our spirits. LF

Deep Roots

24 MAY

Let not your wisdom exceed your deeds lest you be like a tree with many branches and few roots.

MISHNAH[22]

Learning itself does not suffice unless it is anchored in fundamental convictions about using it for the proper purposes. Learning itself, without applying it to the enhancement of one's spiritual life and the betterment of society, can be vain and useless. We need roots to give us that kind of support that will anchor our wisdom to meaning and worth. Life is not an aimless pursuit of distraction; it has very definite purposes. These purposes are revealed by the articles of faith that give us a continuing source from which to draw inspiration and strength.

Unless we have the roots that give us the proper hold on life, we become like the tumbleweed, which drifts and wanders aimlessly, driven by every wind.

RABBI BERNARD S. RASKAS[23]

Working Hard

25 May

Rabbi Isaac said, "If a person tells you, 'I have labored and not found,' do not believe that person."
TALMUD[24]

Why would Rabbi Isaac advise us not to believe what a person says? Weren't we all taught to accept what others say, particularly those who are in authority or are older than we are? Shouldn't we assume that when someone tells us something, he or she is speaking the truth? Is this the cynic in Rabbi Isaac speaking or is he telling us something else?

The Talmud is presuming that we are all asking the really difficult questions in life: Why am I here? What am I supposed to be doing? What is my real work here? And how do I find my way to the Divine? What should I be doing with my life? What does God want of me? If you have not found the answer yet, then you are not working hard enough at asking the question. To place it in today's jargon, "Don't take someone's 'no' for an answer."

If we dig deeply into ourselves, we will find the answer. And if we have not yet found it, then dig deeper. Perhaps we are just not asking the right questions. Or maybe we are searching for answers in the wrong places. KO

Our Dreams and Our Children

26 MAY

Who is rich? One who sees a portion of her dreams fulfilled in her lifetime, and half her dreams fulfilled in the lifetime of her sons and daughters.

RABBI NINA BETH CARDIN[25]

We all have many dreams which we hope to fulfill during the course of our lives. These dreams spur us to learn more, to become involved, to pursue new avenues, and to expand ourselves. Along the way, we may actually fulfill some of our dreams. We may attain certain educational degrees, reach our professional goals, build a family, and become part of a community. However, we may also have dreams that we can only plant the seeds for, and hope they will take root and come to fruition during our children's lifetime. For the feminists during the early part of this century, their conviction that women should receive equal treatment and equal opportunities was such a hope. They labored tirelessly to lay the groundwork for the future generations to reap the benefits of a more egalitarian society. Similarly, Theodor Herzl had a dream that he did not see fulfilled: The creation of a Jewish homeland. However, later generations did witness the establishment of the State of Israel. The dreams of the early suffragists and the early Zionists, though very different in nature, were far-reaching and transformative. Our lives have been unalterably changed because of these brave and courageous dreamers. As Henrietta Szold, the founder of Hadassah, once said, "Dare to dream, and when you dream—dream big." Let us dream big dreams and set in motion their fulfillment in the coming generations.   LF

Bridging the Spiritual Gap

27 MAY

Remember God who created you.
MOSES MAIMONIDES[26]

There is a myth about a meeting in the spiritual realm of great Sages from the world's great spiritual traditions. They worked out a beautiful spiritual program that they had all reached for and dreamed of independently for millennia. Each tradition added its special gift. All the pieces now seemed to be in place, so they took it to God. God reviewed the wisdom and said, "Yes, this is wonderful. Only one piece is missing: the bridge between the spiritual and the material. Someone must bring this wisdom to earth. This is the task of the Jews."

Our special talent begins with the reconciliation of the spiritual and the material. It implies a sense of wonder in the everyday, a sense that the material world and the spiritual world are two incarnations of the same ultimate reality: Godliness. It is a notion not unlike what Einstein would later articulate for physics when he quantified the relationship between matter and energy. So it is with the spiritual and the material: They are ultimately one and that one is God. Our purpose, then, is to perceive the Divine as It dwells within everything. "Where does God dwell?" the Kotzker Rebbe asked his students. "When one lets God in." This is a radical act of perception because the world does not always evidence its Godliness on the surface.

RABBI JAMES STONE GOODMAN[27]

Seeing the Light Clearly

28 MAY

Light is not recognized except through darkness.
ABRAHAM BEN SAMUEL HA-LEVI HASDAI[28]

We all have dark periods in our lives. It is part of the challenge of being human. We fail. We sin. We suffer. People whom we love die and are taken from us and we feel helpless. And we recognize that we too will eventually die. And yet the human spirit does not give up. We continue to hope, to pray, to work toward a more perfect time in which there will be no sickness or death, no pain or suffering. Hasdai teaches us that in order to appreciate that future time, what is called *mashiach-zeit* or the time of the Messiah, we have to carry the burdens of this world and of this time. It is another way of saying something that experience teaches us: We can appreciate the intensity of the light only when it illumines our darkness. And only in the light of the Divine do we see light.   KO

The Pursuit of Honor

29 MAY

If you pursue honor, it will elude you. But if you flee from honor, it will pursue you.
TALMUD[29]

Everyone likes to be honored. When our passion and dedication are recognized, we feel good. However, we must learn to pause and examine our motivations. Do we contribute to our communities because we truly care about the issue at hand, or because we feel our work will bring us honor? Some people actively pursue honor and are disappointed when their efforts are not adequately noticed. Their motivations are self-serving from the start. Others work tirelessly because they are passionately committed to their work. They never think about whether they will receive honor or status from their efforts. Their motivations are pure. These are the individuals we should look to honor.

A similar concern is taught in the book of the Rabbis' favorite aphorisms called *Pirke Avot* (4:1) where we read, "Who is honored? Honor comes to those who give it away." In other words, we should look to honor others, not ourselves.

Through these two teachings, the Rabbis guide us to focus on the work at hand, not on our need to be recognized. This is easier said than done. However, if we incorporate this idea into our spiritual practice, honor will come to us when we least expect it.   LF

Struggling toward Wholeness

30 MAY

Turn us, our Parent, to Your Torah; bring us close, our Sovereign to Your service, and return us in full teshuvah before You. Blessing flows from You, Cause of Being, Who desires teshuvah.

FROM THE LITURGY[30]

Those of us who struggle on the path toward personal wholeness before God, tend to learn one thing soon: We never fully arrive. We are always on the road. Spirituality is not a destination. It is a journey that takes us to many places during our lives. However we get there, the inner posture of personal wholeness before God is an inner turning, not an arriving; it is admitting that God has a claim on us. We Jews call that inner posture, that inner turning, that experience of being claimed and redeemed by God, *teshuvah*. Most of us think that *teshuvah* requires a lot of work. And often, it does. However, each time it only takes a small step to turn and then face another direction. We just have to make sure that we keep on walking.   RABBI MORDECAI FINLEY[31]

Functional Memory

31 MAY

When mentioning a righteous person, add a blessing for that person.
MIDRASH[32]

The first day of spring never varies. It always occurs on the vernal equinox in April. The same used to be true of days like Memorial Day. Now the date varies each year, since it is fixed at the last Monday in May. But for most people, Memorial Day—the last few waning days of spring in May—serves as a doorway to summer. This is particularly the case in northern climes, where swimming pools open on Memorial Day weekend and people begin to focus on the outdoors. Lawn chairs come out. Barbecue grills are lit. One thing remains constant, though: memory. Lots of people have memories of this time of year—time with family, with friends. The school year is nearing completion. Many businesses switch to shorter summer hours. The world seems to slow down just a little for a short time.

Some scholars argue that, for the spiritually oriented person, memory is far more important than history. Rather than being the accumulated record of events over time, memory merges our personal experience with the collective experience of a nation and a people. Memory paves a path for current experience. Memory is not a passive accumulation of past events. Rather, memory is an active experience, because we have to create it for others.

So get ready for summer, and have a memorable time. KO

JUNE

Speaking Above the Silence

1 JUNE

For the sake of Zion, I will not remain silent.
For the sake of Jerusalem, I will not rest.
ISAIAH 62:1

Most prophets spoke to God on behalf of the people, even when they felt compelled—or were directed—to condemn them. Even their words of rebuke reflected a profound love and commitment to the Jewish people. Some prophets tried to run away from their responsibility but eventually learned that it was fruitless to try to outrun the Holy One. So it is no surprise to read the statement above from the prophet Isaiah. But we need to try to understand what his words mean for our times. Whenever he spoke, his speeches emerged out of his dedication to the people. Here the prophet is teaching us something that he has come to learn through his experience with the people: Judaism has made unique contributions to the world. Isaiah is proud of our people, and even prouder to be counted among them.

We have an obligation to follow in the footsteps of the prophets, to speak out like them. Otherwise our ancestors will have lived in vain. When we see injustice, we are obligated to speak out. When we see things that are unfair, we have a responsibility to try to right the wrong. It is part of our partnership with our Creator. When you do this, you will be transforming Eden into paradise once again.   KO

Giving Anonymously

2 JUNE

One who gives a gift to another person must inform that person about it.
TALMUD[1]

There are times when it is appropriate to give anonymously and times when it is not. In giving *tzedakah,* it is preferable to remain anonymous, because we should try to avoid embarrassing the recipient. In fact, according to Maimonides, both the giver and the recipient should be anonymous, if possible. In this way everyone's privacy is protected. This principle does not apply to the simple exchange of gifts between friends. The Rabbis' paramount belief is that we are to embrace each and every opportunity to express gratitude. By doing so, we open ourselves up to the many blessings in the world. By giving an anonymous gift, we deprive the recipient of such an opportunity.

We should seek to spare the recipients of our *tzedakah* any shame; our *tzedakah* should never cause embarrassment. Yet, when possible, we should seek to allow others to express their gratitude. Learning to express and receive gratitude is a central teaching of Judaism. Let us not deprive ourselves, or anyone, of this experience.   LF

Education and Work

3 JUNE

I am God's creature as others are God's creatures; my work may be in the city, theirs in the field; if I arise early for my work, they get up early for theirs; they don't presume to do my work as I don't presume to do theirs; can you say that I accomplish much while they accomplish little? No, for we have learned, it matters not how much you accomplish, so long as what you do is for God's sake.

TALMUD

In the judgment of the Rabbis, whatever we do must be done as though it is for God's sake. We are all called to do whatever it is that we do with a passion that comes from knowing that work—*all* work—is more than mere work: It is our own particular place on God's earth from which we are asked to contribute our share to the world. And who knows whose contributions will matter more? "Save one human being," goes a saying in the Mishnah, "and it is like saving a whole world."

Traditionally, children begin their Jewish education by reading from the book of Leviticus: "God called to Moses," as if to say, "and to you too," for we are all "called"—teachers, lawyers, doctors, parents, clerks, artists, bankers, merchants—regardless of who we are. Although we may not always know it, what we do matters too much for us to consider it "just a job." RABBI LAWRENCE HOFFMAN

Friendship

4 JUNE

*Your friend has a friend and the friend of
your friend has a friend.*
TALMUD[2]

This saying from the Talmud sounds logical. It may even
sound like the Jewish version of the Kevin Bacon game in
which everyone in Hollywood is somehow connected back to
Kevin Bacon. In my social circles, we like to play Jewish
Geography. As soon as you meet someone new, you try to
establish some connection through someone else. "Do you
know _____?" This "game" helps move a stranger into
the field of friendship.

Nothing seems to be wrong with this approach. Women are
particularly good at it. They have an uncanny ability to get to
a know a person quickly, intimately. Pop psycholinguists like
to call the difference between the way men and women
approach such relationships as the difference between Mars
and Venus. I like to spin it differently: "Women are from
Genesis and men are from Leviticus." Genesis is full of lively
family relationships and rich, colorful narratives. Leviticus, on
the other hand, focuses on law after law after law.

The Rabbis understood this phenomenon. Perhaps they
were even afraid of it. Maybe that is one reason why they
fiercely opposed gossip and talebearing. They considered it
like the leprosy that is described in the Torah. Today we
understand this kind of conversational exchange of intimate
details as a way that women get close to one another. Men
don't seem to share such intimate details about their own
lives, even in the locker room. In their prohibition against

gossip, the Rabbis offered a warning: *Some* things should not be shared with others, even if it is about yourself, and certainly not about another person, for words take on a life of their own, and "your friend has a friend . . . " who just might pass on what you have just told him. KO

Forgetting Torah?

5 JUNE

When a fetus is in the mother's womb, an angel teaches him the entire Torah. When the time arrives for him to enter the world, an angel touches him on his lips, and he then forgets all he has learned.

TALMUD[3]

What purpose is there for an infant to learn the entire Torah only to forget it? Shouldn't we exclaim, "What a waste!"? Think of all the time we could save if we knew, from the moment of our birth, all the wisdom contained in the Torah. The commentators, however, teach us otherwise. The fact is that all the Torah's wisdom is within us, not outside of us. It is hidden in the deep recesses of our beings. While we may have forgotten it upon being born, this wisdom is never truly lost. At birth we begin a new process through which we recall and relearn this knowledge and wisdom. In this way, we fully integrate it into our lives. Without the active process of learning, which includes making mistakes and errors, we would never fully understand and absorb these life lessons. Nonetheless, they are not out of our reach. They are lessons we all know but just need to recover. LF

On the Nature of Being Weavers

6 June

*May you reunite us from
the four corners of the earth.*
Liturgy[4]

We Jews are a union of weavers binding our traditions and language, rituals and laws, to the fibers we find from the cultures around us, we weave a personal shawl of Judaism. Some shawls are open and loose, allowing the currents of other cultures to flow easily in and out of it. Others are fine and tight, holding much of Jewish culture in and foreign cultures out. Each adds its flair, its strength, its warmth to the sacred garment of the Jewish people. Our choice of weave determines the synagogues we affiliate with, what we eat, where we live, how we pray, whom we marry, what we do in our spare time, how we educate our children.

Sadly, we too often denigrate one another's craftsmanship. It is true that with too loose a weave, the cloth loses its integrity. And it is true that with too tight a weave, the body underneath smothers. But most of our shawls fall somewhere in between. They complement each other, preserve the secrets of the different weaves for each other, and for future generations. Which is very good, for no shawl can suit every Jew. And yet, while we weavers differ, we should acknowledge that we all work on the same loom, with the same warp holding tight our differing patterns of weft. And that, if nothing else, unites us. Rabbi Nina Beth Cardin[5]

Hearing the Self Speak

7 JUNE

Let your ear hear what your mouth utters.
TALMUD[6]

This is a principle from Jewish liturgy that extends into everyday behavior. Some prayers, which are misunderstood as being "silent," are more accurately called "quiet." This description applies particularly to the traditional recitation of the core prayer in the service, which is usually called the *Amidah* or standing prayer because it is said while worshipers are standing. It helps people (like me) who have a tendency to pray, as well as do other things, very loudly. We speak the words of the *Amidah* so that we can hear what is being said and we can listen to them. This is not a bad idea, in general. It is a lesson that we can carry over to the rest of our lives. Sometimes we say things and do not pay attention to what is being said or the tone in which they are being said or even the volume. When that happens, words that are not meant to hurt, do. And words that are meant to heal, don't.

So watch your words and repeat them to yourself before you share them with others. KO

The Art of Correcting Others

8 June

There are two kinds of ways in which one can correct others and bring them to do God's will. One person corrects them with good words. . . . With such a correction, one can incline people's hearts to God. There are others who admonish with severe words, using phrases calculated to shame. There is a great difference between these two groups.

RABBI LEVI YITZCHAK OF BERDITCHEV[7]

It is always a sensitive matter to be in a situation that requires us to correct or admonish someone. As parents, we do this with our children because we know deep down that it is our responsibility to teach them the correct way to behave. Some of us may also be in this situation in our jobs; if we are in a supervisory position, we are called upon to give feedback to those we supervise, and at times we may have to express dissatisfaction. While we may try to give positive suggestions, there may be times when we are more blunt.

Nonetheless, these exchanges can take on different tones, depending on our motivations. There are many ways to give others "feedback," as it is called in contemporary speech. The language we choose is crucial, for it either allows the other person to hear and receive our comments or, all too often, causes him or her to feel shame. If we shame another person, it is likely that we undermine any sense of trust we have established.

The next time you speak with someone about correcting a behavior or an attitude, let us be mindful about the tone of voice and the language you use, just as Rabbi Levi Yitzchak of Berditchev teaches. LF

Heroes and Heroism

9 JUNE

Who is a hero?
MISHNAH[8]

A culture can be judged by the character of its heroes. Some civilizations celebrate the military man, the conqueror, the inspiring warrior. What constitutes a Jewish hero?

In his autobiography *A Gentleman and a Jew,* Maurice Samuel writes about having grown up in England. He was struck by the contrast of heroes. In English literature, he read about the gentleman: Byronic, dashing, gifted at swordplay and love. The gentleman sees life as a grand game and dies with a smile and a quip on his lips. The gentleman speaks in Shakespearean cadence, cape tossed gallantly over his shoulder, his step as light as his view of life.

As Samuel got older, he saw the Jews around him, hurried and taking life far more seriously. Their humor had bite; their eyes had sadness. When young, Samuel preferred the gentleman. Only as he got older did he see the gravity and worth of the image of the Jew.

Heroism is not only insouciant courage in the face of death, it is also nobility in the course of life. In the ancient eyes of the Jew is a subtle heroism that requires maturity to understand.

As our children absorb different images of heroism, we have a right to worry that many of the images they encounter are negative, even destructive. We should keep before their eyes the image of the Jew, one who believes that morality, sensitivity, learning, and righteousness are what makes a true hero. Perhaps in time, with God's help, such an image not only will become familiar, but will be realized in their lives and in ours'.   RABBI DAVID WOLPE

Real Learning

10 June

Rabbi Hanina taught, "I have learned much from my teachers, and from my colleagues more than from my teachers, but from my students I have learned more than them all."

TALMUD[9]

Many of us who have been out of school a long time figure that anything that speaks about teachers and students must be for children. But Judaism has always had a different take on schooling. In Judaism, education is a lifelong pursuit. Study has the potential to bring you closer to God. For many, it is even a form of prayer. We are very concerned about who it is that taught us something, afraid that teaching something without giving the original source of that insight would be an expression of arrogance. Thus we may begin what we say with "My teacher, _____, taught me the following." Alternatively, we may use the Hebrew phrase, "*Beshem amro,*" "in the name of whom it was said." These unusual cultural forms may be off-putting to some people. But for others, it reminds us of the Ultimate Source of all knowledge and discovery and of the fact that we are merely channels through which these insights come into the world.

When we learn something from a teacher or colleague, it is difficult enough to give that person credit. When we learn something from someone whom we are supposed to be teaching, like an employee or trainee, it is even more difficult. Instead of climbing over the competition, raise them up so that you may both be able to reach higher.   KO

Giving Freely

11 June

*Give of yourself . . . you can always give something,
even if it is only kindness . . . no one has ever become
poor from giving.*
Anne Frank[10]

Anne Frank's profound and wise statements have captured our hearts. Although she was in hiding, she rarely wrote of despair or depression. She even thought about giving to others. If her heart didn't close down while she was living in cramped conditions, then certainly we, who live in a free, democratic society, can keep our hearts open. This is not always easy to do, especially since our society breeds cynicism and that leads to indifference and callousness, not to compassion.

When we hear the word "giving," we may think, "Oh no, what more do they want of me?!" Many of us may receive numerous phone calls or direct-mail letters of solicitation and may have decided to ignore these appeals. Let us hope that these marketing efforts haven't closed our heart. We can touch another person's heart by being present in a moment of grief or fear, by calling or visiting someone who is ill, by sharing our spirit and smile with those we meet during the course of a day. We touch many people's lives when we respond by giving *tzedakah* generously. As Anne Frank, whose birthday is tomorrow, so correctly reminds us, giving of ourselves will never make us poor. Practice compassion and kindness today and see how you yourself benefit.   LF

A Birthday Gift for Anne Frank

12 June

*Parents can only give good advice or put them [children]
on the right paths, but the final forming of a person's
character lies in their own hands.*
ANNE FRANK[11]

It was Friday, June 12, and Anne woke up at six o'clock
ready for her thirteenth special birthday. After an hour, Anne
couldn't contain herself anymore and burst into her parents'
bedroom. Anne was pleased with all her gifts that morning:
books, a jigsaw puzzle, jewelry, and candy. But more than
anything she was thrilled with a hard-cover diary bound in
red and white checkered cloth.

It was Amsterdam 1942. The world was at war. Little
could anyone have known that this present from years ago
would serve as the most famous chronicle of the darkest period of humankind's inhumanity. Anne Frank would write in
that diary for two years before her hiding place was discovered. She died in Bergen-Belsen death camp in March 1945.

Anne's birthday in 1942 and the war which surrounded it
seem so far away, and yet this very morning many young
girls around the world will receive their birthday presents.
No one can know how their lives will be transformed. Will
they inspire and give meaning to the miracle of life? Or
will they suffer a life of hunger and abuse?

Surely those of us who have been blessed with the privilege
of reading Anne's diary, with the ability to study our past, to
learn from it, must affirm on this day that the greatest gift of
all is the gift of remembrance that inspires good deeds. With
each little girl you see today, think of life and of what you

could do to heal the world, not tomorrow but today. That would be a wonderful gift for our special Anne's birthday.

RABBI ABIE INGBER

Changing Places

13 JUNE

Who changes one's place, changes one's luck.
TALMUD[12]

This folk saying from sacred literature sounds best in Hebrew (*mishaneh makom, mishaneh mazal*), but it works just as well in English. It is a well-held folk belief that many of us practice, although we may not have found the words to articulate it quite this way. Instead, we confirm it with our actions or, in the jargon of the times, "we walk the talk." People move to get a new start on life, particularly after a tragedy or misfortune. They change jobs, move to a different house or apartment, or even relocate to a new community. For some people, the move may be the beginning of major changes in their life as they begin—or continue—a spiritual journey. For others, the move is part of how they are navigating through midlife challenges and crises. All this is about turning or returning, as Jewish tradition likes to put it.

Most of the biblical matriarchs and patriarchs made this kind of change. They answered a call, left behind what they had come to know, and took off for a new life. Many of our own relatives followed suit. They left Europe—or were pushed out—to seek a new and better life. In this generation, in communities throughout North America, Jews-by-choice take a similar path. They leave places that are predictable and comfortable in order to chart the unknown.

But *mazal* (literally, the constellation of the stars, but now meaning "luck") is not left to the stars as the Hebrew word implies (a residual element of our primitive folk culture). Instead, "luck" comes from coupling our own initiative with the direction and guidance we receive from the Divine.   KO

The Enduring Nature of *Mitzvot*

14 JUNE

For one whose good works exceed wisdom, the wisdom will endure. But for one whose wisdom exceeds good works, the wisdom will not endure.

MISHNAH[13]

Wisdom and good works seem to be the two things that are worthy of acquiring during our lives. But what is the relationship between them? What if we just acquire wisdom? Or what if we just acquire good works? Is it adequate to pursue just one of these? If so, which one?

The Rabbis favor good works over wisdom and say that if our good works do not exceed our wisdom, then the wisdom itself is fleeting. We could certainly be disappointed by this statement, for who among us wants to lose any piece of wisdom, no matter how incomplete it might be.

Perhaps the Rabbis are here suggesting that enduring wisdom comes when we apply it to nitty-gritty problems and use it to transform even one small corner of our world. Wisdom can never endure if it is distanced from the problems that surround us. We, as Jews, do not escape this world to find wisdom. Rather, we find wisdom by living within it.

What wisdom can we learn today from getting involved in the pressing matters that face us?   LF

Beginning Anew Each Day

15 JUNE

In beginnings, worlds are created. In creativity,
meanings are formed.
ANONYMOUS

Menachem Mendl of Kotzk counseled a Hasid who had experienced "terrible thoughts" by questioning justice and meaning in the world. To every anguished doubt of the Hasid, Menachem Mendl retorted, "And so—what do you care?" And seeing that the Hasid truly cared, he advised him not to worry about his doubts, "For if you care so deeply, you are an honest Jew, and an honest Jew is entitled to such doubts. In beginnings, worlds are created. In creativity, meanings are formed."   RABBI HAROLD SCHULWEIS[14]

Setting Our Sights on Sinai

16 JUNE

Rabbi Joshua ben Levi said, "With each and every word
that issued from the mouth of the Holy One, the entire
world, all of it, was filled with the fragrance of spices."
TALMUD[15]

For the Jewish people, one of the most interesting aspects of the Sinai experience is that it never ended. All you have to do is breathe deeply and inhale its fragrance, for it will be carried from Sinai until the end of days. Sinai might be described by the Torah and marked at a certain point and certain time of our journey from Egypt to the Promised Land. But we prevent the Sinai experience from becoming just a memory by reliving it each time we read Torah in public, each time we study it with a partner or by ourselves. We even keep it alive with such simple and routine table rituals as grace after meals (*birkat hamazon*).

All it takes to relive Sinai is a little effort on your part. So what are you waiting for? KO

Do Not Waste

17 June

This, then, is the first law that is opposed to your presumption against things: Regard things as God's property and use them with a sense of responsibility for wise human purposes. Destroy not! Waste not! Do not be avaricious! Be wise economically with all the means that God grants you, and transform them into as large a sum of fulfillment of duty as possible.

RABBI SAMUEL RAPHAEL HIRSCH[16]

We are often careless with how we use nature's resources to fulfill our own needs. Environmental consciousness is such a contemporary concern that we are surprised when we find earlier writings that express similar sensitivities. Rabbi Hirsch wrote extensively about the Jewish value called *baal tashchit,* which can be translated "Do not waste." This phrase is first found in Deuteronomy, where we read it in regard to cutting down fruit trees in the midst of war. The Torah says: Do not destroy! Though we might feel the need to cut down trees during the moment of battle to punish the enemy and limit their food supply, the long-term value of the trees supersedes this short-term need. Rabbi Hirsch preached publicly about our need to become aware that God, not humanity, is the owner of the earth and its resources. We must not assume that we can recklessly waste God's creation for our own ends.

We are all guilty, to some extent, of wasting needlessly. This is so easy to do in the age of disposable goods. By throwing out items that can be repaired, or using paper goods instead of reusable utensils, we create more and more waste. To value God's creation and to see ourselves as part of the larger whole, let us be more mindful of how we use our planet's resources.   LF

Who Are You?

18 JUNE

Know before Whom you stand.
MISHNAH[17]

Inside many synagogues' sanctuaries, the phrase above hangs over the Ark to remind those present that they stand before God. It is written in Hebrew. Unwritten, but no less important, is the instruction to consider who is the person standing:

Who are you? Do you consider yourself primarily an American? A Democrat or a Republican? A Jew? The truth is that we are complex creatures and each person is the composite of many different and overlapping identities—children to some, companions to others, parents or friends to still others. Each of us takes those many strands of identity and weaves them into a unique tapestry that is "me" by virtue of no one else blending quite the same mix.

At the same time, we also have a clear sense of who we are not, and those rejected identities form the backdrop of the "they" against which our own identities emerge. Between the solitariness of the "me" and the otherness of the "they," we strive to build a sense of belonging and community by reaching out to other similar individuals, by together estab- lishing a "we."

As we look inward, we join Jews the world over in think- ing about how we measure up to our own highest ideals and those of God. The boundaries of a solitary soul can restrict no less than would the requirement to stay inside a single room. By reaching beyond our own personalities, by identify- ing our interests, hopes, and joys with those of a living and eternal people, we shatter our own mortality and our own disappointing limits.

By ourselves we are alone. But as part of a covenanted people, we are part of an ancient and sacred dialogue with God.   RABBI BRADLEY SHAVIT ARTSON

Loyalty

19 JUNE

Entreat me not to leave you and to return from following after you. For where you go, I will go, and where you lodge, I will lodge. Your people will be my people and your God my God. Where you die, I will die and there will I be buried. Adonai will do so to me and more also, if nothing but death parts you and me.

RUTH 1:16

These are among the most moving words in the entire Bible. Ruth says them to her mother-in-law, Naomi, following the death of Ruth's husband. Since she is the Bible's most cele- brated convert to Judaism, she is held in high esteem by cur- rent Jews-by-choice. As an ancestor of King David, who was connected to the messianic line, she is rightfully honored. Her words are read on the festival of Shavuot, which celebrates, among other things, the experience of the Jewish people at Sinai. Like Ruth, who was motivated to cast her lot with the Jewish people, Shavuot recognizes our special individual and collective connections to God. Ruth also teaches us a profound lesson about loyalty. By casting her lot with the Jewish people, she is prepared to take on whatever responsibility comes with it.

How far will we go for those who are close to us, whether they are Jews or non-Jews? Are we prepared to go as far as Ruth went? A well-known Hasidic story teaches the lesson a little differently. The rebbe asks his disciple, "Do you love your friend, [who we'll call "Jim," just to bring the story up-to-date]?" "Of course I do," comes the reply. The rebbe continues, "Do you know what gives Jim pain?" "How can I know what gives Jim pain?" comes the response. The rebbe concludes, "If you do not know what gives your friend pain, how can you say that you love him?"

Loyalty demands love. It also demands that we know what pains our friends. Ruth knew this, and that is why she was prepared to cast her lot with Naomi and her people—our people. Are you prepared to do the same?   KO

The Consequences of Injustice

20 JUNE

The sword comes into the world because of justice delayed, because of justice perverted, and because of those who render wrong decisions.
MISHNAH[18]

This teaching suggests that violence is a consequence of injustice. We all see injustice if we look around us. It is painful to see and hard to escape. If injustice after injustice pile up with no signs of redress, it is not uncommon for people to relieve their outrage and frustration in violent ways. Victims of injustices want relief, not explanations or empty promises.

Of course, many injustices are complicated and cannot be solved immediately. Many go unpunished. As Jews, we have always pursued justice. Whether through legal proceedings, political action, or community organizing, we have stood up for our rights and for the rights of others who have been oppressed. We seek to create a peaceful society, one devoid of violence, one in which justice prevails.

Look around and see what issue has galvanized your neighborhood or community. What can be done to address this grievance or injustice so it can be resolved without violence? Start working on this today!   LF

The Temple: A Place for Moral Vision

21 June

Who shall ascend the Lord's holy mountain? Who shall be permitted to stand in God's holy place? One who has clean hands and a pure heart, who has not taken a false oath by God's life or sworn deceitfully.

PSALM 24:3–4

What accounts for the Temple's hold on the Jewish imagination? Why did Jews pray for its restoration daily for millennia? Why, even now, do people study the dimensions of the building and the laws of sacrifice?

The Temple is a microcosm of the world that Judaism seeks to create. This building was consecrated to life. Inside, no war was permitted; no death or dead body was allowed to enter. No hunger or poverty marred this building. Those who were financially better off were commanded to include the widow, the orphan, the stranger, and the Levite (the assistants to the priests) in their feasts and celebrations.

The Temple was a place of moral purity. All who sought to come in were asked, "Who shall ascend the Lord's holy mountain? Who shall be permitted to stand in God's holy place?" They had to answer, "One who has clean hands and a pure heart, who has not taken a false oath by God's life or sworn deceitfully."

Of course Jews did not always live up to these expectations. Still the Temple remained a model of a better world, a place where each person's better self came out and was lifted to lofty heights by God's Presence. No matter how ethically compromised a person became in the course of living, he or she could return to the Temple for moral renewal, to envision the world as it could and should be—a world of justice and peace. The Jews were oppressed and degraded for centuries, but the dream of being restored and made whole again could not die.

As long as people dream of a better world, they will not yield to the injustice in the world. As long as people can conceive of liberation from pettiness and cheating, from selling out and settling for the status quo, they will seek a better self. The Temple is that once and future shining place where the individual, the people, and the world are all made whole. No wonder the prophet Ezekiel saw it in his vision. No wonder the people lived only for its restoration—and for theirs.

Can we rebuild the Temple in our time? Those of us who say that we no longer believe in sacrifices or the Temple miss the point. Do we not need a microcosm, a perfect place to model the kind of society and people we want to be? Our ability to reach for moral greatness depends on the answer. The answer is in our hands.   RABBI LESTER BRONSTEIN

Lighting the World

22 JUNE

All the children of Israel had light in their dwellings.
EXODUS 10:23

Summer days always seem long and lazy. They continue to get longer until the summer equinox, which occurs today, changes things. Then the days start shortening, ever so slightly, and we begin to realize that summer, like every other time, has to come to an end. Summer does not last forever, much as we might like it to.

As the Israelites traveled for forty years in the desert, they encountered numerous summers. The heat seemed like it would scorch them as they made their way from Egypt to the Promised Land. But during their travel, a light illuminated their dwellings and their lives. This Divine light made it possible for the Israelites to see the path ahead of them. But what is important to note is that while the light may have originated with the Divine, it came from the dwellings of the Israelites. Light that comes from the love and warmth within our homes still promises to guide us as we make our way through the darkness.   KO

The Truth Resides Among Us

23 JUNE

*When God was about to create Adam, the first person,
Truth and Peace argued that God should not create
humanity. Truth asserted that if humanity were
created, the world would be filled with falsehood,
and Peace said it would be filled with strife.
God then cast Truth to the ground.*

MIDRASH[19]

Why did God throw truth to the ground? Because the Holy One realized that truth could not be a lofty ideal existing in the heavens alone, but had to grow from among the people. In other words, truth sprouts from the ground up. This notion is also suggested by the verse in Psalms, "And truth will spring out of the earth."[20]

Many adherents of various traditions believe that they alone have the Truth and that anyone who doesn't follow their prescribed path is doomed. But early on, the Rabbis saw the pitfalls of teaching such an exclusionary, fundamentalist perspective. It is not easy to see that views that differ from ours may have merit and worth, especially if they go against the very grain of our moral system. But this is a spiritual challenge worth meeting.

When was the last time you thought you knew the truth about a particular matter? Were you willing to hear other opinions and other viewpoints? Perhaps we too need to let truth tumble from its lofty heights. Truth dwells among us and between us, and its pursuit and definition lie in our hands.   LF

Created in God's Image

24 June

Rabbi Akiva used to say: "Beloved is the human being—for the human was created in the image of God. God showed even greater love by letting the human being know that he or she was created in God's image."

MISHNAH[21]

God loves human beings and has expressed this love by creating them in God's image. Being created in the image of God means that every human being—man and woman; white, black, and yellow; young and old; famous and unknown; rich and poor; handsome and ugly—has the intrinsic dignities of infinite value, equality, and uniqueness.

Many people are treated as it they were not of infinite value; many people feel inferior; many are treated like numbers instead of like individuals. Therefore God showed even greater love by informing humans through the Torah that they are created in the image of God. Once people know and understand their true dignity in God's eyes, they will demand appropriate treatment and respect and they will show the same to others.

We who are commanded to imitate God should inform the other humans in our lives that they are all created in the image of God and should treat them accordingly.

RABBI IRVING GREENBERG[22]

Healing from Pain

25 JUNE

*If your entire body is in pain, you should
occupy yourself with Torah.*

TALMUD[23]

It is rare that you have the opportunity to prevent an illness
with the same ingredient that is used to care for it. This statement sounds contradictory, but it is not. The ancient Rabbis
believed that "Torah is a healing balm." Its words contain
the secrets of well-being, but they can help you only if you
are prepared to study the sacred text in depth.

Some people are not motivated to approach the Torah
unless—or until—they need it. But truthfully, we all need it,
but not all of us know this fact. So spiritual pain comes to
remind us of Torah. How do we get rid of the spiritual pain
when it emerges? We enter into the text and become
immersed in its cleansing waters. When we enter into dialogue with the Torah, it becomes alive and we become one
with our biblical ancestors as they struggle with their own
faith and their journey toward the Divine.   KO

Today

26 JUNE

*Yesterday and tomorrow are humanity's downfall.
Today you may be aroused toward God. But yesterday
and tomorrow pull you back.*

RABBI NACHMAN OF BRESLOV[24]

We spend much of our time dwelling on the past or worrying about the future. But we can't change the past, and the

future is largely beyond our control. Nevertheless, past and future tug on us continually. We wonder if things would be different had we made different decisions. We might say to ourselves, "What if I had gone to medical school, or married David or Susan, or taken that job offer?" The phrase "what if" only leaves us in the past, stuck and immobile.

Images of the future can obsess us as well. We worry about growing old and about our children's well-being and about our security. Some of these matters we can address in thoughtful ways, but others are beyond us and in the hands of the Holy One.

If our minds are filled with all these thoughts, how often are we fully in the present? Most likely, not often enough. We need to train ourselves to stay focused and to experience fully what we are doing moment to moment. Finish reading this passage, then close your eyes and follow your breath. See how long you can follow your breath and be fully present without being distracted by your incoming thoughts. Probably only seconds. Note what arises in your mind. Is the thought about something in the past or the future? Just take note and return to your breath and the present moment. This meditation shows us where our thoughts take us. It gently teaches us to return to the moment at hand. LF

The Fragility of Trust

27 JUNE

It is better to take refuge in God than to take refuge in your neighbor. It is better to take refuge in God than to trust princes.
PSALM 118:8

The absence or presence of trust can either create or destroy relationships. Covenants are either strengthened or weakened by every word and every act. To be blunt: We either re-covenant or we betray. Every relationship is more fragile than we think it is because the possibilities of betrayal are always lurking.

First, there are betrayals of language. Every time we are insincere, we betray the trust others have in the meaning of words. Second, there are betrayals of responsibility that occur whenever we fail to do what another person needs us to do. Whether failing to be a full partner in a marriage to failing to observe basic rules of safety, we can betray the trust that others put in us. Just to drive is to trust the other drivers; to fly means to trust the pilots and air traffic controllers; to have friends, to build families, to have a community are all leaps of faith and exercises in trust.

Our entire understanding of ourselves as a people depends on strengthening covenants. The establishment of the Jewish people was based on one unique trust, a covenant between God and Israel: On knowing that God will be our God and that we will be God's people. Because of that covenant, we have committed ourselves to living in a sacred relationship and in a sacred bond of trust.

Today how can we strengthen the bonds which underlay the covenants we cherish? RABBI RACHEL SABATH

Walking the Talk

28 JUNE

The essential thing is not study. Rather it is "mitzvah-deeds."
MISHNAH[25]

Most people translate this text differently, substituting the word *mitzvot* or deeds for "mitzvah-deeds." But the translation above, by contemporary poet-author-teacher Danny Siegel, reflects a profound understanding of the intent of the Rabbis who penned this aphorism. "*Mitzvah*-deeds" are those special activities that God directs us to do. By doing them, we are able to raise the level of the world one notch closer to the heavens.

So study hard. Engage sacred text. Teach one another the words of Torah. Don't consider yourself finished until you have ventured out into the world and touched another person. KO

The Beauty of Disagreement

29 June

In truth each person has a unique opinion; everyone who is engaged in a dispute must acknowledge that his companion also has a unique point of view. One should not stay rigidly attached to his own idea, but search for truth. In this way, God will help the eyes see clearly, and peace will come from conflict.
BIBLICAL COMMENTARY[26]

Our world is mired in disputes. Some take on grand, historical proportions while others are petty, inconsequential tiffs. Yet, whether big or small, these disputes drain our cooperative spirits, sap our energy, and depress us. They also feed the cynicism which can pervade our lives. Instead, we need to broaden our minds to provide uplift and hope to resolve these disagreements.

In our personal lives we might also be involved in a contentious relationship with someone. In extreme situations, this can lead to a "family feud" in which we don't talk to a family member for years. In every instance, we can only grow by trying to see the situation from the opposite perspective. Perhaps we will see something new which will allow us to resolve differences that seemed insolvable. Perhaps we will be able to remain in a relationship with others despite existing disagreements.

The world is too small, and our lives are too brief, for us to allow disputes to overwhelm us. Let us commit ourselves to expanding our outlook and working toward peace.   LF

Boundaries and Borders

30 JUNE

You shall call your walls "salvation" and your gates "praise."
ISAIAH 60:18

What did the prophet Isaiah mean when he foretold that the nation of Israel, at the moment of redemption would call the walls around their cities "salvation" and the gates that enter into them "praise"? Could it be that the people would experience impenetrable protection from God as they waged their wars, and therefore their protective walls would be symbols of God's salvation and their sturdy gates cause for divine praise? This doesn't seem to be the case, for the very beginning of this verse predicts that "Violence shall no more be heard in your land!"(Isaiah 60:18).

Rabbi David Kimchi, a medieval commentator, explains that prior to redemption, when war and violence would plague the Jewish nation, the people would climb the city walls to protect themselves from the enemy and would gather around the city gates to share information about the battle. But when salvation comes, when the walls no longer need to be scaled and the gates no longer need to be used as a meeting place for war stories, the people will gather at these places to proclaim redemption and sing praises to God.

We live in a world not yet fully redeemed, in which most of our cities do not have walls or gates. And those that do are hardly able to keep the world out, what with instant global telecommunication.

Yet despite the relative physical openness and accessibility of our world, we continue to build walls and gates made of ideological, religious, and racial divisiveness. Oppression persists as our differences sever us from the human family.

Cultural and ethnic diversity will never disappear. And it shouldn't, for it testifies to the beauty and grandeur of God's creation. Our task in hastening the day of redemption is to celebrate these "walls" and "gates" which define our communities and not let them force others out of our world. We must find a way to promote and glorify that which distinguishes us while, at the same time, appreciate and respect that which is unique about other persons. Only then will our walls become sources of salvation and our gates become causes for praise. RABBI ADINA LEWITTES[27]

JULY

Reaching Beyond Routine

1 JULY

*We naturally like what we have become accustomed
to. . . . This is one of the causes that prevents humans from
finding truth.*
MOSES MAIMONIDES[1]

We all have a routine we like to call our own. Most of us
follow this routine almost every day. It makes our lives predictable and offers a sense of balance, something for which
we all yearn. These routines take all forms. They involve our
use of the bathroom, our eating habits, the order in which we
put clothes on. Some of these basic routines are prescribed by
Jewish tradition. We call them religious rituals. They help us
transcend the mundane. When we are fortunate, they actually
help us on our journey to meet the Divine. Sometimes it takes
many, many repetitions of the same routine before we are
able even to consider the possibility of reaching God.

But because such rituals are repeated in the same way
each day, they also have the potential to be quite limiting.
Since we are used to them, and they fuse with our personali-

ty, we generally do not want to change them. "This is the way that I have always done it," we might say. "This is part of who I am."

The great teacher and medieval philosopher Moses Maimonides taught a certain truth about finding the truth. It is cited above. His advice is no less significant now than when he first offered it almost nine centuries ago. If we are not willing to stretch our souls and grow beyond the familiar, then we cannot find the truth. And it is the truth that we constantly seek. KO

Watching Our Tongue

2 JULY

Keep your distance from falsehood.
EXODUS 23:7

Do you remember when you told your first lie as a child? Did you get away with it, or were you caught? If you got away with it, how did you feel? Telling lies can be insidious. It can be a habit that is hard to break. Lying is one aspect of *lashon hara,* the Hebrew term for slanderous talk and gossip, which the Torah teaches us is as serious as murder. We may lie to protect ourselves or someone we love. Yet one lie leads to others, and before we know it, we are buried under the burden of our lies. Lying eclipses the fullness of our spirit.

Judaism demands that we stop lying and that we keep our distance from those who spread falsehoods or that we change the topic if they start speaking slander about others. Falsehoods have a tendency to spread like fire. They can ruin a person's life. Though it is not easy to remove ourselves from listening to a juicy piece of gossip, we are called on to put the fire out before it starts. Can you distance yourself from such a situation? LF

On Pluralism in America

3 JULY

May there be peace within your walls and security within your gates.
PSALM 122:7

Two great dates of freedom fall in July: July 4th is the anniversary of the U.S. Declaration of Independence, which launched the American Revolution, and July 14th is Bastille Day, the date on which the French people celebrate the fall of the Bastille prison in Paris, an opening salvo in the French Revolution. Each revolution was undergirded by a different cultural model of freedom. Jews have been the direct and major beneficiaries of both revolutions, but the difference between the two revolutions has led to different Jewish experiences of freedom.

In France, the price of equality for Jews was to stop being different. As Clermon-Tonnerre expressed, "To the Jews as individuals, everything would be given; to the Jews as a nation, nothing." In retrospect, equality is not true equality if one group, the Jews, must prove their worthiness by giving up their own heritage. After all, all the other French were not asked to give up their heritage as the price of liberty. Underlying the French grant of freedom was the assumption that there is one model of citizenship and one universal culture and that Jews must earn their freedom at the cost of their uniqueness.

In America, Jews were not fully accepted in America as of July 4, 1776, although the declaration that "all men are created equal" did not exclude Jews. There was also pressure to assimilate in America. As John Quincy Adams said, immigrants "must cast off their European skin, never to resume it." Yet because this was a nation of immigrants, the assumption of one unitary culture was fairly weak from the very beginning. Many churches, synagogues, school systems, and standards of cultural authority grew up in America.

Despite the pressure which any majority generates over any minority in a democracy, the July 4th freedom model pointed a way to a multi-ethnic society. As a result, the Jewish community maintained itself quite visibly, and America has become a more truly pluralistic society.

Pluralism may yet turn out to be the greatest gift American Jewry has given to the United States: Pluralism is the greatest assurance that democracy will be strong and that there will be justice. In fact, the Jewish experience of freedom in America points the way to a universal freedom that truly respects the variety and richness of human culture.

RABBI IRVING GREENBERG

Independence

4 JULY

Proclaim liberty throughout the land to all its inhabitants.
LEVITICUS 25:10

Freedom. Liberty. Independence. Self-determination. These are some of the critical concepts that we associate with the Fourth of July. But they often slip from our focus as we engage in all the other activities of this holiday. Families and friends get together, but they infrequently reflect on the very basic ideas that shape our lives as Americans. We too easily take for granted the liberties that were hard won and the freedom that is ours. Instead of self-reflection or dwelling on the fundamental beliefs of our country, we enjoy parades, fireworks, and picnics, or we go away for a long weekend.

During the days of the Temple in Jerusalem, there was also much sharing of food as pilgrims offered it to the priests to sacrifice on their behalf to God. But then it was understood that the smoke of the consecrated flesh wafted heavenward as penance for sins and as a plea to God for mercy. On July 4th, we don't ask for mercy. Nor do we think too much about our sins or the sins of our nation. But we do gather around campfires and barbecue grills, and smoke does waft toward heaven. As we follow it with our eyes, we can think of the grace which God has shown us and the bounty which the Divine has given our country.   KO

Presenting Ourselves without Pretense

5 JULY

The best thing is . . . to serve God from your heart without falsehood or sham, not giving out to people that you are one thing, while, God forbid, in your heart you are another.
GLÜCKEL OF HAMELN[2]

It can be tempting to present ourselves to others falsely. Sometimes we do this by changing our external appearance and think that no one will look any further. Or we create aliases on the Internet and assume a whole new persona. Perhaps doing so fulfills a fantasy that, for a short time, we can change who we are and become someone totally different. This habit can be seductive. It can give us an opportunity to present ourselves in new ways that others do not allow us to try. In fact, though, it takes a lot of effort to pretend to be someone other than who we truly are. We end up distancing ourselves from ourselves and from others. In essence, what we are doing is denying those parts of ourselves of which we are ashamed and pretending that they will disappear. Alas, they do not.

Glückel of Hameln, a Jewish woman, wrote letters to her children in the late 1600's as a way to give them guidance and direction. Her insight—that we must strive to become whole with who we are and not misrepresent ourselves—is wisdom we can all heed today.   LF

Entering the Sacred

6 July

Behold God is my salvation. I will trust and not be afraid, for God is my strength and song.
ISAIAH 12:2[3]

Legends in the Talmud and Midrash speak of Adam at the termination of the Sabbath when the sun sank and darkness began to set in. A terrified Adam thought, "Surely indeed, the darkness shall bruise me." God inspired Adam to find two stone flints. One was marked with the name *afelah*, which is "darkness." The other was inscribed with *mavet,* which is "death." Adam struck the flints against each other. The friction produced a spark with which he lit a torch. The fire comforted him throughout the night, and in the morning Adam saw the rising of the sun. He then observed, "This is the way of the world."

Out of darkness and death, a spark is created. There is darkness and there is light, the fear of death and the hope of survival. Therefore we recite a blessing over the termination of the Sabbath because the movement back into the regular week was created for the first time. And we begin the

Havdalah prayer, which separates the end of Shabbat from the rest of the week, with a benedictory prologue of courage: "Behold God is my salvation. I will trust and not be afraid, for God is my strength and song."

RABBI HAROLD SCHULWEIS[4]

Finding True Happiness

7 JULY

The best way to attain happiness is not to seek it.
MOSES MONTEFIORE[5]

The promise of happiness fuels the advertising industry: If we buy a certain car or house, we will find happiness. The advertisers prove this either through pictures of smiling people or through personal testimony. The entire industry of infomercials is based on this theory. We are so desirous of happiness that sometimes we buy some things whether or not we need them because they seduce us with their alleged potential to bring us joy.

For a fleeting moment we might find what we perceive is happiness through these products. Then reality bites and we are back where we started. And we still have the problem we were trying to escape.

Summer presents us with all kinds of opportunity. It is more casual and less pressured than the rest of the year. We can take things a little easier and use the opportunity to think through our ideas on happiness. By its very nature, happiness is elusive, maybe because we pursue it so relentlessly. Instead we should simply appreciate the fact that we wake up every day; the happiness that accompanies that event should frame our day. That's why Jewish tradition includes two long prayers and a series of short blessings that are said shortly after arising. In summary, these blessings read, "Thank God, I am alive. There is much work to do. Come let's start our day together." KO

Learning from Life's Circumstances

8 July

To young and old, then, the same advice must be given: Turn every trial to account, however trifling in its character, to make of it as a polishing instrument that will change the roughest stone into the jeweler's prize.

RACHEL SIMON[6]

It is easy to say we must learn from everything that happens to us. This is the kind of refrain that we have resented hearing from our parents since childhood. Yet it is true. Nevertheless, it is difficult to put this advice to the test. It takes great courage to do so. Whether we lose our jobs, break up with our beloved, or suffer the death of a loved one, it is often impossible to think there is a lesson in these tragedies. On such occasions we find ourselves asking, "Why me, God?" To our dismay, there is not always a good answer.

Our life is made up of big and small incidents. We can ignore them—or we can use them as opportunities for growth. We can learn from each event, the good and the bad. Many times it is beyond us to change the situation, but we can be conscious of how we respond to it and, in this way, learn to respond differently in the future should a similar situation arise. Then we can grow beyond it. LF

The Mixture of Life

9 JULY

In this world there is no perfect joy unmixed with anxiety,
no perfect pleasure unmixed with envy;
but in the future the Holy One will perfect
our joy and pleasure.
MIDRASH[7]

All of us experience joy and pain in the course of our life-time. Sometimes our suffering seems total; we cannot recall the moment of joy, nor can we summon hope for the future. At other times our joy is so great, our hearts so full, that we cannot imagine that we may yet again know dullness, doubt, or depression. This modern midrash reminds us that our lives are a mixture of both suffering and joy:

When Abraham was called to sacrifice his son Isaac on Mount Moriah, he had a vision of the future of the Jewish people. He saw a long, dark tunnel with Isaac standing at the front and Isaac's son Jacob behind him, and behind Jacob were Jacob's children—Dina and all the tribes—and all the generations lined up behind them, stretching back through the generations. All Abraham saw in that dark tunnel were the pogroms, the oppression, the genocides against the Jewish people. So he decided to raise his knife and slay Isaac in order to prevent all that suffering from happening. But at that moment another tunnel appeared before Abraham. This time it was a tunnel of light. He saw Isaac standing at the front and Jacob behind him, and Dina and all the tribes behind Jacob, and all the generations lined up behind them, stretching back through the generations. But in this tunnel all Abraham saw were the beautiful Shabbat celebrations, the festive dancing on the holidays, and the songs that reached to heaven. Overcome with the beauty of this vision, he decided that he should not slay Isaac. He realized that the suffering and the joy would come together, and that to get rid of one would be to get rid of the other.　　RABBI NANCY FLAM

Hearts and Hands to Heaven

10 JULY

Let us lift our hearts with our hands to
God in heaven.
LAMENTATIONS 3:41

This selection from Lamentations is more than a statement of faith that is read on Tisha b'Av, which commemorates Jewish historical tragedy, particularly the destruction of the ancient Temples in Jerusalem. Tisha b'av occurs anywhere from the middle to the end of the summer, depending on when it occurs on the Gregorian calendar. In the playful heat of the summer, it forces us to take serious note of those who have come before us. It has an uncanny way of coloring the entire month in which it falls. The attitude it encourages us to adopt can inform all that we do.

By lifting our hearts to God, we pray that God will direct Divine attention to us. There is more here than turning our hearts to God. By doing so, we are taking initiative. We are not leaving the solution to any problem we may be facing to God. Instead we are enacting our part of the covenant and exercising our responsibility in the partnership.

So take action. Use your own strength and lift yourself up. Then you can be lifted up even more by God.　　KO

Embracing Life

11 JULY

I am filled with confidence, not that I shall succeed
in worldly things, but that even when things
go badly for me, I shall still find life
good and worth living.

ETTY HILLESUM[8]

Perhaps the essence of knowing that we have developed a spiritual core is being able to see and embrace the good even when surrounded by suffering and horror. The words above were written by Etty Hillesum on July 11, 1942, while she was living in Amsterdam under Nazi occupation. A young woman in her mid-twenties, Hillesum diligently recorded in her diaries her personal and spiritual response to the collapse of the life she had known. In the face of pure insanity, Etty didn't despair, but rather found the grace to hold onto life as good.

We all experience painful, trying times. We all know sickness, death, financial insecurity, and family problems. It is all too easy to throw our hands up when we hit the bumps in life's journey. But the question always remains, "Can we still find the good, the blessing, the love in the midst of our travails?" Etty Hillsum never lost her love for life. Even after she was deported to Westerbork (the main transit camp for Dutch Jewry during the German occupation of Holland, located in the northeastern Netherlands), and later to Auschwitz, where she died in 1943, she never denied that life held insurmountable good although she was living amid unmitigated evil.

In her memory, let us commit ourselves to see the good in our lives even when our hearts are heavy. Let us infuse ourselves with the confidence that we will succeed, despite our struggles. Behold, life is good and we embrace it.   LF

Seizing Freedom

12 JULY

You think that wealth will make you free.
But I say this: freedom is not bought but seized.
Freedom is not the last step, but the first.
AFTER ECCLESIASTES 5:9

There is no path to freedom. There is no technique to get clear of the things that hold you fast. Moses tried to talk Pharaoh into letting his people go. It didn't work. Then he threatened him with plagues. Still Pharaoh refused. Finally Moses, at God's behest, just decided to leave Egypt.

Look at the story carefully. Many people think that Pharaoh let the Hebrews leave because the death of the firstborn Egyptians was too much for him to handle. His spirit was broken, at least momentarily, and he relented. But this is not true.

Moses instructed the people to leave before the final plague. He was taking them out of Egypt regardless of Pharaoh's response to the mass murder of his people. They were packed and ready to go. The fact that Pharaoh agreed only made it a bit easier to leave, but they were leaving regardless.

Freedom cannot be granted by another person. It cannot be bestowed. It is proclaimed and lived, or it doesn't exist. Don't wait for someone to grant you freedom. Seize it wherever you find it and don't let it go!   RABBI RAMI SHAPIRO

Sparks of Holiness

13 JULY

Everything created by God contains a spark of holiness.
BAAL SHEM TOV

Since everything has been created by God—even those things crafted by human hands—everything has a spark of holiness in it. This sounds great, but what happens when we encounter something that does not seem very holy? Do we just write off this one thing or this person as void of a holy spark? Perhaps an individual can loosen the holy spark from him or herself by performing certain horrible deeds. And maybe there are some inanimate objects, or even animals, that do not have holy sparks. Perceiving the world in this way would certainly make it easier to understand the world as being either good or bad. Or so it would seem. But the Baal Shem Tov's statement is a challenge to us rather than an outright description of reality. The Baal Shem Tov is trying to teach us that we have an obligation to find that spark of holiness in *each* individual and in *everything* that has been created. And when we can't find it, we just have to look harder.   KO

Grasping for the Real

14 JULY

Worldly pleasures are like sunbeams in a dark room. They may seem solid, but one who tries to grasp a sunbeam finds nothing in his hand.
RABBI NACHMAN OF BRESLOV[10]

Our culture advocates material consumption. It often succeeds in convincing us that our worth is connected solely to our possessions. "The more we have, the better we are" is a message advertisers convey to us time and time again. Surely we have all been seduced at one time or another by glitzy advertising. This is not easy to resist. Many of us have also experienced the thrill of buying the newest gadget or item only to say to ourselves the next morning, "Do we really need this? What was I thinking yesterday that I thought this was so essential?" Many things bring momentary excitement that passes in due time. What, though, brings long-lasting contentment?

When we know deep down what is truly lasting, then we can ask ourselves if we are striving for the right things. Do we exert ourselves for elusive thrills or for deep and sustaining joys?

Consider what three things have given you a sense of contentment and wholeness in the past month. Are they easily disposable? Do they bring you into meaningful contact with others? Do they isolate you from others? As Rabbi Nachman explains, so often our grasping is for the hollow instead of for the holy. Reach for the holy!   LF

The Wisdom of the Wilderness

15 July

Wisdom can only come by way of a willingness
to accept truth from any source.
Solomon ibn Gabirol

Apparently, for the first year following the liberation of the Israelite slaves from Egypt, they had begun to move into the wilderness. There they would spend the next 38 years continuing their travels and their intimate dialogue with God, a dialogue that would form the roots and essence of our Torah.

For the generation of liberation and wandering, the bulk of their lives was spent in the wilderness. Why? What is so significant about the wilderness? According to one midrash, our Rabbis taught that Torah was given with three things: fire, water, and wilderness. Why, the Rabbis ask, is the giving of the Torah accompanied by these three features? Their answer indicates that just as these three things are freely accessible to humanity, so too are the words of Torah free and available to all.

In other words, the wisdom in the Torah is the property of all humanity, not just the Jews! No one owns the wilderness, since it stands outside the boundaries of any nation. And no one owns God's love, loyalty, or concern in a way that others do not. Claiming to possess a monopoly on God's love diminishes God's grandeur and is a form of blasphemy and human arrogance.

The Torah was given in the wilderness to warn us not to mistake this gift as exclusively ours, to declare that the possession of Torah does not make us more worthwhile, more valuable, or better than others. The wilderness, then, is a reminder of the accessibility of God and of God's will to all people. Moreover, just as the wilderness is open on every side, taking in travelers from any direction, so too the religious seeker must be willing to listen to all—not with an ear for converting the speaker to one's faith, but rather for extracting whatever insight, truth, or wisdom that speaker might transmit.   Rabbi Bradley Shavit Artson

Admitting Arrogance

16 JULY

The haughtiness of the individual shall be made to bow down. God above shall be exalted on that day.
ISAIAH 2:11

I admit it. While I try not to be arrogant, sometimes certain behavior that marked my adolescence creeps up on me. It is *yetzer hara* (inclination to do evil) that maturity helps me keep in check. So I turn to the prophets for inspiration, guidance, and loving rebuke.

Our daily liturgy constantly repeats this notion of Isaiah. The daily recitation of these prayers centers me and focuses me each day. They are a further reminder that God is above and we are below, reaching heavenward. They remind me of our relationship with God, of the responsibilities implied by our covenantal relationship, of the need to be humble and modest. So each day, I look to the sky and then bow my head in reverence until that final messianic day comes when all our heads shall be raised up and there will be no one and no thing that will force our heads to be forced down.   KO

The Need for Vision

17 JULY

When there is no vision, the people perish.
PROVERBS 29:18

Moses had a vision. Theodor Herzl had a vision. Ghandi had a vision. Martin Luther King, Jr., had a vision. The power of their visions changed history. Moses liberated an enslaved people; Herzl inspired a new country; Ghandi led a nonviolent revolution; and King dreamt of a land free of racial bigotry. These leaders would never have succeeded in rallying hundreds of thousands of people, even millions of people, to effect change without having a powerful vision. A leader without a vision will quickly disappear. Each of us needs a vision for our own lives to inspire and motivate us.

Our families need a vision to maintain a sense of belonging, and our communities need a vision to create a sense of cohesion. It takes work to develop a vision. Through study, discussion, meditating, and prayer, we can develop a vision for our lives that will be both clear and compelling. We need to articulate this for ourselves so it becomes alive and integral in every being. Prophets used to be society's visionaries. Today we each need to be a prophet to fill the world with inspiration and hope.   LF

Acting in Sync with the Moment

18 JULY

Thus I understand the simple truth of life:
There is nothing better than for you to rejoice in every deed
done in harmony with the moment.
For doing is your purpose; in doing is your meaning.
Leave the result to those who come after you, and attend
solely to doing well that which must be done at all.
AFTER ECCLESIASTES 3:21–22[11]

Doing in harmony with the moment is Ecclesiastes' key to tranquillity. He has already told us that each moment has its own integrity: a moment for birth, a moment for death, a time for building, a time for tearing down. Our challenge is to discern the integrity of the moment and act in sync with it.

Intuitively you know this to be true. Think back to any time you found yourself in conflict with another person. At the root of the problem was an inability to fathom what was needed in the moment. What the moment called for was an admission of error and a sincere apology. What you offered was an excuse or an explanation. What was called for was a healing silence, acknowledging the real grief. What was offered was a hollow homily on why this must have happened for a reason.

We tend to act not in harmony with the moment, but in harmony with our own story or our own need for reason and understanding. We project our supposed need onto the moment and act from that, when what we really need to do is to let go of our projections and stories and perceive what the moment calls forth in and of itself.

Strike a bell with its clapper and it rings true the first time and the hundredth time. It is always true to its own nature. It could be the same with us. We too have a true nature from which we could respond to the moments of life. But we don't. Why? Because our true nature is fleeting and we desire something permanent. It is our fear of impermanence, our fear of emptiness, that blinds us. Try letting go of impermanence today and act in sync with each moment.   RABBI RAMI SHAPIRO

Raising Spirits

19 JULY

As water flows to the lowest level, so Torah finds its way to the lowliest of spirit.

TALMUD[12]

For some people, summer is very difficult. Not because of the heat or the humidity. During the rest of the year, people are always busy working. Some people even take their work home with them at night. There never seems to be enough time in the day to do what needs to be done. Yet often work is a camouflage for loneliness.

Then comes the summer and people join their families or their lovers or friends on trips that they have been planning and looking forward to for months. They visit exotic places or do simple things like sleeping late, reading books, taking long walks, drinking good coffee, or taking in a movie.

Especially for those for whom summer is lonely, we recommend study. Why? For "Torah finds its way to the lowliest of spirit" and raises you up.   KO

Shabbat Saves the World

20 JULY

To really observe the Sabbath in our day and age!
To cease for a whole day from all business, from all work,
amidst the frenzied hurry-scurry of our age!
To close the stock exchanges, the stores, the factories—how
would it be possible? The pulse of life would stop beating
and the world perish! The world perish?
To the contrary, it would be saved.

RABBI SAMSON RAPHAEL HIRSCH[13]

While Shabbat takes place only on Friday evening through Saturday evening, and occurs every seven days—never changing from year to year regardless of the date—it is the prism through which we count each day of the week. Rabbi Hirsch wrote the passage above in the mid-1800s in Germany. Imagine what he would say today. If he thought that his life over a century ago was fast-paced, then our lives today would seem like a frantic tumult to him.

Shabbat is a unique concept which the Jews gave civilization. It taught us that we could step back from our engagement with the world for one day a week to renew our spirit and relationships. Though we are called human *beings,* most often we are human *doings.* Shabbat returns us to our true state, one in which we are not driven to create, change, or alter anything in God's world.

Many of us are afraid to slow down. We wouldn't know what to do without constant activity. This fear is a sign that we are distant from our inner selves. We are afraid to be by ourselves and uncover what we think and feel in the quiet of nonactivity. Once we quiet down, we can become reacquainted with ourselves and with a more relaxed pace of being.

Shabbat means we draw boundaries and say "No" to the many things that take up our time and attention for six days a week. By embracing Shabbat, we say "Yes" to our friends, families, and ourselves, with whom we get to spend uninterrupted time. LF

The Fear of Hope

21 July

In Judaism, faith is . . . the capacity of the soul to perceive the abiding in the transitory; the invisible in the visible.
RABBI LEO BAECK[14]

I learn most of my theology, not from my teachers but from my children. When my daughter was three years old, each night shortly after I tucked her into bed and she would scream, "Daddy! There's an alligator under my bed!" I would calmly return to her room, turn on every light, and look under the bed. "No alligator. No monsters. Now go to bed.

Tomorrow is a new day and you've got to get some sleep. Everything is safe. Good night."

We did this dance for an entire year until one night I asked myself the question: Who is right? Whose description of the world is factually correct? The child afraid of alligators under the bed, or the father who reassures her that everything is safe and tomorrow is surely coming? The beginning of spirituality is our experience of God's presence. An adolescent can proclaim his disbelief. It's easy for him—he doesn't put children to bed each night. He is isolated; there is no one whose life and hope depend upon him. But those of us who live with others, who live for others, we know better. Having children, raising children, loving another with all our soul is an exercise in spirituality.

Spirituality is not something added to life. It is underneath life, just beneath the surface of consciousness. It represents the answers to the ultimate questions of our lives—questions we may never have consciously asked but whose answers ring through our daily actions. Why do we get out of bed every morning? Where do we find the hope, strength, and inspiration to go on each day? How do we cope with all that is terrifying in life?

Judaism is a way to ask these questions consciously. It is a way of sharing the answers of the generations that have come before us. And it is a discipline for facing our fears, listening to the questions, and searching out the answers.

RABBI EDWARD FEINSTEIN

Study Trips

22 JULY

*If you are alone on a journey, you should occupy
yourself with Torah.*

TALMUD[15]

Since summer is a time for vacation, many of us find ourselves traveling this time of year. Sometimes our travels take
us far from home. Wherever we travel, we should remember
the words of what Jewish tradition calls the Traveler's Prayer,
available in most traditional prayer books. This prayer asks
God to watch us as we venture out into the world, away
from the protection of our home and community. Say it
before you leave and encourage others to do the same. Keep a
copy in your pocket or in your bag. Then when you get to the
place you are going, remember to bring words of Torah along
with you. Each Friday evening and Saturday morning, we
must *remember* Shabbat even if there is not a community in
which to *observe* it.   KO

How to Reach Out to God

23 JULY

*One who does charitable deeds is greater than one who
brings sacrifices, as it says, "One who does justice and
charity is more dear to God than one who brings burnt
offerings on the altar."*

TALMUD[16]

Sacrifices seem far removed from our present way of life. Yet
at one time sacrifices were the central means of worship in

Israel. The Temple in Jerusalem was the center of the ancient Jewish spiritual world. People came from all over Israel to offer sacrifices. The teaching above was written after the Second Temple was destroyed. Then, without a Temple, sacrifices were no longer a viable way to communicate sorrow, praise, gratitude, or remorse to God. The Rabbis of the new era had to direct the people creatively to new modes of religious expression. They taught that acts of justice and charity took the place of sacrifices.

Thankfully, acts of justice and charity are not a thing of the past. We can each participate in such acts by visiting someone in the hospital, volunteering at a homeless shelter, giving *tzedakah* (charitable giving), and working for social justice issues. There are many additional ways to embrace just and charitable action. Look around: What are the specific needs of your own community? Doing these is one way to form a living relationship with the Holy One.   LF

The Letters of Our Lives

24 JULY

A person is like a letter of an alphabet: to produce a word, it must combine with another.
BENJAMIN MANDELSTAMM[17]

There is an old Hasidic story, recounted by Martin Buber, of the disciples who gathered to learn from their rebbe, the Baal Shem Tov, the founder of Hasidim. After the evening prayers, the master would go to his room where candles would be lit and "the mysterious Book of Creation" lay open on the table. All those seeking advice from the Baal Shem were then admitted in a group to hear their teacher, who would speak late into the night.

One evening as the students left the room, one apologized to the others for monopolizing so much of the Baal Shem's attention. Throughout the entire audience, the master had spoken to him personally. His friend told him not to talk such nonsense. They had all entered the room together and, from the very beginning, the master had spoken only to him. A third, hearing this, laughed and said that they both were mistaken, for their teacher had carried on an intimate conversation with him alone for the entire evening. A fourth and fifth made the same claim: The Baal Shem had spoken to them personally to the exclusion of everyone else. Only then did they realize what had happened and all fell silent.

So it is with us when we read scripture. The biblical text speaks intimately and demands an intensely personal response. As Harold Bloom has said of reading "strong poetry," the interpretation evoked "insist[s] upon itself . . . and the text are one." Because the words of the poem speak to me, I am not free to comment dispassionately on them, for I am in them. They are me. What you say of the poem you say of me.

RABBI LAWRENCE KUSHNER[18]

Running toward God

25 JULY

Let us know, let us run to know God.
HOSEA 6:3

It seems that we have two choices: running toward or running away from God. So let's examine why we would choose one path over the other. In the book of Genesis we encounter Adam hiding from God after doing precisely what he was told not to do. God seeks Adam and calls out, *"Ayeka?"* "Where are you?" This is probably more for Adam's benefit than for the benefit of God. Of course God knows where Adam is hiding. Later in the Bible the prophet Jonah actually tried to run away from the task God set before him. He boarded a ship to Tarshish. According to the Bible, he did not get very far. He ended up in the belly of a big fish, with lots of time to reflect on his actions. Thus his running away caused him unintentionally to get closer to himself and to the Divine forces in his life that were directing him.

Running away does not always demand a change in physical space. Often it means retreating inside the self, which is one of the places where God can be found. So in running away, we are actually running toward God.

Some people try to run away from responsibility. Or they face a crisis and try to leave it behind. Doing this often creates much emotional debris. And unfortunately, there are those who try to leave responsibility behind permanently by taking their own lives.

This is the bottom line: The only direction to run is *toward* God. Any other running has no direction.   KO

Our Uniqueness

26 JULY

Every single person is a new thing in the world and is called upon to fulfill his or her particularity in the world.
MARTIN BUBER[19]

Each of us has unique qualities through which we relate to others and to our surroundings. Some of us are artistic, others are great organizers. Some of us are musical, while others are business-minded. Through a mysterious process, we are each dealt certain gifts at birth, which we can choose to nurture and develop as we mature. A *midrash* illustrates this matter by saying that each time a king mints coins, they are all identical; yet when God creates a human being, he or she is unique. No two of us are totally identical, not even twins.

What are your particular strengths and gifts? Are you a good listener or planner? Are you humorous? Through these God-inspired gifts, we have unique ways to touch others and transform the world. Embrace your specialness and shine in your uniqueness.   LF

Discovering Our Own Purpose

27 JULY

All beginnings require that you unlock new doors.
RABBI NACHMAN OF BRESLOV

For four hundred years, the Hebrews dwelt in Egypt. It was a dark, dark time. Who were we? We had no Abraham, no Sarah, no Joseph, no Torah. Did we even know God? Had we been passed over? Our people knew their names; they knew their tribes. Though genealogy sustained them, they became slaves of Pharaoh and the Egyptians. They were isolated, without meaningful identity.

Then the plagues struck. The darkness did to the Egyptians what the Egyptians had done to us. Our centuries of pain became theirs; our losses became their losses. But we followed the pillar of fire through the wilderness until we reached Sinai and received our own light—Torah. We had identity. Now we became a people of purpose. We had a future.

The Rhiziner Rav wrote that "every Jewish soul has a spark from the Light Above. However, much depends on where Jews live. One can compare Jews to precious stones that, when mixed in sand, are not discerned as being valuable." Perhaps we are set in sand, unable to discern our value and Torah's light. Do we know how to live as Jews? Are we merely bound to one another tribally, or do we see purpose in our presence? Do we have a future?

American Jews are on a journey, even now. The Torah is our map. Make certain to unfold it so you can discover your route. And when night comes, you'll be amazed at how well that map radiates light. RABBI ELYSE FRISHMAN[20]

Seeing Life through Others

28 JULY

Happy are they who take refuge in God.
PSALM 2:12

Life is tough. There is no way of getting around it. Sure, for some it looks easier than for others. As a matter of fact, it always looks easier for others, since we are not the ones who have to live their lives. We can only see their life from our perspective. And until we have lived the life of the other, we can never know it.

As hard as we try to figure out why life appears easier for one person than for another, we still are clueless. Even were it possible to find some sort of logical answer to life's challenges, we would remain unsatisfied with the answers we might find. Such knowledge does not necessarily imply that we can change a situation. This problem happens frequently in medical science; physicians may be able to describe an illness or disease, but naming it does not give physicians control over a disease. It merely gives them insight.

So we get up each day and confront the world, looking for insights from the experiences we had the day before. There seems to be no other way to live.

We do not do this alone. Some of us are fortunate to have family and friends to help us bear the burdens we carry and to face the challenges of daily living. But too many of us feel alone, isolated and estranged from others. None of us, though, is truly alone. That is what the Sinai covenant was all about, the covenant that our people entered on our behalf thousands of years ago in the wilderness during their journey from Egyptian slavery.

All of us have God who can help. All of us can take refuge in God, for one of the names of God is *HaMakom,* which means "the place". It is only *there* where we can indeed find true refuge. KO

Friendship

29 July

One who finds a faithful friend finds a treasure.[21]
APOCRYPHA

From childhood friends to college roommates to colleagues at work to next-door neighbors, we all meet many people on our life's journey. We call many of these individuals our friends. For a short while our lives are intermingled, and we share happy and sad occasions with them. We need these friendships for support, companionship, and intimacy. But, as we all know, friends move in and out of our lives. People move, change jobs, remarry. It is the rare friend who remains in our lives over the decades and with whom we share our deepest doubts and burdens. Not many people will be honest with us for fear of hurting our feelings or losing our friend-ship. Our true friends are the few individuals who honestly reflect back to us our strengths and weaknesses and guide us back to the right path when we waver. They are our best cheerleaders and advocates. These friends are to be loved and cherished. With them, we will grow old and look back on the tapestry we have woven stitch by stitch in the making of our lives. The summer is a great time for renewing friendships that may have diminished somewhat during the rush of the rest of the year.

So be a faithful friend. Stand by the side of your friend and help put their life in perspective. LF

Withholding the Vision

30 JULY

Please let me cross over and see the good land that is beyond the Jordan, that good hill country, and Lebanon.
DEUTERONOMY 3:25

What the Torah doesn't tell us is that Moses was supposed to die ten times in the Wilderness but that he had beaten that fate, and at the end of forty years, as Moses stood on Mount Nebo and gazed at the Promised Land in the distance, he argued his case with God in a private language, mostly hand signs and grunts.

Moses distrusted spoken language, yet he was a natural storyteller. He could tell stories with few words, and everyone would understand him. He talked with his hands a good deal, and with his eyes. He could speak a whole story without words, and everyone would nod with understanding and delight.

He was able to talk this way because his soul was bound up with the people to whom he spoke. That was his power as a leader. The people would sit around the fire at night and he would speak their inner life. He would describe how they felt, and he was almost always right. His soul was so bound up with the people that when they were withheld from the Land, it was only natural that he be withheld too.

RABBI JAMES STONE GOODMAN[22]

Endings that Precede Beginnings

31 JULY

Better is the end of a thing than its beginning.
ECCLESIASTES 7:8

Most people acknowledge that beginnings are difficult. Our tradition has a variety of ways of expressing that sentiment. Writers generally do not attempt to explain the reason, because so many people readily resonate with the experience. However, few people talk about how difficult it is to end an experience. Sure there are those who might explain how to end a relationship or how to bring closure to an unpleasant encounter, but few are willing to teach us how to stop a pleasant experience. Perhaps this is so because ending seems counterintuitive. Why would someone want to discontinue something that brings pleasure? Simply put, we cannot live in a world of peak experiences. Generally, they cannot be maintained. Instead we nurture them in such a way as to bring continued pleasure and insight into the mundane. Some we even translate into ritual. But for most, we have to find a way to bring them to an end—and then move on with our lives.

Consider the journey of the Israelites through the desert. Although we may long to go back to the desert experience, convincing ourselves that the joy is in the journey, the Israelites eventually reached the Promised Land. But the journey did not really end at the entrance into Canaan. Rather it took a different form. It was transformed. Thus, unlike beginnings, endings are difficult only when we are unwilling to reframe them—and begin again. It is not easy to do this. The first step is often treacherous, but we only have to take it once.   KO

AUGUST

Seeing Yourself in the Eyes of Those You Love

1 AUGUST

I am to my beloved and my beloved is mine.
SONG OF SONGS 2:16A

The verse above is often recited during wedding ceremonies; some people even have it inscribed on wedding bands. While it is not apparent in the English, the first letter of each of the Hebrew words from this well-known verse spell out the word *Elul,* the name for the month that falls at the end of the summer, the month that precedes the fall holidays: Rosh Hashanah, Yom Kippur, and Sukkot. As might be expected, the Rabbis deduce a lesson from this notion and see it as a lens through which to view the entire month. This month of Elul, which generally coincides with August or early September, is devoted to intense introspection and self-evaluation, to what Jewish tradition calls *cheshbon hanefesh.*

For those who have already spent a good deal of time peering into their own souls, regardless of the time of year, they know that this process can be difficult and often painful. Many of us avoid the process entirely because of the inner turmoil that it can cause. Perhaps we are afraid of what we may find. We may be even more afraid of what it will be necessary for us to do in order to mend what we have found. That's why the message of this text is so important at this time of year. Although you may be engaged in a process of self-scrutiny that turns your world upside down, God calls out to you, as if to say, "Don't worry. 'You are my beloved and I am yours.'" The *Hasidim* suggest that, while we spend most of the year looking for God, God comes looking for us during this season, maybe because of what we are involved in this time of year, and because we are so spiritually spent as a result. Perhaps God understands that through the process, you may become disenchanted and give up on life entirely. Always remember: God is there, right by your side, in order to make sure that does not happen.

But there's more: Our tradition realizes that you will realize things about yourself and your relationship with others during the process of *cheshbon hanefesh* that you did not fully realize before. You may also realize that you have done things to hurt other people, so now you have to make the repair. You have to fix what is broken. Again God comes to teach you this text to remind you about the relationship that we each have with God. The philosopher-theologian Martin Buber suggested that our relationship with others should mirror our relationship with God. In the context of such profound love, anything is possible. KO

Choosing Life

2 August

*God does not predetermine whether a person shall be
righteous or wicked: that God leaves to us.*

MIDRASH[1]

Judaism teaches that each person has free will. Judaism also
teaches that everything is foreseen by God. This seems self-
contradictory, but it is not. It is part of the logic of the spirit.
We can each still decide on the path we pursue in life. I like to
frame my spiritual search as trying to figure out what God
wants me to do, because God already knows what I am going
to do—I just have to discover it for myself. Each of us has a
particular genetic makeup which influences our development
and decision-making. We also know that societal forces play
an important role in our growth. This debate of "nature versus
nurture" has yet to be put to rest. Despite the crucial role that
both genetics and culture have in shaping us, Judaism teaches
that we all have the ability to set our own course.

But we are not fatalists. We do not believe that our life-
course is predetermined. Instead we are partners with the
Almighty in this process. In the course of our life's journey
we will each be faced with many decisions. Some of these
may be relatively minor, but each contributes to the path we
take in life. In this respect, every decision we make—even
those that appear to be inconsequential—are in fact potentially life-changing. Certainly, the decisions about whether to
marry and whom we marry and whether to have children and
then how to raise them are basic, yet monumental, life choices. Other choices are whether to pursue healthy or unhealthy
habits, or how we spend our time and with whom, or our

work and what its role in our lives will be, and whether it renews or drains our life spirit.

Reflect about where you are today. What changes do you need to make to pursue life and blessing for yourself and your family so that you can "Choose life so you and your children may live"?   LF

Embracing the Light

3 AUGUST

Adonai is my light and my salvation.
PSALM 27:1

This verse from Psalms begins with the image of God as light. The text is taken from the psalm that we read daily for personal reflection for the entire month prior to Rosh Hoshanah and Yom Kippur, and in some communities through Hoshanah Rabbah (the month that usually coincides with August, although it may fall in September or even into October). The image of light evokes the notion of being visible: Both we and God see who we are and what we have done. None of us can hide in the dark, either from God or from ourselves. God's light is more penetrating than the light of the sun, since nothing remains hidden in God's light. When we see ourselves in God's light, our true selves emerge, complete with blemishes and imperfections. In some respects, God's light is the harsh light of truth, but it is simultaneously the healing light of God's Divine Presence. There is a healing quality in taking an honest look at ourselves, in appraising ourselves in the light of God's standards and God's concerns, for that light is forgiveness and healing for those who follow to completion the process of repentance, *teshuvah*.

We associate light with the ultimate redemption as well. Regarding the verse "God said: 'Let there be light!'" the Zohar teaches that this is "the first light God made before making the sun and the stars. God showed it to David, who burst into song. This was the light Moses saw on Sinai! At the creation, the universe from end to end radiated light, but it was withdrawn and now it is stored away for the righteous, until all the worlds are again in harmony and all is united and whole. Until this future world is established, this light, coming out of darkness and formed by the Most Secret One, is hidden. "Light is sown for the righteous" (Psalm 97:11).

Teshuvah is a redemptive process, and the light of the righteous is ours. It illuminates our path, step by step, when we engage in *teshuvah*. Do not fear the light.

RABBI AMY SCHEINERMAN

The Power of One

4 AUGUST

For the sake of one true penitent,
the whole world is redeemed.
TALMUD[2]

This is an amazing notion. We are worried about ourselves and our own well-being, convinced that we can do nothing about others. In other parts of the tradition we are even advised that we should not focus on others, because they are not our responsibility. When my children complain about someone, I usually advise them not to worry: "In the end, he or she has to live with himself or herself. You don't." Alternatively, I might say when people are attending an important event (and others are not), "At least, they are here, aren't they?" This tends to deflate the intensity of a complaint about the way someone dresses or behaves.

It is hard enough to try to make repairs on our own selves. But read the above text closely. It does not say that we should try to correct others. Instead, the Rabbis teach us that by repairing ourselves we provide an opportunity for others to do the same. When we approach others to make amends, we give them the opportunity to forgive us. And even if they are not yet able to do so, perhaps they will learn from our actions that it is possible to change what they have done.

When we make amends with other people, we are helping to repair a fractured world. We are doing our part to collect the shards of the vessels of light that were broken at the creation of the world, according to the legendary mystic Rabbi Isaac Luria. When we repent, we affirm our belief in the spiritual structure of the world. Because of our personal acts of repentance, God maintains a belief in humankind. With each act, we prove to the Divine that we are worthy, that God should not give up on us. Jewish tradition teaches that *teshuvah* (repentance), *tefillah* (prayer), and *tzedakah* (righteous acts of charitable giving) can avert the severe judgments that might take place during Yom Kippur and then sealed for the year to come.

Next time you see a friend engaged in *teshuvah,* even if the act of repentance has nothing to do with you, tell your friend, "Thanks, you just saved the world. And you saved me too!"   KO

Judging with Care

5 AUGUST

Judge your friend justly.[3] *This means that you must always*
give another person the benefit of the doubt
and judge favorably.
TALMUD[4]

We are all quick to judge others. Unfortunately, at times we do this instinctually. We see someone walking toward us and our mind jumps to assess how they are dressed, how they walk, how they hold themselves. We all know that body language speaks loudly, yet how much do we constrain our tendency to judge others unfairly? How different our world would be if we saw the positive aspects of others before noticing their imperfections.

We also tend to jump to conclusions without necessarily having complete knowledge of a situation. We must give people the benefit of the doubt even when we suspect wrongdoing. This principle is part of the core of the American legal system: All individuals are innocent until proven guilty. In courts of law strict rules of procedure are maintained. However, as we know, the standards we apply in ordinary life are not as stringent.

We often judge those closest to us the harshest. Our partners and children often receive the swiftest of judgments. The talmudic teaching above reminds us to give others the benefit of the doubt, especially those we love, for the manner in which we judge others will, in turn, be how we ourselves are judged. LF

Going with What We've Got

6 AUGUST

One who endeavors to perfect oneself succeeds.
TALMUD[5]

During Elul, the month that precedes Rosh Hashanah, there is an ancient custom of blowing the shofar each morning as a means of preparing us for *teshuvah,* the process of repentance which is expected of us at the new year. So each Elul I take the shofar which sits on our living room coffee table and put it to my lips each weekday morning before we all run out the door to begin our busy days. My daughter will say, "Daddy, I don't want to hear that noise now," and indeed, I may be ruining her lovely morning by sounding my pinched *tekiah.* "Too bad," I say, and blow away. She may not want to hear it, but she stands fixated while I do the strange deed. Then she wants to try it. And then my wife takes a shot at it. Sometimes we chuckle, acknowledging that we sound like a goose chasing a child with bread crumbs.

What is happening here? Perhaps in some subliminal way we are psyching ourselves for what any rational observer would call the futility of starting over. All through childhood we are naively led to believe that breaking bad habits and honoring new commitments is as easy as "just say *teshuvah.*" We are taught that by searching our deeds, sincerely apologizing to those we have hurt, and resolving to be more honest, religious, moral, and loving, we will actually change our lives. Because we know these are venerable ideals, we even go through the motions and say all the words to try to bring about a truly "new" year. In this context, a finely executed shofar blast infuses us with a confidence and a sense of well-being about our ultimate goodness.

The shofar tells the truth. It strips away our delusions of grandeur. It reminds us that for all our talent and good looks we are less than impressive, and that for all our money we are poor in deeds, as the liturgy puts it. The one thing that we know for sure is that if we are granted another year of life, we will be looking at ourselves next Elul and making most of the same self-criticisms. We simply do not have what it takes to change completely.

Yet in some inexplicable way, we cherish our lives just as I cherish my less-than-perfect shofar blowing. Something drives us to give ourselves a chance to work toward becoming the beings we profoundly want to be. Thus during these holidays we will say the ancient words with sincerity in spite of ourselves. We will ask the One who set impossible standards to accept our best efforts whether we believe that the source of acceptance is distant or deep within.

And I will continue to sound my mediocre *tekiah*. From this, I pray that I learn to value improvement over perfection.

RABBI LESTER BRONSTEIN

The Challenge of Judging

7 AUGUST

Do not seek to be a judge.
APOCRYPHA[6]

Ben Sira, a Jerusalem sage and scribe who lived around 170 B.C.E., was surely talking about the position of judge in a community when he wrote the warning above. Perhaps he was afraid that such a role placed individuals in difficult and dangerous circumstances, since they were close to the sort of power that has the potential to corrupt. Maybe he was afraid of developing relationships with the kind of people who might seek out judges in order to influence their decisions, to manipulate their authority in the community to suit their own personal gain. Surely people would seek them out to tempt them with bribes. Or maybe Ben Sira thought that those who sought such a position were the sort who relished judging others and were unwilling to scrutinize themselves.

The responsibility of judging others makes it difficult to judge the self. After all, if you spend each day doing one thing, it is hard to change directions for a short period of time. But that is exactly why this entire month has been dedicated solely to this pursuit in the religious calendar. Maybe those who judge should start the process by judging themselves.

So judge yourself this month. And let others do the same to themselves. KO

The Supportive Power of Love

8 AUGUST

Many waters cannot quench love,
neither can floods drown it.
SONG OF SONGS 8:7A

As Jews, we don't speak of the sustaining nature of love often enough. In fact, many people may say that love is not a Jewish value. For too long, Judaism has been portrayed as being solely a religion of law and ritual. However, Judaism also teaches love, kindness, and generosity of spirit. The Psalmist correctly reminds us that, without love—that unexplainable mysterious feeling we have for one another and for life itself—the world would collapse. Some of us might say that without commerce, without innovation, without cooperation the world could not stand. While these activities and qualities are certainly needed to maintain our global world, we must also nourish our sense of love.

How we can hold onto the feelings of love when we realize their presence? How often do you tell your children, your partner or spouse, or your parents that you love them. Too often we dismiss our feelings, even our loving feelings, and do not embrace them. So help sustain the world: Embrace love as it appears in your life and give it away freely!   LF

Living to Create a Legacy

9 AUGUST

Humans were created to learn wisdom.
ABRAHAM IBN EZRA[7]

All good parents worry about their children's well-being. In life, parents worry about providing their children with the character and the skills to earn a decent living and to maintain a long-term love relationship, so the children will be cared for when the parents are no longer there. The last thing a parent can give a child is an inheritance.

What is it that we leave our children? In America, it is customary to draw up a last will and testament, in which parents leave all of their earthly goods to their children. We leave our children cars, homes, artwork, and money, as if those were the possessions of ultimate significance. But does anyone really believe that security and well-being are to be found in owning more things?

The truth is that money is just about the least important thing we can will to our children. As Jews, we possess something far more precious and more nurturing that we can give to our children during our lifetimes and after we are gone. In leaving a legacy of Judaism, we can provide eternal care upkeep to sustain our children and theirs through whatever challenges they face.

In deciding to transmit a spiritual gift, Abraham gave his son, Isaac, the ability to summon up blessing from those he met and those he loved. This is a model for us too. Often in life we perceive others through their own insecurity, our own need or shortcomings. We turn an encounter that could be a blessing into a conflict or a missed opportunity for friendship. Abraham's gift to Isaac was to see blessing in others and to cultivate the capacity to bring blessing out of every encounter.

Like Abraham, we can pass something on to our children in addition to money and property. In thinking of what we want to leave our children, surely our heritage should seem precious in our eyes. But we cannot leave someone what we do not ourselves own. Only if we make the effort to truly learn Judaism's wisdom and to live its truths can we act as worthy executors.

RABBI BRADLEY SHAVIT ARTSON

Choose Life

10 AUGUST

I have set before you life and death, the blessing and the curse. Therefore, choose life.

DEUTERONOMY 30:19

This seems like an obvious statement. But everything in the Torah has profound significance. Each word, each letter—even the spaces between the words—teaches us something. Our challenge, particularly in this postmodern era, is to set rational criticism aside and try to discover the spiritual message that lies sparkling beneath the surface of the text. What is it that was being conveyed to our ancestors and to us?

When the Torah outlines our choices and then guides us toward making the right one, we realize that the choice may not be so obvious. There are indeed those who would choose death over life. Life is not an appealing choice for some people. But the Torah is addressed to all of us for whom life is constantly challenging.

Always choose life. This idea runs throughout all aspects of Jewish life. We are even permitted to transgress all of Jewish law if our life is threatened, although we still cannot take another life, or have illicit sex, or engage in idolatry. But we all engage in some self-destructive behaviors. Consider what we eat and drink (as well as how much), how we take our bodies for granted until they don't work exactly or as willingly as they are supposed to or once did. But do we stop these self-destructive behaviors? Generally not without urging from those close to us or after a visit from the angel of death, who constantly hovers in our midst looking for someone who is vulnerable.

The options are constantly in front of us. God is telling us the right choice to make. Life, however difficult, is indeed a blessing. KO

How Our Actions Are Connected to One Another

11 AUGUST

Hasten to do even the slightest mitzvah, and flee from all sin, because one mitzvah will lead to another, and one sin will lead to another.

MISHNAH[8]

We are conditioned by our behaviors. The psychologist B. F. Skinner proved this with his famous psychological experiments which became the basis of behavioral psychology. Our habits can become so familiar and comfortable that breaking them takes effort, persistence, and a change of attitude. It is not always possible to use will power alone to do this. Perhaps this is why as parents, we guide our children to choose their friends wisely: We know that the habits they pick up in their youth can be hard to leave behind.

The Rabbis who lived centuries ago were also well aware of this facet of being human. So they teach that if we consistently practice doing *mitzvot*, they will become an inherent part of who we are; alternatively, the Rabbis teach that if we engage in destructive behaviors, these will define us. Thus, many times we have to do *mitzvot* even when we don't particularly feel like it. The Rabbis believed that the practice of doing good takes constant training. The next time someone asks you to participate in a mitzvah, don't stop to ponder and analyze the situation. Say "yes!"   LF

How God Addresses Us

12 AUGUST

Rabbi Levi said: "The Holy One appeared to the people at
Sinai as a statue with a thousand faces on every side.
A thousand people might be looking at the stone, but it
would appear to be looking at each of them. So, too, when
the Holy one spoke, each and every person in Israel could
say, 'The Divine World is addressing me.' . . . The Divine
Word spoke to each and every person according his or her
particular capacity."

MIDRASH[9]

Using a blasphemous metaphor—comparing God to an idol—Rabbi Levi teaches that at Sinai people experienced

God so individually that standing there one might have said, "God is addressing me!" This midrash moves in the opposite direction of our usual understanding of what happened at Mount Sinai. We think of it as a communal experience. This interpretation suggests something radical: A deep relationship between our own individuality, our place in life, our culture and world, and the kind of connection to God we might experience. If the Sinai experience is so individualized, then certainly in ordinary human life, where God is far more hidden and where we must strain to hear the still small voice, the experience of God flows from who we are and what we really expect from the experience.

In other words, each person in each age finds the understanding of God appropriate to his or her needs and circumstances. No one image of God will ever be appropriate for each time and place in our own histories. There is instead an ever-changing human perspective in which the many images of God speak in the moment in which they make sense. Sometimes God is Father, King, Lover, Husband, Friend, Place, Queen, or Mother. Which image of God speaks to you today?   RABBI IRWIN KULA[10]

Short Term Memory

13 AUGUST

Remember not the former things.
Consider not the things of old.
ISAIAH 43:18

It is easy to remember all the people who wronged us over the course of the past year, as well as everything they did. We could spend time making lists and getting angry at this person or that person for this act or that act. Some may even take pleasure in such an activity. It is much more difficult to remember all the things that *we* might have done wrong, as well as all the people whom *we* might have wronged these past twelve months. In an effort to make an accounting of those people who wronged us, it's easy to forget what we have done. Some people think that forgetting is simply a negative aspect of memory. If we don't remember something, then we are forgetting it. But forgetting can be active when we are attempting to void what we did to wrong other people. At this time of year, as we think about all of these things, we first ask people to forgive us. Then we ask God for forgiveness. And while we stand before the Holy One of Blessing, we ask God to remember all of the things that we—and our ancestors— did to make us worthy of such forgiveness.

Forgetting and forgiving is part of the circle of repentance. The prophet Isaiah teaches us not to dwell on the past. He asks us to focus instead on the ultimate future. It is that notion that illumines the present. KO

Respect for our Bodies

14 AUGUST

Respect your body as the receptacle, the messenger, and the instrument of the spirit.
RABBI SAMUEL RAPHAEL HIRSCH[11]

We think about our bodies more during the summer than during other times of the year, especially if we live in northern climes. During the winter we can cover up with layers of clothing, but during the summer we wear less, particularly if we enjoy the outdoors. Some religions elevate the spirit and denigrate the body. Judaism teaches that our physical bodies and physical needs are holy and sacred. They should not be disregarded. If we are to free our spirits, we must be mindful of our physical well-being. In the Torah, we are taught that we should not violate our bodies with tattoos or any other markings, since we manifest part of God's holy creation through our physical bodies. If we ignore our bodies, we cannot serve God fully. While we do not worship our bodies as an end in themselves, as the ancient Greeks did, we do need to respect and care for them. Today we know that means exercising, eating properly, and relinquishing smoking, recreational drug use, and heavy drinking. It does not mean living an ascetic life, for Jews do not deny the pleasures of this world. It does, though, suggest that our bodies and spirits are partners which we must equally respect.

What have you done to take care of your body lately?   LF

Becoming a Full Human Being

15 AUGUST

Each person is obligated to give new life to one's own being. . . . Repentance . . . is an act of creation—self-creation.
RABBI JOSEPH B. SOLOVEITCHIK[12]

When I was young, I had an unfailing indicator of my spiritual health. Whenever I recited the *Al Chet,* the confession of sins on Yom Kippur, the more alive I was both religiously and ethically, the more sins I was able to recognize for the past year. From the opening admission of wrongdoings committed "unwillingly and willingly" and "by hardening the heart" to the closing misdeeds done through "breach of trust" and "confused hearts," so many of them applied to me. I saw that not just obvious acts, but also much subtler attitudes and feeling, were being judged. But as I stood before a loving but all-knowing Judge, my self-deceptions fell away. I could admit the truth and I could work to change my life.

As I matured, however, I began to see that by focusing on my misdeeds, I was missing a deeper truth in Judaism. The greater issue was not just turning from sin, but rather becoming a full human being. The focus on wrongdoing allowed me to overlook all the standard good actions, the routinized daily behaviors which fell short of what I could, and should, be doing. The issue was not just misdeeds, therefore, but mediocrity. Could I change? Could I grow? The Days of Awe challenged me to reshape myself, to improve relationships, to become a more vital person.   RABBI IRVING GREENBERG[13]

Raising the Self

16 AUGUST

A righteous person falls seven times and rises up again.
PROVERBS 24:16

It is true that the number seven (and multiples of seven) is special in Judaism. Some even call it a holy or a mystical number. Think about it: Seven days of creation; seven times seven days (or forty-nine days) between each Jubilee year; and forty-nine days to count the *omer* from the second day of Pesach to Shavuot, when we wait anxiously for God's revelation at Sinai—the list goes on. The sentiment of the statement above affirms the significance of this idea. No matter how many times you fall or fail, you have to pick yourself up again, even if you fall as many as seven times. Knowing that failing seven times is rather disappointing and disillusioning, the Rabbis feel the need to offer this advice. Perhaps the ability to rise repeatedly is even one of the indications we can use to gauge the righteousness of the individual.

What is it that motivates the individual to raise the self up after failing? Usually we think of the person who continues to fail as being a failure. We may even exhibit pity, thinking that person is somehow "jinxed." But that person, instead, deserves our praise. It is easy to stumble and get back up. It is more difficult to do so time after time. Rabbi Abraham Isaac Kook, the first chief rabbi of Israel, recognized the difficulty when he noted that the path to repentance is not straightforward but rather it is circuitous. People who want to straighten their lives out, who want to make changes in it, may not necessarily accomplish all that they want to do the first time, or the second, or the third. . . . the challenge is to keep going.

KO

The Temptation of Bribes

17 AUGUST

Do not take a bribe, for a bribe will blind the eyes of the wise and distort the words of the righteous.

DEUTERONOMY 16:19

People use bribery in many ways. Of course, we immediately think of monetary bribes and how judges, public officials, and others with power can be tempted to sway a decision when large sums of money are offered. As the Torah teaches, money tends to blind us from following what our heart knows is the correct path. If we walk a spiritual path and keep our values front-and-center, then, let us hope, we will not be tempted. However, bribes are not always monetary. People are also guilty of using information as bribes. In our competitive world, information is often more important than money.

The essence of bribery is to undermine a system that is created to work for the benefit of all of us. While some might say accepting bribes is a victimless crime, there are no victimless crimes. When we undermine justice in any way, we are wounding others and society at large. Every day we find ourselves in situations where we make decisions. Let us use caution and not be swayed by ulterior motives. Rather, search for what is just and compassionate.   LF

Dealing with Mortality

18 AUGUST

Everything in this world has an end.
MIDRASH[14]

Life, too, has an ending. We are all going to die, some sooner and some later, but all of us nonetheless. All life is flux and change: birth and death and new births. If we cling to any one part of life, if we seek to dam the flow of time and events, if we become attached to any one stage to the point where we cannot let go and move on, life will tear the moment from our grasp and we will be miserable. Life is tough, and there is a natural suffering that comes with that toughness. But why add to that natural suffering with the unnecessary suffering that arises when we refuse to let go when there is no way we can hold on?

There are two corollary truths to the fact that life is temporary. The first is: Don't take life so seriously. It's only temporary. We are all too serious, casting our most ordinary lives as extraordinary dramas. We produce and direct and star in a movie that plays over and over in the theater of our mind. The extent to which we get trapped in this theater is the extent to which we miss out on real life. Even the pop-corn is stale. Life is happening around you as well as within you. Pay attention. Get involved. We are life's way of getting things done. There is always something that needs doing right here and now. So do it.

The second corollary is the preciousness of each moment. You've heard this a million times, but listen once more: We are all destined for a guaranteed termination. No one has ever beaten the system. Every moment of life is valuable. As Dr. Dennis Hensley wrote, "Once time is gone, it's gone for-ever. You can't buy it back, borrow it back, bribe it back, or even pray it back. A wasted moment is irretrievable." Who has time to waste?   RABBI RAMI SHAPIRO

The Key to Below and Above

19 AUGUST

Speak gently, control your temper, promote peace even with a stranger in the street so that you may be beloved above and below.

TALMUD[15]

Is this the beginning of a list of moral virtues? Or is it the entire inventory? Maybe by controlling certain tendencies, we will be able to control all of our behaviors. If it were my list, I might add humility, since lack of it is the scourge of the current generation. We raise ourselves up—at the expense of others—in what appears to be a survival mechanism. We are critical of others because it takes the focus away from ourselves. I like to think that the short list of items outlined above by the Rabbis contains the answer to dealing with the *yetzer hara,* the tenden-cy to do evil. It is this tendency that tugs at both the strengths and weaknesses of our personalities.

If you were making a list of virtues, what would be on it? Since your list probably reflects the challenges to personal repair that you currently face, what are you going to do about them in this season of self-reflection and self-scrutiny? Start with one item at a time. The Rabbis realized that after so many years, we would be unable to repair everything quickly. But full repair is eventually possible, since the repair of even one item leads us to the path to complete repentance and renewal.

Just remember one thing: It is the honest attempt at personal repair—not its immediate success—that brings us closer to self, to others, and to God.   KO

Prayer and Natural Light

20 AUGUST

Pray only in a room with windows.
TALMUD[16]

Why do the talmudic Rabbis care about the architectural layout of the rooms where we pray? If we are sincere in our prayers, why does it matter? Perhaps we work in a room with no windows. Does that mean we cannot pray at our desks if we are so moved? The Rabbis' concern for praying in a space with a window reflects a sensitivity to the power of light. Maybe their aging eyes required just a little extra illumination. Remember, they did not live in an age of electricity. For the Rabbis, natural light was precious. It was also a reflection of the Divine and was felt more in the summer than in any other season of the year.

The Rabbis wanted to ensure that people did not pray in a dark, depressing place, since surroundings influence how we address God. Thus we should take care to pray in places that are open to natural light and through which we can remain in contact with the natural wonders of the world. If we lose contact with nature, we shut ourselves off from one path to God.

So open a window. Look outside. Pray. LF

Reading the Soul of Torah

21 AUGUST

*Let not the Torah seem antiquated which nobody minds,
but new to which all run.*

MIDRASH[17]

We live in a world with tremendous technological power. Why do we read the Torah from a scroll—a handwritten parchment, no less? There have been at least three "information revolutions" since the tradition of the reading of the Torah began. In the eleventh century, the books as we know them were introduced to replace scrolls; in the fifteenth century Gutenberg perfected movable type; and today we have entered the third revolution. On many of our desks sits a computer that processes several million "bits" of information per second. Attached to the computer is a CD-ROM device, in which we can insert a disk and have immediate access to whole libraries of knowledge. One disk contains the Bible, the Talmud, and all the major commentaries of Midrash. A lifetime—several lifetimes—of learning come up instantly on our screens. Ask it to find any word, any concept, any name, and it accomplishes a year's worth of bibliographic research in seconds. Will our children look upon books as we look upon a scroll—as a relic, honored by tradition, but of limited efficiency?

Still, we read Torah from a scroll. And we will read from a scroll long after CD-ROMs are replaced in the next revolution. We do so not just out of stubborn adherence to ancient tradition, and not just as a symbol of the authenticity of ancient truths, but precisely because the scroll is so inefficient, so slow, so linear. Only by reading in that format does each word remain real and important. Written slowly and carefully. Read slowly and carefully. Each information revolution has put us in touch with so many more words so much more quickly; but each has compromised the depth of the words we touch. To know the soul of Torah is to read deeply, and slowly, and reflectively. RABBI EDWARD FEINSTEIN

Standing Upright

22 AUGUST

I have broken the bars of your yoke and made you go upright.
LEVITICUS 26:13

While the statement above is a quote from the Torah and helps us understand the consciousness of the biblical period, it optimistically reflects a sentiment that echoes throughout the Jews' journey through history until the establishment of the modern State of Israel in 1948. It is a fundamental idea in Judaism, we feel it coursing through the daily liturgy. For example, in the blessing that begins and concludes the first prayer of the *Amidah,* which is the core of the three daily worship services, we are taught to bow at the knee, then bend forward for *Barukh ata* "Praised are You," and then stand upright when we say *Adonai.* Through the choreography of prayer, we are affirming our belief that once we enter into a relationship with God, then whatever has been yoking us will be broken so that we can stand upright.

It is ironic that the text intentionally chooses the word "yoke," the same word that is used to describe our connection to God's instructions (or *mitzvot*) and the same word that is sometimes used to describe Israel's subordination to the nations that conquered it in the ancient world. One would think that we are simply going from one yoke to another. But it is a different kind of yoke, not the one that is described in these other contexts. It is one of those notions in spiritual logic that is not self-evident. It is this different yoke that allows us to go free. I invite you to put it on. KO

Wisdom and Radiance

23 AUGUST

A person's wisdom makes his or her face shine.
ECCLESIASTES 8:1

There are some people whose aura is magnetic. We say their faces shine and their eyes sparkle. They are joyous to be around. We are drawn to them. The author of the book of Ecclesiastes, the collection of wisdom attributed to King Solomon, states that a person's wisdom is responsible for this luster. What *kind* of wisdom, though, Solomon, doesn't say. Is it academic knowledge? Is it business acumen? No. King Solomon is talking about a deeper wisdom that comes with life experience. Perhaps that is why Bezalel was chosen to be the chief designer of the desert Tabernacle. Not only does his name mean "in God's shadow," but he is described as *chokhmat lev,* "wise of heart." Bezalel's wisdom enabled him to be a vehicle for God as he designed the first home for the holy tablets that Moses brought down from Sinai. Moses, too, is described as having a shining presence when he descended the mountain after his forty-day commune with the Holy One on Sinai.

Those of us who have experienced prolonged silence sitting in deep meditation, can identify with Moses' altered state of consciousness upon returning to the Israelites. When we quiet down and turn off our mind's normal chatter, we can listen to the wisdom which arises from within us. From this experience, we return to our daily lives invigorated and newly aglow. Search for lasting wisdom that will nourish your spirit in sustaining ways, and watch your face shine.   LF

The Original Soul

24 AUGUST

All souls in the world, God's handiwork, are mystically one;
but when they descend on earth, they are separated.
ZOHAR[18]

The wilderness is just not a desert through which we wandered for forty years. It is a way of being. A place that demands being open to the flow of life around you. A place that demands being honest with yourself without regard to the cost in personal anxiety. A place that demands being present with all of yourself.

In the wilderness, your possessions cannot surround you. Your preconceptions cannot protect you. Your logic cannot promise you the future. Your guilt can no longer place you safely in the past. You are left alone each day with an immediacy that astonishes, chastens, and exults. You see the world as if for the first time.

Now you might say that the promise of such spiritual awareness could only keep one with the greatest determination in the wilderness but for a moment or so. We would live our lives in but a few hours and die of old age. "It is better

for us to serve the Egyptians than to die in the wilderness"
(Exodus 14:12). And indeed, that is your choice.

RABBI LAWRENCE KUSHNER[19]

The Challenge of Power

25 AUGUST

Power buries those who wield it.
TALMUD[20]

It may not seem so, but we all have the potential to abuse power. We may think that power is limited to the elite, since the common folk have no access to it. It may also be true that power corrupts. But we constantly exercise power throughout our lives in the form of the responsibility we have for other people, particularly those whose care is entrusted to us such as children or aging parents.

Moreover, we exercise power over people we encounter in our everyday routine: the people we work with; those we encounter in the streets; even the people who serve us in a restaurant or a grocery store. How we interact with them contributes to the shaping of their lives. Sometimes it is because we may wield little power in our work that we unintentionally try to wield it elsewhere. That is when it really has the potential to bury us. So raise yourself above it. Share your power. Make people your partners. We will all be strengthened in the process.   KO

Greeting the Messiah

26 AUGUST

*If you have a sapling in your hand and someone should say
to you that the Messiah has come, stay and complete the
planting, and then go to greet the Messiah.*

COMMENTARY ON THE MISHNAH[21]

Judaism teaches us that an era will come when war, strife, disease, and injustice come to an end. Traditionally, Jews believe that one person—the Messiah—would usher in such a time. During our history there have been many false messiahs, individuals whose messianic claims were exposed as being untrue. We have become more skeptical when someone makes such a claim. Instead we use our own energy, wisdom, and passion to try to transform the world and rid it of its social evils.

Rabbi Yochanan ben Zakkai, in whose name the text above is taught, was the chief architect of the rabbinic Judaism which took hold after the Second Temple's destruction in 70 C.E. He prodded those who survived Jerusalem's collapse to help reconstruct Judaism. He did not want them to wait passively for a savior. His message—to finish planting a tree before greeting the Messiah—teaches that we are, first and foremost, responsible for finishing the task before us. Planting a tree is a sign of involvement and a statement of hope for the future.

At different moments of our lives we may hope that our struggles will be lifted by the intervention of a savior who will miraculously lift our burdens. However, if we wait on the sidelines, we will not even have the satisfaction of participating in building the present and contributing to the future. What is before you that you can finish and will be your statement of hope for transforming the world?   LF

Listening and Calling Out

27 August

God called to Moses and spoke to him.
Leviticus 1:1

Why does God call to Moses before speaking to him? According to Rashi, all oral communications from God to Moses, whether they are introduced by the words *daber, amar,* or *tzav,* "speak," "say," or "command," were preceded by a call in order to prepare him for the forthcoming message. Why would Moses need such preparation?

Rabbi Abraham Twersky, in his book *Living Each Week,* answers by focusing on the internal changes that Moses faced in order to meet each of God's new tasks and challenges. He draws a correlation to lobsters growing until they become too tight in their shells, then going to the bottom of the ocean and discarding their shells, then growing a larger one. So, too, Moses needed to journey deep within and discard old, dysfunctional behavior to be able to grow and stretch.

Midrash HaGadol also addresses this question by saying that the Torah is teaching us *derekh eretz,* courtesy and civility, for we should not speak to another person unless that person has called to us. When we are called by another person, we bring focused attention to them. Such relationships require us to retract attention from ourselves to make room for the other and for God.

Will we listen and attend to those who call us so that what we give and offer can be from our innermost selves, not merely rote actions and behaviors? Will we truly hear and then respond through genuine two-way dialogue so the arrows of connection can fly in both directions?

Will we be listening for God's voice, ready to stretch ourselves to meet God and bring the Holy One into the world through our minds, hearts, souls, and actions?

SHARON L. WECHTER[22]

Singing Praises

28 AUGUST

Let another praise you, not your own mouth.
PROVERBS 27:2

Since childhood, most of us have been taught to look out for our own well-being and to speak up on our own behalf. This commonly held wisdom suggests that this is the only way to succeed. This approach usually does succeed. We may think that if it works for the advertising executives of Madison Avenue or the spin doctors of Washington, then it can work for us, and so we get in the habit of self-aggrandizement.

But the author of the book of Proverbs, whom Jewish tradition suggests is the wise King Solomon, spun this idea quite differently. He wants truth to speak on its own—and to endow us with a more humble spirit. The next time you are motivated to say something about what you have done, say it on behalf of somebody else instead. When the time comes, perhaps he or she will do the same for you.   KO

Darkness and Light, Harmony and Chaos

29 August

Let us bless the source of life, source of darkness and light, heart of harmony and chaos, creativity and creation.
MARCIA FALK[23]

Judaism teaches that Abraham was the first person to recognize that One God was responsible for both the good and the evil in the world. This understanding stood in stark contrast to other Near Eastern religions, which believed in many gods, each responsible for different realms. But it is not always easy to believe in One God who is responsible for everything. Why would God want us to suffer or allow evil in this world? Why not just create everything good and leave it at that?

God created all possibilities: darkness and light; harmony and chaos. As human beings, we have the *yetzer tov*, creative impulses, and *yetzer hara*, destructive impulses. It is up to us to balance the pull and the tug of these forces on our inner life.

Hasidism teaches that when we are caught in the midst of darkness and chaos, we can raise these sparks back to God, the Holy Source and, thus, transform them to light and harmony. How have you been able to transform bad to good, pain to joy, suffering to appreciation?   LF

Finding God in Your Place

30 AUGUST

God is in this place and I didn't know it.
GENESIS 28:16

Jacob awoke from his dream with these words. They are a way of describing the paradox of God everywhere, all the time, and a child dying, a war happening, an earthquake, a disease, a famine, a curse. It's a way of authenticating the whole grand scheme—it is what it is, and it is still full of God. Not either/or, but both. All of the above. Don't I know this about life? I do know it, but I don't have words for it. Neither did Jacob, so he said, "God is in this place, and I don't know a darn thing." A feeling so expansive it drives everything else out, all the contradictions, gone.

God is in this place, this moment. The rocks are God, the ground is God, you and me are God. Light and darkness are God.

No place is empty of God. When Jacob felt that, all the illusions collapsed into one long affirmative embrace that pushed all his prior notions out of him. And he said, "Surely God is in this place, and I don't know a thing." This is the beginning of wisdom. Now Jacob was free to be taught the truth of the world. As are we.

RABBI JAMES STONE GOODMAN[24]

Private Space

31 August

What is improper in public is forbidden in secret.
TALMUD[25]

The postmodern era has given us new notions about privacy. Some people have cases before the Supreme Court dealing with the extent to which the private domain is off limits to societal censure or control. And some people try to keep their activities private by disguising them. They may use different names or private postal boxes, in an effort to keep their activities private and sometimes even anonymous. Today people are permitted to do almost anything they want in the privacy of their homes. Access to new forms of electronic communication such as e-mail has taken this idea to levels we had not previously contemplated. But in their wisdom, the Rabbis have a rather simple take on this idea: If it is inappropriate to do something in public, then it is equally inappropriate to do it in private. I like to add that if you have to think twice about whether you should do something, then you should not be thinking once about doing it either.   KO

SEPTEMBER

Redirection

1 SEPTEMBER

*You need not complete the work but you are
not free to desist from it.*

MISHNAH[1]

With the first days of September, even for those of us who can stretch our vacation a little beyond Labor Day, it's really the end of summer. There's a palpable change in weather. Children are going back to school. Adults are going back to work. And everyone is thinking about the upcoming Jewish holidays. The demands on our lives return, nearly overnight, in full force. Even after we finish school or think we are done raising school-age children, the seasonal calendar continues to shape our lives. Then Labor Day comes and summer is officially over—even if the scientists wait a few more weeks to mark the occasion on the calendar on September 21 with the autumn equinox.

So we brace ourselves for the change in seasons and the change in attitude. The relaxed attitudes of June, July, and August are over. There are no more short days, long lunches, or early office closings on Fridays. It's back to the hectic pace of regular work weeks. But with the stress comes the sweet satisfaction of purpose, the joy that we experience through our work regardless of our chosen field of endeavor. Vacations are nice, but it is the real work we do in the world—volunteer or paid—that gives meaning and direction to our lives.

KO

Have a Heart

2 September

The Torah begins and ends with loving acts of kindness. It begins with, "Adonai made clothing of skins for Adam and his wife, and God clothed them" (Genesis 3:21), and it ends with, "And God buried Moses there in the valley" (Deuteronomy 34:6).

TALMUD[2]

The core teaching of Judaism is that we strive to be a people who perform acts of *chesed,* loving acts of kindness. These acts—small and large—range from providing clothing for those in need to burying the dead. They also include many additional *mitzvot* such as feeding the hungry, providing shelter, caring for mourners, and visiting the sick. In Hebrew all these actions are called *gemilut chasadim,* loving acts of kindness. In the rabbinic collection of pithy sayings called *Pirke Avot,* we are taught that the world is sustained by three pillars: Torah study, prayer, and loving acts of kindness. Without these loving actions, the world could not continue. So love, in Judaism, is not abstract. It is primarily not about feelings but rather takes shape and form by the actions we weave into the fabric of our lives. That is why synagogues open their doors to shelters and food kitchens for the homeless and the hungry and why many congregations have groups of congregants who visit the sick and provide *minyan* for those who are in mourning. That is why many Jewish communities support Hebrew Free Burial societies.

The Torah begins with the letter *bet* and concludes with the letter *lamed*. These two letters, when reversed, spell the word *lev* which means "heart." While the Torah may have 5,845 verses and 79,976 words, let us remember that its core message is contained in one core word: Heart. May we maintain our hearts by caring for others.   LF

Judging the World and Ourselves

3 SEPTEMBER

*The world is judged by the majority of its people, and
an individual by the majority of his or her deeds.
Happy is the one who performs a good deed: that may tip
the scale for him or her and the world.*

TALMUD[3]

When the sun goes down on the first evening of Rosh Hashanah, the Jewish soul goes up. Rosh Hashanah is the time to find out who we are and what we have done and whom we have pleased and whom we have offended. It begins ten days of repentance that culminate in Yom Kippur, when our efforts to repair what we have been must cease, for judgment has been made. We have ourselves to account to for the judgment, because even in God's mercies, justice must balance the good and the evil, the mundane and the rare, and what we have done returns to us in equal measure and equal weight.

This is the time when we must humble ourselves as we have never been humble before, to confront ourselves as we have never done before, to let our own personhood fade into spirit and our spirit fade into God. Everywhere around us is a mirror of who we are and who we might be and who we could have been—and the choice is forever ours of the reflection we will find in the mirror, not just at the end of the year but at the end of our lives, when the sum of each moment and each breath is duly noted and we discover that we have been far more—or far less—than we ever expected or set out to be.

So when the sun lowers on Rosh Hashanah, there will not be a dimming of light, but a brilliant showering of it for the potential of all that we have been. The choice is ours: To embrace the brilliance, or to be swallowed by darkness.

ARTHUR J. MAGIDA

Looking Forward

4 SEPTEMBER

Look to Adonai for hope. Be strong and of good courage.
Look to Adonai for faith.
PSALMS 27:14

This is the way the twenty-seventh psalm ends. This psalm accompanies our daily prayers during the month of Elul, the month of introspection that precedes the fall holiday season. In this verse are the ingredients for a prayerful life: hope, strength, courage, and faith. Seems simple enough. But how do you develop such a perspective? The answer: Through a prayerful life. This is the reasoning of spiritual logic. If you lead a prayerful life, you are led to these soulful qualities. And finding any one of them will lead you on the path toward a prayerful life, where you encounter the other three qualities. That's the way a life of prayer works.

On the Saturday just prior to Rosh Hashanah (or the previous week if Rosh Hashanah begins on a Sunday) we gather for penitential prayers (called *Selichot*) at midnight. As a community, we offer up our prayers, gaining strength from one another at a time when we need it most. There in the darkness of night, we realize that the source of it all—hope, strength, courage, and faith—is indeed the Source of all of it.

KO

Taking on Responsibility

5 SEPTEMBER

Do not separate yourself from the community.
MISHNAH[4]

This teaching from the collection called *Pirke Avot*, well known for its many clever aphorisms written by the Rabbis, is a fundamental value, since it speaks to our responsibility for becoming involved. It is particularly important to think about this around the time of the Sabbath of Return (*Shabbat Shuvah*), the Sabbath that punctuates the fall holiday season by marking the time between Rosh Hashanah and Yom Kippur. It is particularly relevant now because Jewish communities in North America come together this time of year more than any other time and in greater numbers. It is also noteworthy that we change our perspectives this time of year as we turn our backs on summer and again immerse ourselves in the work of our communities. This text teaches us that we are obligated to participate in the work of the community even though we are not required to see its completion.

Some among us may wonder why this is a value. One could claim that serious involvement with the Jewish community requires staying the course. Certainly such an attitude is often needed for short-term endeavors. However, for long-term enterprises such a perspective provides a ready excuse for many people to remain uninvolved. This Jewish value gives us no justification for ability to justify remaining on the sidelines. It correctly recognizes that our efforts are valuable even though others will succeed us and add their own contribution to what we have done. It wisely reminds us that some undertakings require the participation of many individuals. Think of how many worthy projects have been started by one group and continued by others. In fact, we should feel pleased when others continue our work, for it speaks to the power and worthiness of our vision.   LF

Hearing Our Cry

6 September

We are groaning from our bondage and our cry rises to God and God hears our moaning and remembers the covenant with Abraham, Isaac, and Jacob.
Exodus 2:23–24

Is this the moment that God enters the liberation drama in a very personal way? Is that what the text is saying? The midrash, however, takes us back to the moment of decision when Moses moves out of his complacency and defends his brother Hebrew and cites that moment as the moment God, so to speak, moves out of God's complacency, precisely because of Moses' example.

But there is something more subtle here that is taught in the name of Reb Levi Yitzchak of Berditchev. He asked the question, "When does out freedom saga begin?" Like all questions, this questions is designed to move us out of complacent ways of thinking. Freedom is infinitely regressible. That's what the midrash is reaching for by taking us back to Moses' action, because when he goes out to his brothers, we ask the same question of our lives: What preceded this action? What did Moses learn at his mother's breast to bring him out of complacency at that moment? What did his mother receive from her people to have transmitted this to Moses? Who said what to you, when, that slipped the message past your psyche, snuck it by the guardians of your equanimity? Who taught you to resist? Who led you to believe that you could transform, that you could be free? Who was it? What teacher? What voice?

Freedom is infinitely regressible. Each act in the chain of behavior which leads to freedom is built on a previous act. Every act contributes in some partial way to freedom. No deed is done, no thought is thought, no dream is dreamed, for nothing. Everything contributes in some inscrutable way to freedom. When does freedom begin? It may begin today, with this thought. This thought was preceded by the dream the day before. Back beyond today. Every act, every thought may be a gesture for freedom. Every act has a liberating potential of which we may be unaware. No deed wasted, no thought for nothing. When did we get free? When we paused, when we resisted, when we dream it. Back beyond, way beyond, before it came to be.

RABBI JAMES STONE GOODMAN[5]

Royal Roots

7 SEPTEMBER

Don't forget that you are the child of a king.
RABBI SHLOMO OF KARLIN[6]

Throughout the liturgy of the High Holy Days, we are reminded that God is a Sovereign Ruler. Some would prefer a gentler conception of God that is not rooted in the hierarchy of royalty. However, most of the choreography of prayer blatantly reflects this theme, which is only hinted at during the rest of the year. It is most poignantly demonstrated in what is called the Grand *Aleynu* when, in most synagogues, the leaders of prayer prostrate themselves on the floor in front of the Ark. During the rest of the year, and at other times in the service, we simply bend the knee and bow our head in reverence. This time of year is different. We even change some of the language of prayer, replacing phrases like "the Holy God" with "the Holy King." The liturgy frames our relationship with God in various ways. Nevertheless, we are God's subjects.

Rabbi Shlomo of Karlin reminds us that we are not just subjects of a royal ruler. We are God's children, as well. That makes all of us the child of a king.

As we go about our business and leave the precinct of the synagogue after the holiday season, let us remember that we are children of royalty. Let us act accordingly.   KO

Beginnings

8 SEPTEMBER

All beginnings are difficult.
MIDRASH[7]

Beginnings—there are so many in our lives. As children we began each school year wondering who would be our teacher for the year. Would he or she be kind or strict? Who would our classmates be? As the years pass, we face even more beginnings. We start new jobs, begin new relationships and friendships, move to new places. Some of us may follow our own personal rituals when we approach the many beginnings that punctuate our lives. But we should also make sure we pay attention to the ending that precedes each beginning, because endings are just as important as beginnings, and no less difficult. Through them we say good-bye to one chapter of our lives and open the door to the next.

Many of us may experience beginnings as difficult. One spiritual response to this feeling is to realize that personal growth often follows beginnings. If our routine never varied, life would be unbearably monotonous. We can welcome these beginnings and embrace the challenges they present. What new beginnings have you recently faced? Reflect for a moment on how you dealt with them.   LF

Yom Kippur—Tailor Made

9 SEPTEMBER

*Master of the Universe, I beg of you to redeem Israel.
And if you do not want to do that, then redeem
the rest of the world.*
THE REBBE OF KOZNITZ[8]

Sometime this month or next we will mark Yom Kippur, the Day of Atonement, the holiest day of the Jewish year. The period is characterized by penitential prayers and fasting, synagogues with standing room only, and haunting melodies of ancient days.

It is also a time when simple stories often succeed where sermons fail. So here is a story for our week of preparations:

A tailor in the Old Country chanced upon a great Hasidic master. When the tailor mentioned that he was illiterate and couldn't read the prayerbook, the great rebbe asked him what he does if he can't follow the prayers. "Well, last year," said the tailor, "I spoke to God and said, 'The sins for which I am expected to repent are minor ones and inconsequential. I might have kept a little leftover cloth, or been too busy to recite an afternoon prayer. But You God, Your sins are really grave. You have allowed children to become deathly ill, You have pitted brother against brother in battle, You have created a world where so many hunger for food and shelter. So let's reach an agreement. If You pardon me, I'm ready to pardon You.'"

The rebbe looked at the tailor angrily and replied, "You not only are illiterate, you are foolish as well. You were too lenient with God last year. You should have insisted that God bring redemption to the entire world."

So when we pray this Yom Kippur, wrapped tightly in our prayer shawls like simple tailors, may each of us add to our pleas for atonement a heartfelt petition that God redeem not just us, but the entire world this coming year.

RABBI ABIE INGBER

Undoing the Past

10 SEPTEMBER

What's done cannot be undone.
TALMUD[9]

It may be true that once we have done something, it is part of the historical record of the world. Moreover, it becomes part of our life script. But the fact that something cannot be undone does not mean that it cannot be fixed or changed. Once we repair what was broken as a result of what we did, then our relationship with what happened changes as well. And then we change. We are not the same "we" who did it. Perhaps the action remains the same, but the person who did it is no longer the same. So go out and fix what is broken. In doing so, you will find that you have changed the past.   KO

Inscribe Us for a Good Year

11 SEPTEMBER

*This is the day of the beginning of creation . . .
the day on which the universe was conceived. . . .
May all humanity join together as one, to do Your will with
their entire hearts. Inscribe us in the book
of life, blessing, and peace.*
LITURGY[10]

How many of us say each year, "Rosh Hashanah is early this year." Or "The holidays sure seem late this year." These days of awe can seem so inconvenient, often coming just as we return from summer vacation and are busy getting ready for another year at school or work. Some of us might like to postpone the High Holidays until the first week in November so we can have a couple of more months to get organized and planned.

It is precisely that fantasy that the holidays challenge. Yes, it might be nice to feel more prepared. It would be wonderful to have more control over the weather, our children, our spouses, our life. But reality, not fantasy, must be acknowledged. Rosh Hashanah and Yom Kippur are not flexible or avoidable. They demand that we allow reality in. The New Year is *here,* they exclaim. Life is complicated, distracting, confusing. We do our best and still we make errors and mistakes. We are more willing to blame our failings on circumstances than on ourselves. We are more willing to rush around, out of the best motives, and postpone a confrontation with ourselves and the reality of our lives. And were it not for these days, during which we slow down and reflect, we might even do more to avoid the inevitable self-confrontation.

But beginning with Rosh Hashanah and concluding with Yom Kippur, there are no excuses. Whether we are ready or not, the holidays come. They are a challenge and an opportunity. They demand that we face reality and come to terms with what we have and who we are. We are given the chance to acknowledge that all of us are less perfect than we had hoped to be, but perhaps more able to move on than we had feared. Seen in this way, it seems that the holidays do us a valuable service. Perhaps coming at the end of the summer, they come at the right time after all! LF

Redemption

12 September

For it is a spiritual disquiet, much more than a guilty feeling, that makes us feel the urge to take a look back. Indeed, we feel we are no longer the right person in the right place, we feel we are becoming outsiders in a world whose scheme of things escapes us.

Rabbi Adin Steinsaltz[11]

Teshuvah is the ever-present possibility, urge, and gesture of returning to our Source, the Holy One of All Being. Through *teshuvah,* all life is returned to its source. As Rabbi Abraham Isaac Kook, the great mystic, teaches, it flows unnoticed throughout creation. *Teshuvah* is not simply apologizing or making right the damage we have done—though these surely are prerequisites. It is only this; The Return. *Teshuvah* is the hardest thing in the world: To fully make *teshuvah* would bring the Messiah. But it is also the easiest thing: It has only to occur to you to make *teshuvah* and you've already begun.

More than just an individual gesture, *teshuvah* is a great world-yearning that flows through and animates all creation.

Through attempting to repair and heal what we have done in the past, we set it within a larger context of meaning and effectively rewrite the past. What was once only some thoughtless or wicked act, now—when viewed from the perspective of our present *teshuvah*—becomes only the embarrassing commencement of this greater healing now realized.

RABBI LAWRENCE KUSHNER[12]

Ready, Willing, and Able

13 SEPTEMBER

I am ready to fulfill this commandment.
LITURGY[13]

This statement from the prayerbook serves as an introductory statement for many mitzvah-motivated activities. It serves as a sort of *kavannah*, a bit of sacred writ which focuses us on the activity we are about to perform. In some cases the *kavannah* is repeated over and over, perhaps as a chant with or without words. It is especially helpful in prayer as we make the transition from the secular to the sacred. By saying this verse aloud, so that the ears hear what the soul intends, we are centering ourselves for our holy work in the world, whatever it may be.

What does it take to prepare for such sacred tasks? Moses was asked to remove his shoes before he could approach the burning bush and there encounter God. The Israelites had to wash and then sustain from sexual relations for a few days so they would not be distracted when receiving the Torah at Sinai. Some people prepare for an encounter with God with silence. Others prepare with song. Some study. Others pray.

How do you prepare for such important tasks? Perhaps it is the preparation that helps you understand how really important is the task you are about to perform.   KO

Celebration

14 SEPTEMBER

Remember that life is a celebration or can be a celebration. One of the most important things is to teach people how to celebrate.
RABBI ABRAHAM JOSHUA HESCHEL[14]

Whenever the human spirit is free, people celebrate. All cultures commemorate what makes them distinctive and worthy in their own eyes. In celebrations, people often affirm the joyous outpouring of their spirit. What are the occasions in our lives that we celebrate? Among the prominent milestones are birthdays, marriages, anniversaries, graduations, and promotions. Why, then, does Rabbi Heschel suggest we need to teach people how to celebrate? Because it is too easy for us to go through life and get caught up in the sameness of our everyday commitments. Have you ever said to yourself, "Oh, this birthday is not so important. I'll just skip it this year." Or "What's the big deal that we've been married nineteen years? Next year we'll celebrate when we reach the big one." Such statements easily dismiss important personal milestones. When we stop and mark the special moments in our lives, we pause to put our most recent growth and effort into perspective. We can reflect where we are today and how far we have come. Life is full of challenges and sad moments. Let us remember to embrace moments of joy and celebrate with friends and family.

We also celebrate communally at different points of the year. Rosh Hashanah, Hanukkah, and Passover are just a few of the holidays that punctuate our calendar. These annual holidays anchor us in time and space. They connect us to our history and to a larger community. Let us bring communal celebrations into our life just as we embrace our personal joys.   LF

Combating Loneliness

15 SEPTEMBER

By virtue of their nature, people seek to form communities.
MOSES MAIMONIDES[15]

Jews privilege community. Ten of us are required to recite blessings; we need organizations to provide our religious needs; and our entire religious experience depends upon our identification with a community, historical and current. What then is the function of loneliness in the development of our spirits? Perhaps it is the very communality of our religious lives that makes us feel so lonely when we find ourselves alone. Rabbi Soloveitchik is right to insist that it is not aloneness which is the starting point, but it may be closer to the start than we realize. As we grow older, we may feel more lonely and even want to be alone, at the same time that we yearn increasingly for community, and as we grow older, religious life becomes more important, in both the communal and private senses. We need to be alone to face who we are, and we ought to be in community to learn who those about us are. What really matters may happen in the inner places where we are alone: Our rooms of work and the rooms of our hearts. But that may be why we so desperately seek community as an antidote. Community, where we come to know each person's name, is the place where we share the fear that comes as we continue to focus on the night, dark and alone. Like God, we are alone. But God is the only being Who may never feel lonely.   RABBI WILLIAM CUTTER[16]

Heart and Spirit

16 SEPTEMBER

O God, create for me a pure heart, and renew within me a just spirit.
PSALM 51:12

A pure heart and a just spirit. These are the goals of every human being who reaches for spiritual renewal at this season and throughout the year. From the Psalmist's sentiment above, it is clear that this goal cannot be reached alone. It takes a relationship with God, the commitment of covenant. It also demands work for both partners. The individual has to be willing to enter into a relationship with God. But there is more work to be done. In order to make room for a pure heart and a just spirit, we have to empty ourselves of the puffy haughtiness of self that sometimes fills us up, leaving no room for anything—or anyone—else. Then and only then can God do what God has to do, and that only God *can* do. So start emptying yourself of ego and pride.   KO

Finding Time to Study

17 SEPTEMBER

Say not, "When I have leisure I will study."
Perhaps you will never have the leisure.
MISHNAH[17]

How many of us gather brochures of adult learning courses each fall and spring only to toss them away because we can't make room in our busy schedules to take a class? We might even circle courses that interest us or ask others about the instructors. Yet in the end, we say to ourselves, "Not this year. I'll do this next year when my kids are in school" or "I'll do this in five years when I retire." Our time seems to fill up, if not with work, then with family and communal commitments. It is never easy to find regular time to pursue new avenues of study unless we weave it into the fabric of our lives, even when we are very busy.

There are ways to commit ourselves to study by taking bite-size pieces of it. Some people read a *mishnah* (a segment of the Oral Law) a day because these are short and concise. Others study a page of Talmud a day, called *daf yomi,* or they read the weekly Torah portion. You can even participate in this incremental study by joining a study group on the Internet. If you commute, use some of your time in the car or train to study Torah, read a religious book, or listen to a tape on a Jewish topic. If we think creatively, the possibilities are endless. Don't wait for leisure time to study. Make time to do it today.   LF

The Freedom of Humanity

18 SEPTEMBER

*Humanity has freedom, we can choose God or reject God,
we can lead the world to perdition and to redemption. The
creation of humanity with such power of freedom means that
God has made room for co-determining power alongside
God's self. Humanity is the crossroads of the world.*

RABBI HENRY SLONIMSKY[18]

The theme song "The Circle of Life," from Disney's *The Lion King,* may reflect humanity's most popular idea. Nature is all circles: day and night; the turning of the seasons; the revolutions of the planets; birth, growth, maturity, decay, death, and rebirth. If life is a circle, then death is not an end. Death is only an invitation to rebirth and renewal. This is the "myth of the eternal return"—the phoenix rising from its ashes. No wonder so much of humanity finds comfort in this idea.

In Judaism, however, you find no circles. Jewish tradition rebelled against circles because it perceived the deadly implications of this belief. Life as a circle is closed, its pattern fixed, and nothing new can enter. Can there be a more hopeless idea than history, like nature, bound to repeat itself in endless cycles of war, holocaust, plague, and destruction? Can we never learn? Can we never change?

Judaism passionately rejected the Circle of Life. It offered a radical new idea: *Bereshit,* "The Beginning." We are a people obsessed with beginnings. Our High Holidays commence with Rosh Hashanah, the new year. Twelve times each year, *Rosh Chodesh,* the arrival of a new month, is celebrated. The Torah opens with the word *Bereshit,* "In the Beginning."

We believe in beginnings because we believe the world can change. We believe that people can change. Destiny is not fixed. And personality is not fixed. You have the freedom to choose to be the person you would be. We have the power to create the world as we would want it. No force of human nature or of heaven can rob us of that freedom, and none can relieve us of its responsibility.

We believe in beginnings because we believe that the human individual is precious—brought into this world to add something totally new and unprecedented. We have expectations for each one. Each of us carries one word of God's message. Only with each of our words, each of our contributions, will the message ever be intelligible and will the world be complete.   RABBI EDWARD FEINSTEIN

Repentance with a Warranty

19 SEPTEMBER

*What is repentance? The One who knows all
that is hidden will testify that the individual
will never again repeat this sin.*

MOSES MAIMONIDES[19]

How can God testify that once we have repented we will
not commit a particular transgression again? We might argue
that all is foreseen to God, therefore God knows what will
happen. Other people will argue that the only real repentance
comes at death and that once you die, you can, of course, no
longer transgress on earth. Or so we think. Still others might
say that since most of our life is lived in routine, we can follow people on their daily routines and discern whether they
are tempted to transgress again. Those activities that are
beyond daily routine may be beyond the possibility of transgression, since we have no prior experience with them.

I like to think of Maimonides' insight this way: God can
peer into the soul of the individual and make a determination
about our proclivity to sin even when we think that we cannot do so on our own. This is accomplished through the light
of Divine illumination. When we make use of this Light, we
can find the recesses of self. Then we can more fully know
the self.

Why this talk about transgression and repentance at this
time of year? It's true that opportunities to realign our lives
are presented to us throughout the year. But then there are
other distractions. Only at this time of year does Jewish tradition focus on helping us see ourselves clearly and helping us
grow beyond where we are at this moment.   KO

Being Fully Ourselves

20 September

Before his death Rabbi Zusya said, "In the coming world,
God will not ask: Why were you not Moses?"
They will ask me: "Why were you not Zusya?"
MARTIN BUBER[20]

Many of us may fantasize from time to time that we are someone else. We may wish we were a famous actor or singer, or a starter pitcher for our favorite ball club, or that we were taller or thinner. These dreams may be harmless if we still remain true to who we are and what our core values are in our professional and familial relationships. They become worrisome only when we let them rule our lives and overshadow our sense of self. We have all encountered people we look up to, whom we might strive to imitate in some fashion. They play an important role in showing us we can stretch beyond our initial dreams. However, we can never become them. What we can become is fully ourselves. So while we may learn from those we look up to—our teachers, our parents, our mentors—let us strive to uncover our full selves and embrace all we offer to ourselves and others.   LF

Effecting Real Change

21 SEPTEMBER

*We do not know the extent of our own power
to change and to effect change. But we must act;
that is in our power. We have to do our part
and we have to hope that God is indeed attentive.*

RABBI BARUCH BOKSER[21]

Pagan religion inhabits a universe in which everything happens within circles of return. From days to months to years, from dreams to events to lifetimes, sooner or later, everything happens again and again forever. The task of religion in such a system is therefore to rehearse and celebrate those cycles—surely a noble and even sacred task. But there is more.

Judaism, especially as taught by the Hebrew prophets, brings to this world-view of cycles the linearity and non-repeatability of history. Some things, some very important things, just happen once. You only get one shot at them. For this reason, serious religion also necessitates politics. Yes, meditation in the prayer hall is vital, but equally so is taking to the streets. We are obligated, even commanded, to take responsibility for what is set before us, to step forward into our destiny, to try as best as we can to influence the way others behave and the way things happen. If we don't, someone else will.

Each day sets before us unique, unprecedented opportunities and challenges. More than a few of these have our names engraved on them. Most of the time, we are too busy or too conveniently self-deluded into thinking that our decision will have no consequence. Yet every now and then, we feel compelled to act. Each one of us are messengers on a sacred mission. The world depends on it! RABBI LAWRENCE KUSHNER[22]

Atonement

22 SEPTEMBER

They will eat them [the offerings] and will be forgiven.
EXODUS 29:33

It seemed rather simple to atone for one's sins in ancient days. All you basically had to do was bring your sacrificial offering to the priest at the Temple in Jerusalem. He would take care of the rest. While this process of expiation was available to people most of the year, there were certain times when the activity was encouraged and thought to be even more efficacious. Going to Jerusalem may have been a difficult and expensive journey for some, but once they got there, their responsibility essentially concluded.

The Temple and its sacrificial system came to an end nearly 2,000 years ago in the year 70 C.E., so we are now left with the obligation to atone for our sins fully on our own. Teachers like Moses Maimonides have outlined the process of atonement rather succinctly: regret, remorse, confession, and restitution. Then comes the most important element: A commitment not to do it again. The Rabbis suggest that we know if it is an effective atonement only if, when we are confronted with similar circumstances, we don't sin again. This is the only test that we need. Actions speak and, in this case, so does inaction.   KO

The Seasons of Our Lives

23 SEPTEMBER

It seems to me I have lived not one life, but several, each one bearing its own character and insignia. I find that, old as I am, in a certain sense I have not stopped growing. While my intellect is an organ of narrow limitations, my inner world—perhaps it is my world of feeling, of instinct—expands.

HENRIETTA SZOLD[23]

As we look back on our lives, we see that they consist of many different periods. We may feel that we have lived many lives, each characterized by its own unique qualities, relationships, and accomplishments. They might be marked by marriage, children, different careers, and other significant projects.

Think back over your life and see if you can distinguish how many distinct epochs you detect. What stands out in each period? Is there a common passion, theme, or concern?

We can see our lives as a process that continuously unfolds. Yet our growth never ends. From time to time we may reach plateaus, and these too are part of growing. They allow us to regroup and prepare for the next growth spurt. As we move through one period to the next, let's be conscious of our inner life so we can experience a deepening and an expansion of our spiritual natures. LF

Quality Time

24 SEPTEMBER

If you are too busy to spend time with your children, then you are busier than God intended you to be.

RABBI MENDL EPSTEIN[24]

Depth and intimacy require lots of time . . . and who has that? Try an experiment: Call someone you would confide in—a friend, a member of the family, a colleague—and ask this person for a full hour of undivided attention. When can they see you? Tomorrow night? Next Tuesday? Not until the last week of the month? You know how things are! Family pressures, tax season, tickets to the symphony we've waited years for . . . You understand I'm sure! If you find someone who will share an uninterrupted hour with you upon a moment's notice, give thanks—you have the rare gift of a good friend.

For so many who share our culture, the characters in television fantasies become more real than the flesh-and-blood people who fill the real world. A child who spends seven minutes each day with a parent still spends about three hours in front of the TV. Who is more real to that child—his family or *The Simpsons?* Who are my people? Those members of my household from who I feel so distant, or the happy gang of *Friends,* the compassionate staff of *ER,* the intimate circle of *Seinfeld?* They always have time for me!

What an irony: This generation invented FedEx, fax, e-mail, pagers, cell phones, and the Internet. We can connect with anyone, anywhere, anytime. But there just isn't time or energy to really share.

Each Friday night in my home, we shut off the TV, draw the family together into a tight circle, and share Shabbat together. I explain to my children that the things people collect that are most precious are moments—moments of closeness, moments of sharing, moments of inspiration, moments of wholeness. We stop the world to hold one another, to hold the moment, to hold onto the peacefulness of Shabbat, and to hold onto what's real. Let us refuse to be made strangers to one another.   RABBI EDWARD FEINSTEIN

Full Forgiveness

25 SEPTEMBER

*I hereby forgive everyone who offended me or angered me
or sinned against me.*
LITURGY[25]

Why does Jewish tradition insist that we recite this phrase
before retiring at night? Perhaps it is necessary for the full
restoration of the soul that comes in the morning following a
night of sleep. Maybe it lets us sleep comfortably because we
have let go of everything that might otherwise preoccupy us
during the night. Perhaps it is a recognition of our vulnerability while sleeping because sleep seems to simulate death. Or
maybe it is a fear that should we die, while sleeping, God forbid, anyone who may have sinned against us will not be able
to make full atonement. We should not take such forgiveness
to the grave—and we never know when death will come
upon us.

Practice reciting the phrase above regularly. It will change
your entire outlook on life. It may help others do the same
as well.   KO

The Sacredness of History

26 SEPTEMBER

*For others, a knowledge of the history of their people is a
civic duty, while for the Jews it is a sacred duty.*
MAURICE SAMUEL[26]

As Jews, why do we believe that history is sacred? Our people have survived some of the most atrocious incidents ever

committed against humanity. We have been exiled, expelled, excluded. We have been victims of mass murder. One might think that we would want to forget our history. Who wants to remember one tragic event after another? But the Jewish response has been the exact opposite. We believe that history is not predetermined. By embracing what happened in our past, we believe we can affect the future.

We follow Abraham's lead when he left his father's pagan home and followed the One God. In doing so, Abraham asserted that he could take a risk and become an active player in history. By recounting our history to ourselves, our children, and others, we remember the past and pledge to ensure that atrocities are never repeated. If we forget our past, then we are at a great risk that historical amnesia will numb our ability to act and cry out at the injustices around us. Also, all of us have personal pasts which we either embrace or deny. By brushing aside the painful parts of our personal histories, we may be burying information that can actually liberate us. We might be immobilized by those areas of our lives that we are afraid to confront, to look at squarely and deal with in a direct manner.

Our past is a crucial part of our inner lives, as individuals and as people. Do not forget the past. It is an important lens through which to understand the present. LF

Dwelling With God

27 SEPTEMBER

Make Me a Sanctuary that I may dwell among them.
EXODUS 25:8

That pretty much sums up the religious enterprise: You have to do something, so that God, who is not there, can be. The tabernacle is a metaphor for the religion we "construct," an exercise we perform to alter our consciousness.

Or, to put it another way: If God's everywhere, then why can't we find God anywhere? If God made the world and, as Menachem Nahum of Chernobyl teaches, the presence of the Creator is within each created thing, then why can't we find it? We have this nagging suspicion that God is ubiquitous; we just can't seem to find God.

According to Shneur Zalman of Lyadi (founder of Chabad Hasidism in the middle of the eighteenth century), it's not that there is a world and God is everywhere within it. It's that there is God and the world is everywhere within God. There is nothing, absolutely nothing, that is not already God. It's all God. You, me, the trees, the murders, the children, the sewers the blossoms of springtime, the toxic waste dumps, the tabernacle—it's all God. At the end of Job, God says, in effect, I'm the whole kazoo. Not just the sunshine and bluebirds, but even in the lions tearing gazelles, vultures eating carrion. Everything. Everywhere. God. God. God.

And how do you get to that awareness? It has something to do with how you behave as a human being. Being a decent human being increases the chances that you'll find it, that it'll dawn on you, just as being a louse gradually seals you off from it. It's not that you're religious to be good; it's that you're good to be religious!

But suppose you want this awareness more of the time: that it's all God, that the presence of the Creator is everywhere. Suppose you say, "I want to be aware of the presence of the Creator more than just sporadically." What do I do? That's where religion comes in. That's the constructive advice of those who have come before us on how to attain it. Sure it doesn't always work. Sure it can easily be perverted. But the "hit rate" is way ahead of whatever is in second place. So

God says, "You build me this sacred place, just as I've told you, so that I can dwell among you" (Exodus 25:8). Whenever you perform a religious deed with devotion and reverence, then you get it. Every time. It's all God.

RABBI LAWRENCE KUSHNER[27]

Praise

28 SEPTEMBER

I shall not die but I shall rather live to tell of the deeds of God. God has indeed chastised me, but has not surrendered me to death. Open the gates of righteousness for me. I will enter and praise God.

PSALM 118:17–19

This verse is taken from a group of psalms known as the Hallel Psalms (Psalms of Praise) because they overflow with praise for God. They help shape the liturgy for holidays such as the fall festival of Sukkot. Almost every verse of these psalms becomes a paean of praise in its own right. Many of these verses have melodies that we closely associate with certain holidays. This selection above captures much of the psalms' intent: In order for me to praise God, I must live. And for the blessing of life, I praise God. I have done some things wrong, and for these I accept my punishment—as long as it is not death. Open the gates of righteousness for me so that I can dwell with God and continue to sing God's praises. That is when I am most happy.   KO

Words of Torah

29 SEPTEMBER

*Words of Torah need each other. What one passage
locks up, the other unlocks.*
MIDRASH[28]

One of the surprising and satisfying aspects to Torah study is how one verse—or even one word—unlocks an array of meaning for verses found elsewhere. We never read Torah in isolation.

We bring to our study of it the insight and comments from previous generations. No wisdom is ever isolated. When we attain a deep, penetrating understanding of a particular situation, we can see connections where we thought none existed. We gain insight and wisdom by understanding things in their proper context and looking for ways to relate them to each other. Wisdom is not about isolating facts but rather about joining together unspoken, and at times intangible, truths.

In our personal lives we can never be sure what will release a blockage in our spiritual lives. We might think a solution will come from one direction, when lo and behold, relief comes from an unexpected place. Just like Torah, which has interconnections among its many parts, so too does our inner life reveal an intricate web of connections. Never rule out that one insight is limited in nature or scope. It may give rise to many additional insights.

This teaching reminds us that learning can never stand alone but needs to be continually deepened through additional study and exploration. In this way, we can further see the hidden connections and unlock the richness within.　　LF

A Parent's Blessings

30 SEPTEMBER

A father's blessing establishes his children.
APOCRYPHA[29]

September 1, 1939, is a day remembered well in my family. My father was nineteen years old when the Nazis invaded Poland, the country that had been his ancestral home for generations. By the end of September my father and his two older sisters had left their parents' home and begun their journey through the hellish night of the Holocaust. They were never to see their parents again. The last thing my father recalls, after the words of final instruction, was my grandfather taking my father's hand in his and kissing the back of his hand. This touch was to stay with him throughout the war years.

Very few of us will ever have to reflect on this kind of a final touch, on this kind of separation, although each of us at one moment or another is privileged to be so embraced. Often this final touch comes in the form of a bedside blessing, a patriarchal gift that links life and death.

Parents care for their children at their most vulnerable time. Yet it seems equally essential that children should care for their aging parents when the parents are most in need of compassion and assistance. While we embrace the young child as it begins its life and we respond to its every need, we often abandon the older parent.

How sad this is. The beginning and the end could frame a life that has meaning and purpose. My father often shared with me that he could still feel the ache in his heart for how his parents must have felt on that September night when they looked at the three empty beds in their small apartment in Poland. With that sadness in their hearts, my grandparents died.

Just one kiss on the back of the hand, just one final blessing.   RABBI ABIE INGBER

OCTOBER

Vanity

1 OCTOBER

Vanity of vanities. All is vanity . . . the striving after wind.
ECCLESIASTES 1:2, 14B

These words from Ecclesiastes help us understand why the entire book of Ecclesiastes is read during the festival of Sukkot, which usually falls in October. Those synagogues that read only a few lines or perhaps sing the refrain from the 1960s folk song "Turn, Turn, Turn" (whose words come from Ecclesiastes) miss the profound insight of the author of this book. The requirement for reading this volume may be a way that the Rabbis made sure that we have read most of the entire Bible by the time we have concluded a complete calendar cycle. They frequently play out this educational theme in the liturgical life of the synagogue.

While I used the standard translation of the Hebrew to translate the verse above, I prefer to translate the word usually read as "vanity" as "a wisp of wind." Such a translation reinforces the notion that *hevel* (the Hebrew word translated as "vanity") has no substance. There is no value to it. It is totally void of anything of worth. As we take note of the fall harvest of crops and revel in our bounty, all in preparation for celebrating Sukkot—whether as farmers or as city dwellers—we consider the produce of our labors. And doing that can make us cognizant of the harvest of our lives, especially as we approach middle age and beyond. But this life's harvest does not have to be the striving after "a wisp of wind" that the author of Ecclesiastes would have us believe. Life need not be as flimsy as the reeds that hold our sukkahs together. Instead, life becomes significant when we do something significant with it.

Some people find the Book of Ecclesiastes depressing. It's true that some sections, if read as isolated excerpts, can be disillusioning. Nevertheless, I have always found the book to be inspirational because of its profound insights. Its words give me a unique perspective on the world by helping to focus me. When I take myself too seriously, I am reminded that it is vanity (a "wisp of wind") that is driving me. When I spend too much time working and not enough time enjoying the blessings of my family, I am reminded that it is the pursuit of wind that may be fueling me. When I worry about things in this world without regard for the next, I am reminded that it is vanity that is pushing me forward—and that I have to push back.

But Ecclesiastes does not conclude with the same sentiments that began the book. Modern scholars argue that the end of the book was written by someone different and that the Rabbis required this other ending before they were willing to accept the book into the canon. The opening words provide the author, who is known as Kohelet, with the necessary prism to review his entire life. And in the end, after he has experienced great wealth and power, he concludes that a relationship with God is what it takes to change the perspective we have on our lives. In the pursuit of God, there is no "wisp of wind." There is only a "still small voice" that we hear in our silence.   KO

Hope

2 October

Where there is life, there is hope.
TALMUD[1]

Our embrace of life is inextricably bound up with our ability to nourish and sustain hope. Hope in the midst of even the worst situations will renew our spirits and give us the ability to walk into the unknown despite all our fears and concerns. There have probably been times when we have all lost hope in ourselves, in others, and even in life itself. When such despair overcomes us, it is necessary to reconnect with the spirit that resides within each of us, though we may think it has been extinguished.

How have you recovered in the midst of despair? Holding a baby, touching the earth, taking a walk in the woods, playing with a child, laughing deeply are all ways to stir a dormant spirit. Without a sense of hope for the future, our lives wither, our spirits dampen, and we shrivel.

Hope is like a candle's flame. It may waver, but as long as there is both wax and wick, its flame will burn forever. The national anthem of the State of Israel is called *HaTikvah,* which means "The Hope." For two thousand years we kept alive the hope that we would once again be a sovereign people. Without our enduring hope, this national and religious dream would have long faded away. Protect your sense of hope. Do not let it diminish. Share it freely with others to keep it strong and alive. LF

Leaving Egypt

3 OCTOBER

I will dwell in the midst of the Israelites and will be their God. They shall know that I am Adonai *their God, who brought them forth out of the land of Egypt so that I may dwell in the midst of them.*

EXODUS 29:45–46

The Book of Numbers, the fourth book in the Torah, describes the Israelites' forty-year journey through the desert on their way to the Promised Land. Why devote an entire book to the desert experience?

The desert journeying represents an important stage in the journey of a people from slavery to freedom. The wilderness, far beyond its geographic or historic reality, enters the Jewish experience as a central metaphor for understanding who we are and what we must do. By devoting an entire book to the wilderness experience, the Torah provides an important insight into the real achievement of freedom. Leaving Egypt in a moment of pure triumph is far easier than wrestling with burdens of establishing a functioning community. Here we see a people dealing with the mundane frustrations of gathering goods, pitching tents, establishing new rules and customs, as well as defining leadership.

Despite the problems and murmuring of dissent about which we learn, this slave people raises a new generation of freeborn children. Here is a deeper understanding of the Exodus—the maturity of a people responsibly meeting the daily challenges of life in freedom.

The true goal of the Exodus is to take Egypt out of the Israelites. The experience of the seemingly endless journey transformed a people who were crushed, frightened, subservient, and dependent into a people with initiative, self-respect, and anger at oppression. The Israelites at the Jordan River are a different people from the ones who left Egypt. They are ready to fight their own battles. They are a community committed to one another and to the covenant that binds them together.

The desert experience reminds us that wherever we live, there is a better place, a world more attractive, a Promised Land, but the way to that land is through the wilderness. There is no way to get there except by joining together and marching day after day. RABBI IRWIN KULA[2]

Comprehending Our Life's Work

4 OCTOBER

As the eye needs light to see, so the soul
needs labor to comprehend.
PHILO OF ALEXANDRIA[3]

I am someone who loves to work the soil. I did it with enthusiasm on a kibbutz in Israel, and I do it with a passion in my own backyard. Perhaps it helps me return to our ancestral plane, where agriculture provided the original rhythm for the Jewish calendar. Maybe that is precisely why I enjoy the change of the seasons since I moved north from the sunny south. Whatever the reason, my amateur farming helps me more fully understand this text. To me, there is nothing more wonderful than to see a plant rise from the soil after it has been lovingly cared for. I marvel at its development. Whenever the plant bursts through the soil, whenever it blossoms, I am overwhelmed by the awesome beauty of nature that I experience through its order. Even the simple activity of planting spring flowers helps me understand God's work in the world and my relationship to it.

Gardening serves a secondary purpose as well. It also helps me do my part in affirming order in the midst of apparent chaos; it is a way to acknowledge life in a way that I might fully understand it. While my gardening may have a ritual quality to it, my backyard forays are more routine than ritual. That routine is what places me firmly on the earth. Religious rituals, on the other hand, help make spiritual ideas less abstract and more concrete for me. I then use them to help me pave a path to God.   KO

The Theology of Life

5 OCTOBER

The Divine test of a person's worth is not theology but life.
TALMUD[4]

How do we live our lives? We can spend a lot of time philosophizing about life and seeking answers to our deepest questions. At times such an in-depth inquiry can be most helpful. It may give us fresh ways to think and new strategies to use as we proceed down life's unpredictable path. At other times, though, we may use philosophical and theological discourse as an escape from reality. It can become a way to avoid making necessary life changes. Our head can be full of abstract ideas and our actions can be empty.

As a common saying claims, "Actions speak louder than words."

Put aside for today your theorizing and look closely at each of your actions. What are they saying? Do they communicate what you want to be saying? If you want to be compassionate, are you engaged in acts of compassion or are you just thinking about doing them? If you want to be learning new things, are you engaged in pursuing a plan of study or just thinking about opening a book or attending a class? We create our lives through the simple acts we do every day, through those acts that we repeat day in and day out and that often escape our attention. It is our daily acts of care, not our grand thoughts, that others remember. No matter what your theology, are you living them out? LF

It's All God

6 OCTOBER

God, open my lips so that my mouth may declare
Your praise.
PSALM 51:17

It seems odd that as a prelude to the central rubric of Jewish liturgy, the *Amidah*—a bouquet of prayers of praise, petition, and thanksgiving—the most intensely conversational script of the entire prayerbook, begins with this verse from Psalms.

Wouldn't it make more sense to say something like, "Here I am God, ready to begin our conversation," or "Permit me to introduce myself," or "I know we haven't always seen eye to eye on certain things." For there to be a conversation, there must be two discrete parties. It takes two to tango.

In much (but not all) of the Hebrew Bible and the prayerbook, God and people are separate, distinct, discrete, autonomous, independent, and apart from one another. God says this, we say that. God does this, we do that. God's there, we're here. The energy of the whole thing comes precisely from our being separate from one another. So why begin our personal prayers with a denial of that mutual autonomy and free will?

The psalm says, "God, would you please open my mouth." Hey, who's working my mouth anyway, me or God? Who's praising God, me or God? What's going on here?

What's going on here is another spiritual paradigm, one in which God and people are not only distinct from one another but are literally within one another. God is the ocean and we are the waves. In the words of Hasidic thought, *Alles is Gott,* "It's all God." My mouth is God's mouth. My praises are God's words. In the words of Rabbi Kalnoymos Kalmish Shapira of Piesetzna, "Not does God hear our prayers, God prays them through us as well!"

The words of the *Amidah* may sound like they come from me, but in truth they come from a higher source. Prayer may ultimately be an exercise for helping us let go of our egos, which are hopelessly anchored to this world where one person is discrete from another and from God, and soar to the heavens where we realize there is a holy One and which we have been an expression of all along. "God, open my lips so that my mouth may declare Your Praise."

RABBI LAWRENCE KUSHNER[5]

Sowing the Seeds of Peace

7 OCTOBER

The disciples of the wise increase peace in the world.
TALMUD[6]

I will never forget Yom Kippur of October 1973. The scene seared a permanent image on my soul. I was sitting in the synagogue when the rabbi announced early in the services that he had just received word that Israel had been attacked. While most Israelis were searching their souls in synagogue, Israel's neighbors assaulted her on all sides. Israel was ill-prepared for a response. Perhaps it was overconfident. Perhaps the post-1967 Six Day War euphoria gave Israelis no cause for alarm. The whole episode made me think of the Amalekites who attacked our people from behind as they made their way early on in the desert journey from Egypt to Israel. For me, Yom Kippur has never been the same. Neither has October.

I could easily write off the incident as just another attack against our people. I could use it as a barrier for advocating peace. But what kind of spiritual lesson can I derive from such an event? It reminds me of humanity's general predisposition toward hatred. It would be easy to blame Israel's neighbors and walk away from any potential for peace. But that is not the way that we can bring about a better world.

Few of us are government officials, representing Israel or the United States around a conference table, where the lines of peace are hopefully drawn. But we can turn strangers into friends by extending our hand to them. And if they do not take it, we just have to reach out further, again and again.　　KO

The Fragility of Life

8 OCTOBER

*You know that whether people live in huts or in palaces,
it is only as pilgrims that they dwell; both huts and palaces
form our transitory home. You know that in this pilgrimage
only God is our protection, and it is God's grace
which shields us.*

RABBI SAMUEL RAPHAEL HIRSCH[7]

Our homes are important to our well-being. They provide us with much more than basic shelter. For many of us, our homes become an expression of our deepest selves. We decorate them to reflect our taste and create a warm, loving environment for our families and friends. Some of us may move often, while others of us may stay in the same home for decades. When we purchase a house, we inquire about its structural soundness. We want to make sure it is solid and stable. It is not surprising that we often forget that our homes are temporary dwelling places. While they may suggest permanence, they too are transitory.

Yearly on Sukkot we are reminded that the world is a most fragile place. On this holiday we leave behind our comfortable homes and dwell in huts similar to those of our ancestors. The *sukkah* is a simple structure open to the rain and wind, easily shattered and broken. It becomes our home so we can remember that the world is a delicate place and that impermanence is the way of all things. Sitting under an open sky, we are closer to the understanding that life is full of changes and unexpected turns. We never fully control what tomorrow will bring. Our task, then, in a world forever fragile is to make meaning, to set purpose, to discover the joys of living without illusion. Sukkot is our reminder of fragility.

On Yom Kippur we ask, "*Who* shall live?" On Sukkot we become aware of the fragile nature of life, of love, of hopes and accomplishments, and we ask, "*How* shall we live? What shall we do? What shall we value?"

All of us deep in our hearts know that when we share ourselves and our abundance with others, it is we who gain. By giving, we restock our internal wells of joy and abundance. When we give of ourselves—to those closest to us and to those who are distant from us—we renew our life's meaning in this transitory and fragile existence.   LF

True Leadership

9 OCTOBER

A nation needs its guides and shepherds, its scouts and leaders of the flock, who will carry out the function of leadership: the ability to feel and the power to think.
RABBI ADIN STEINSALTZ[8]

Every day the newspapers splash a photograph of some important world leader doing some important act of diplomacy: attending an elegant state dinner, participating in a formal treaty-signing ceremony, introducing legislation, engaging in fundraising. These are the activities of the busy and prominent.

When posing for official photographs, world leaders sit with pen in hand, or by a globe, or with a phone next to their ears. These are the symbols of power, the subtle way of saying, "This person is important."

One world leader always impressed me as somehow different. Hubert Humphrey stood out because of his commitment to the little guy. Able to mingle with the high and mighty, he still remembered that everyone counts.

One of the greatest leaders of our people was our ancestor Jacob. He too was able to interact with the great and the powerful (God and Pharaoh, to name just two). Yet what characterizes his leadership as particularly remarkable was his insistence that leadership is measured not by how you treat the great, but by how you treat the least powerful. When Jacob goes to meet his brother Esau after many years of separation, Jacob walks not at the front of his entourage but at the back. Unlike most commentators, who think this reflects cowardice, some suggest that Jacob is walking at the pace of the slowest child because his leadership is one of inclusion and of nurturing. Only as the slowest child can proceed will Jacob's entourage move forward.

We too need to measure greatness by a different beat: Not by how often a person speaks with a head of state, but by how well this person cares for the young, the elderly, the sick, and the poor. In caring for those who cannot care for themselves, we show ourselves to be true leaders.

RABBI BRADLEY SHAVIT ARTSON

Who We Really Are

10 OCTOBER

The longest distance is to the pocket.
YIDDISH PROVERB[9]

How do we figure out who we really are? How do we express to others the essence of our inner selves? Some people say, "You are what you eat." Everyone seems to have their own perspective on this question. Commentators on the Torah suggest that when the Israelites responded to God about their commitment to the Torah, they said, "We will do and we will hearken." It was an odd construction of language, but it clearly expressed the sentiment: "We are what we do." It determined an approach to Jewish life and law: If you follow God's instruction by fulfilling the obligation of a particular ritual requirement, even if you do not understand it yet, you will eventually come to understand it. I think it may be the Jewish spin on the well-known parental refrain, "Don't do what I do; do what I say."

Like most folk expressions that emerge out of the common daily lives of people, the Yiddish expression above—"the longest distance is to the pocket," which is certainly one of the favorites of my grandparents' generation—speaks of how difficult it is for people to express themselves through money. It is hard for them to reach into their pockets and give their hard-earned money to someone else. That is why it is an insightful measurement of an individual.

Ask yourself these questions as you consider reaching into your pocket or your purse: How often are you willing to give to someone in need? What do you find yourself buying regularly? Are you more likely to buy something for yourself or for someone else? Do you shop for pleasure or for purpose?   KO

God Lives within Us

11 OCTOBER

A person should always measure their actions as if the Holy One dwells with them.

TALMUD[10]

In Genesis (5:1–2) we read that man and woman are made in God's image. For Jews, this does not mean that our physical appearance or form imitates God, since God is infinite and formless. While God may be invisible, God is not intangible. What may be called the "tangible Divine essence" is what dwells in each of us. This sense of the Holy can be either diminished or enlarged depending on how we relate to this Divine part of ourselves. If we ignore God's essence, we violate an important part of our soul. While it may become dormant, however, it never disappears. When our yearning for connection with this innate part of ourselves becomes strong enough, we then have the task of recovering and reestablishing our connection with it.

It is also true that we share many characteristics with animals. We eat, procreate, and create ways to live with each other. We can engage in all of these actions mindlessly—or with full awareness of our holy nature. By doing the latter, we raise them from their animal nature to a divine level. With this perspective we can interact with ourselves and with others in a new manner. Do we care about the divine image that resides in each of us? Do we denigrate those feelings, expressions, and experiences that allow us to touch our divine selves? Or do we embrace them and draw them into our everyday consciousness?

One path to self-care is to realize that how we treat ourselves reflects how we care for—or how we abuse—God's image which resides in our very depths. It is entrusted to us so we not only protect it, but use it to guide us in life.   LF

How Long Will It Take?

12 OCTOBER

How long, Adonai, will You ignore me forever?
How long will You hide Your face from me?
How long will I have cares on my mind,
grief in my heart all day? . . .
But I put trust in Your faithfulness.
My heart will exult in Your deliverance.
I will sing to Adonai, for God has been good to me.
PSALM 13:1–3, 6–7

This psalm repeats the cry over and over: *Ana Adonai,* "How long?" And that "long" of the "how long" expresses the longing, the yearning of the Psalmist. There is grief and anguish. There is fear of defeat and death. Most of the psalm expresses pain and is focused on urgent questions. It seems right to me that we must dwell on such questions for a long time, that they must be voiced in their full urgency. But there is also an affirmation that a time of deliverance will come. In the end there will be rejoicing.

As I stand with people who are experiencing acute suffering, at times God feels hidden. If God were fully present, this could not be happening. *How long will You hide Your face from me?* You are so mysterious, we cannot understand. We demand that You come back and allow us to feel Your presence. We reserve the right to hide our faces from You. We are made in Your image, *b'tzelem Elohim,* the image of God. As You turn from us, we can turn from You.

It can happen that as we voice our despair, as we call out to God, we coerce God into being present, even if only as an absent presence. And maybe that is as far as we get for a long time. Just as our being created *b'tzelem Elohim* enables us to hide from God, our being created *b'tzelem Elohim* enables us to comfort others as they suffer. As we turn from God, we turn, God willing, to one another. And in that turning toward people, we have the potential, over time, to discover God's presence once again. RABBI MYCHAL SPRINGER

Centering the Spirit

13 OCTOBER

Pleasant sounds, sights, and smells put one in good spirit.
TALMUD[11]

Although it is not always possible to do so, most of us would probably prefer to live a life of inspiration. This is certainly the case for the creative people among us. Regardless of our passion for art or music or dance or writing, we all want the uplift that others boast about. However, it may not be realistic or always possible to be constantly inspired. Our lives are not marked primarily by hills and valleys. They look more like the endless plains of the west. Yet our spiritual goal should be balance, not the peak experiences that we are occasionally privileged to know. Sure, the mundane and the everyday have their downside. So we fend off depression that might threaten us, particularly during life's transitional moments. That's probably why all of us are in the market for the key ingredients that help guide us to a "good spirit." Take a look around. Bookstores abound with titles that promise inspiration. Even things like aromatherapy have become mainstream. But the Rabbis quoted above are not talking about constantly raising us to the peak of the mountaintop. The Sinai experience was enough to carry our people throughout its journey. What is needed instead, argue the Rabbis, is for us to *center* our lives, to be here in this moment with deliberate concentration. This balanced life lets us reach the holy.

The rabbis are suggesting three basic things to help us do this: pleasant sounds, sights, and smells.

What are those sounds? We might begin with the sounds of nature to help center us away from the cacophony of the city, but the Rabbis prefer the sound of children studying and of men and women in a passionate discussion about Torah texts. And for the sights that help balance our lives, how about the sight of families walking together to synagogue? Or perhaps a sukkah in each backyard? Or Hanukkah lights proclaiming the miracle of the season? As for the smells that can take us to the level of "good spirit," the Rabbis prefer—as do I—the smell of holiday cooking wafting through the house.

It may not seem so easy to acquire these qualities. They're not sold in stores. Furthermore, we don't all live near our families or even near Jewish communities.

Start simply. Study with a friend. Celebrate with a neighbor, or gather together ten people to make a minyan. Together you can build a bridge back into the community—or you can create your own.   KO

Details Are the Stuff of Life

14 OCTOBER

I am writing down these many details, dear children
of mine, so you may know from what sort of
people you have sprang, lest today or tomorrow
your beloved children or grandchildren come
and know naught of their family.
GLÜCKEL OF HAMELN[12]

How do we learn where we come from? Some of us may have heard stories from parents and grandparents which anchor us in the long chain of tradition, which stretches back centuries and, will, let us hope, continue centuries into the future. If we forget our family and our people's past, we become spiritually orphaned, for no one exists in a vacuum, detached from the particulars of their past. Each of us asks existential questions at some point in our lives: "Why are we here?" "Who came before me?" "How is my life connected to the past?" "How did my family end up here?" "Is there wisdom in my people's past to guide me?" When these questions arise, we ask others with more life experience to help us understand the inextricable intertwining between our lives and our history.

In order to have a vision for the future, we have to acquire a knowledge of—and a perspective on—the past. Just as we search out repositories of our own past, so too will we be called upon to assume this role for future generations. The role of family historian passes to us for our children and our grandchildren. We are the ones who can anchor their questions in a rich past in hopes that they can have a meaningful future.

What stories illustrate the core values that you want to pass on to future generations? In her diary, Glückel of Hamln, a seventeenth-century Jewish woman, recorded for her descendants the rich details of their lineage. We can do the same. What would *you* record for posterity?   LF

A Full Vessel

15 OCTOBER

The way of flesh and blood is not the way of the Holy One. In the way of flesh and blood, the empty vessel holds; the full one does not. But in the way of the Holy One, what is full holds and what is empty does not.

TALMUD[13]

We know a world where matter obeys the laws of physics so that when a vessel is filled to the brim it will not hold anymore; it runs over. Volume is a finite thing. But there are containers created in the world to which the limits of volume do not apply: the heart, the mind, the soul. When these are full of love and wisdom they can hold more love and wisdom. When these vessels are empty, they cannot hold anything. When a heart is full of anger and resentment, it can continue to fill with anger and resentment. When it is empty of anger, it doesn't fill up.

There are times when the vessels created in the way of the Holy One are empty and we try to fill them as we would fill a stomach sometimes, even with food. And of course they don't fill up, because they exist in another realm of being where the empty vessel cannot hold. The way of the Holy One describes what is. So when we examine a full stomach from the human point of view we say, "I can't eat any more." From the Holy One's point of view we say, "I am satisfied."

Our lives bring us face to face with many kinds of empti-ness and fullness, longing and complacency. May all of us have wisdom in measuring our cups and knowing how to fill and empty them.   RABBI VIVIAN MAYER

Mystery

16 OCTOBER

The secret things belong to Adonai *our God.*
DEUTERONOMY 29:28

When I was an adolescent, I was convinced that I knew everything—or at least that I would soon know everything. In those days I thought that few people could teach me much of anything—especially my parents and teachers. So I went to Israel looking for someone who could teach me. I dared some-one to teach me. Each time I met someone, I never expressed this idea directly, but it was clear from the way I said it. I was challenging them to teach me something that I didn't already know. What I really was saying was, "Teach me something that is really worth knowing."

I found my first teacher there. He took me on my first desert journey and taught me the value of opening myself up to the potential for learning, what he called "making my life a desert," as the Rabbis suggest. We probed the mysteries of life together, studying texts that few have the courage to enter. And after a year of study, this is what he ultimately taught me: Some things I will never know because "the secret things belong to *Adonai* our God." That was clearly the case, although I discovered something else in the process: There are many things that I didn't know and would never know. It is from this knowledge that I gain most comfort.   KO

Permanent Growth

17 OCTOBER

Slow growth is the surest guarantee of success. For the perfect fruit, we need a slow ripening—sunshine as well as rain, failure as well as success.

HENRIETTA SZOLD[14]

How many of us are impatient with our spiritual growth? It is not uncommon to want to rush to some preconceived finish line that we have set for ourselves. Spiritual discovery is not a sprint for which there is a stopwatch or a one-minute guidebook. We are in it in for the long run and have to adopt attitudes that marathon runners use. Slow and steady is a good rule of thumb, since at some point we realize that rushing is counterproductive.

We miss so much when we are hurried. One lesson in spiritual deepening is to slow down our quick, harried pace. If we pace ourselves when integrating new insights, practices, and truths into our lives, they will take hold of our inner spirit and lay down sustaining roots. Slow growth allows us to pay attention and notice all of our various experiences and emotions, those we enjoy as well as those we resist. We even learn that when we stumble, we can pick ourselves up, brush our-selves off, and continue.

The journey of spiritual growth and awareness has no end. There is no finish line. It is not a race we run against others. On this path, when choosing between being a turtle or a hare, be a turtle. LF

Laughter and Skepticism

18 OCTOBER

God has brought me laughter;
everyone who hears will laugh with me.
GENESIS 21:6

When Sarah, Abraham's wife, was old and supposedly infertile, her response to hearing that she would have a child was detached and bemused: "Give me a break, God. Even when Abraham was my devoted young lover we couldn't pro-duce a child, and You're telling me that now, after we have wasted our lives crying bitter tears, You are finally going to make us parents. Well thanks a lot, but next time get Your timing right!"

Sarah's words echoed the experiences of Jews throughout the generations who have waited for promised redemption and have cried angry tears over the losses of our people and all people who have suffered during the seemingly endless wait. Were the messianic age to dawn tomorrow, we would turn to God and ask, "So long, so long. Why did You wait? What did it all mean?"

Today all Jews are in Sarah's position: We are all in the position of our mothers and grandmothers. Today we no longer hear God's message spoken directly. At best, we are like Sarah: We catch glimpses of a divine plan by peeking through curtains. And whenever we do, we are unable to relax. Every time we hear of a Jewish leader of high moral purpose, an Abraham Joshua Heschel who marched for civil rights in the 1960s, a Natan Sharansky fighting tirelessly for his sisters and brothers in the Soviet Union, we also hear of corrupt Jewish businessmen on Wall Street who head Jewish philanthropies or of a Rabbi Kahana spreading hate in Israel in the name of tradition. Not for us is the faith of Abraham marching with a knife held high for his Lord. We have learned to be more skeptical of those who act in God's name. We have grown more skeptical of God.

But even with skepticism, let us return to the place where we began: Sarah's laughter. Sarah laughed at God's promise and then named her son Yizchak, which means "he will laugh." As heirs to this tradition, we are heirs to laughter—dubious laughter, surprised laughter, the laughter of wonder. And if some of us have lost faith in the promises of a supernatural God, we may yet be made to wonder at our own capacities for miracles. Sarah teaches that the pleasure of renewal comes in age as well as in youth and that a Divine Presence may burst forth unpredictably in the form of an ordinary human event. Let us watch and wait.

RABBI LEONARD GORDON

Singing the Song of Your Soul

19 OCTOBER

The song shall testify before them as a witness.
DEUTERONOMY 31:21

Not everyone is blessed with a good singing voice. I certainly don't have one. But I do like to sing. As a matter of fact, I can't control my singing. It just comes out, wherever I am and whatever I may be doing, even in the most inopportune of places. And I don't sing quietly or just to myself. I sing loudly and forcefully, for I recognize that my songs have become witnesses to my faith. When I sing, I continue the work of the Levitical choir that used to sing on the steps of the ancient Temple in Jerusalem. They were the sweet singers of our people who turned personal poetry into song.

But not all songs are set to music. There are also the songs of the heart that emerge from a passionate belief in God. These songs are woven from the days of our lives. Wherever you are, whatever your voice, "Sing a new song to God" (Psalm 96:1a).   KO

Aspirations

20 OCTOBER

No human being leaves this world having achieved even half of his or her material aspirations. If one has achieved one hundred dinars, he craves two hundred. If one has two hundred dinars, she craves four hundred.

MIDRASH[15]

There is no end to our desire for more and more material possessions: a bigger home, a fancier car, a luxury vacation. Society tells us that the more we own, the more successful we are. Our sense of self-worth gets tangled up in our possessions. How can we resist this strong societal tug? We walk around feeling insufficient because businesses, in order to sell us newer and more sophisticated products, have to create a constant sense in us that we don't have enough. It is an insidious message. It keeps our minds and our spirits less than content. We get caught up in judging and comparing ourselves with our neighbors, friends, and co-workers. What would it be like to feel totally filled up, lacking nothing? Could you say, "I *now* have enough"?

The spiritual path is to know that possessions and money alone are not a measure of our self-worth. They will never fill our spiritual longings. Anyone who spends all their time pursuing more and more possessions truly misses out on much of the texture and depth of life. Judaism teaches us to balance the desire for material things with commitments to community, learning, and the quest for spirituality. If we shift our focus onto these latter goals, the insatiable craving for possessions will gradually lessen.   LF

Sweet Joy

21 OCTOBER

A soul sings at all times, joy and sweetest are her garments;
high-minded tenderness envelopes her.
RABBI ABRAHAM ISAAC KOOK[16]

Rabbi Abraham Isaac Kook's soul sang. Born in 1865 in Poland, he was a leading light of religious Zionism, moving to Israel in 1902 and ultimately becoming the first Ashkenazi chief rabbi of Palestine. Kook saw that the great difficulty in the world was alienation, and that the only way that alienation could be overcome was with joy and sweetness. But how is this possible? How can you overcome a sense of separation and aloneness with song and tenderness. Kook believed that there was a great song that was always being sung at the level of the Universe. He had a sense of cosmic harmony. But this harmony resided only at the widest levels of the imagination.

Think about a song with a complex harmony. If you listen to one strand, it could be monotonous or even dissonant. Two of those strands taken alone might be in conflict and produce a harsh sound. But then in your mind add some more voices. Hear a wide variety of people all singing a tune which they think is their own but which, heard together, forms a chorus.

Kook grew up in the world of the *beit midrash,* the study house. A *beit midrash* is a place where many different people study together in pairs, out loud. In the European world where Kook matured, he might have sat in a room that had a hundred pairs of voices all in their own worlds but together producing the sound of energy, satisfaction, and delight.

When Kook first came to Palestine, he found secular Jews. Most Jews from Kook's world were unable to hear the song of these pioneers. But Kook had an ear attuned to song, and he discovered that these souls also sang all the time. He could see the sweat of their labor as a garment of joy. How could he put these two songs together? In the Land of Israel, Kook expanded his mind and felt a sense of high-mindedness, of an awakening reality. In the Land of Israel, he felt something new was in the air. He could hear the songs beyond the human soul, the song of the Land itself, and ultimately the song of the world. The song became a symphony with myriad parts, and each individual line precious and critical to the majesty of the whole.

When we feel alienated, we must know how our song resonates into the world at large. We must know, like Kook, that our soul sings all the time and that our line of melody or harmony is part of the great fabric of the sound of the Universe. Hearing the whole song will help us overcome our loneliness.   RABBI MICHAEL PALEY

Timeliness

22 OCTOBER

It would be correct to say that the world was not made in time, but that time was formed by means of the world, for it was heaven's movement that was the index of the nature of time.

PHILO OF ALEXANDRIA[17]

Toward the end of the month of October most of North America changes its clocks to standard time. Some of us dread it, especially since it still means that it gets dark before most of us arrive home from work. Traditional Sabbath observers, whose pattern of observance are determined by the sun, moon, and stars, generally like daylight savings time because it means that the post-*Havdalah* Saturday night comes nice and early. And everybody loves Saturday night! Nevertheless, three states still refuse to implement daylight savings time. As a result, for half of the year these states are an hour different from those who live in the same time zone.

For many people this situation is no big deal. For others, it is a major nuisance. But it just goes to prove one thing: While we may think that we can order the world, we can't even agree on how to measure time.

Philo had it right. The only real measurement of time is determined by the heavens. We can only try to order our lives by it.

KO

Directing the Heart

23 OCTOBER

The difference between the wicked and the righteous is that the wicked are controlled by their hearts and the righteous have their hearts under control.

MIDRASH[18]

Just how much should we let our hearts dictate what we do? Some would say we should give our heart free rein and live out its every desire. Others say that our heart can lead us astray with irrational emotions and that it is better to follow our rational mind. We are all aware that we cannot sever our heart and our mind from each other, since the connection between them is powerful. Our mind influences how we feel, and our heart influences how we think. Our attitudes and outlook result from the ongoing combination of heart and mind.

The midrash above says that it is wise to have control over our hearts. But why is control needed over our heart and not our mind? This teaching calls those whose hearts control them "wicked." This view may seem harsh, but the spiritual teaching here is about the positive nature of self-control. Letting our emotions spill over is not a helpful way to negotiate life. We walk a thin line between embracing our emotional life and having it run, and in some cases ruin, our lives. While we do not want to suppress our emotions, we also don't want to give them free rein in all circumstances.

Some emotions do have to be kept in check, and all spiritual practices teach some degree of self-control. Judaism does this through *mitzvot,* the actions by which we live our lives in relationship with God and others. Feelings without any control can lead to chaos. What emotional spillage can you rein in today?   LF

Honor

24 OCTOBER

*Honor your father and mother that you may live long in the
land which your God is giving you.*
EXODUS 20:12

At the very center of the revelatory moment at Mount Sinai
is the principle of reconciliation between parents and children. Before this moment, the Torah had set the stage by
focusing on the struggles between father and son: Abraham
and Isaac, Isaac and Jacob, and Jacob and his children. Each
of these relationships were filled with strife, followed after
many years with a moment of healing and reconcilement.

After Sinai, prophet after prophet will point to the parent–child relationship as essential for achieving redemption.
The most famous of their prophecies is spoken by Malachi,
the last of the prophets, in the words, "Behold, I will send
before you Elijah, the prophet, before the coming of the great
and dreadful day of God. And he will turn the heart of the
parents to the children and the heart of the children to
the parents" (Malachi 3:23–24a).

Each of us, when dealing with our parents, and later with
our own children, must acutely confront our own mortality
and our desire for immortality. When we look at our children, we see the transitory nature of our physical selves. As
they grow up, we see ourselves aging. We rebel. We futilely
play God and attempt to shape our children into ourselves.
Rather than encourage them to find God's Presence in their
own lives, we often insist that they relive our lives. By doing
this, we think we are denying our own mortality. Yet as
children, we fled from the mortality of our own parents,
asserting that somehow we would be different; *we* would

live forever. When our parents offer us the wisdom of their mortality, when they attempt to teach us about our helplessness without God in the face of mortality, we reject both.

And so the misunderstanding of one generation after another continues. Only redemption itself, an act of God, can break this cycle of misunderstanding. Our struggle is to prepare this world for redemption and that requires that—in this world too—parents and children attempt to see beyond their disappointments and delusions regarding one another.

RABBI IRA STONE[19]

Friendship

25 OCTOBER

A needle's eye is not too narrow to hold two friends who agree.
RABBI DAVID KIMCHI[20]

Do we seek friends who agree with us? Agreement may be what brings people together. That is why two friends who agree can fit in a needle's eye.

So what about friends who don't agree? Maybe you have a friend or two with whom you don't agree. (We all do.) The challenge is how to disagree with them and still keep them as friends. The Rabbis embraced a notion called *tokhechah*, which means "rebuke." They learned it from the prophets. Here they left little room. They said that we have an obligation to rebuke our neighbors and that doing so is an obligation of friendship. But the challenge remains: How do we disagree and still keep them as friends? Maybe we don't disagree over a lifestyle issue: Perhaps they smoke too much or drink too much or treat their spouse or children or employees poorly. Maybe we are worried about their self-destructive behaviors.

We are constantly afraid of losing a friendship, especially if friends are difficult to come by. Better to risk a friendship by intervening and rebuking when necessary than to *lose* a friend to a self-inflicted death. Hope that they do the same for you.

KO

Miracles in Waiting

26 OCTOBER

No one should depend on a miracle to save them.
If a miracle has saved you once, you must not depend on a
miracle to rescue you a second time.

ZOHAR[21]

What do you consider to be a miracle? Some of us see the miraculous in everyday events: the birth of a baby, falling in love, the budding of the first flower after a winter's frost. Others leave the miraculous to the more mysterious. They think of the burning bush or the parting of the Red Sea that we read about in the book of Exodus. However we understand the word "miracle," the quote above from the Zohar, a Jewish mystical book, tells us not to depend on a miracle to save us. Surely, Divine intervention would be welcome when we feel overwhelmed by life's tribulations. However, it is one thing to be open and receptive to out-of-the-ordinary experiences and another thing to expect such an event to save us. We cannot sit back and wait for miracles to fix our lives or give them meaning and purpose.

By being actively involved in life and grateful for the opportunities that come our way, each of us can be the bearer of small miracles for others.

LF

Spiritual Fire

27 OCTOBER

The Torah was written in black fire on white fire.
ZOHAR[22]

Mystical commentaries abound with images of the Ten Commandments being written with fire. The Talmud itself teaches that the tablets were carved in such a way that the same carving could be read on both sides. While I can't quite understand how this worked in regard to these stone tablets, what I do understand is that people are written on both sides, for we are three dimensional, etched by God's hands. I can also see the real *mitzvot*—the commanded actions, attitudes, and realities—being written on both sides. Fasting on Yom Kippur can be good, or it can go over to the dark side. Keeping Shabbat can be a liberation from the workday week, or it can be a kind of solitary confinement. Context and meaning can change each mitzvah. Giving *tzedakah* can save a person's life or it can be a manipulative exercise of imposing one's will on others. Fasting on Yom Kippur can make you humble and let you really live your inner life: It can be all light. Or, it can turn to a shell. Fasting can become an Olympian event, an excuse for competition, pride, hurt, and darkness. Everything has two sides, the holy and the unholy. Mystics call it the *sitra achrah*—"the other side."

In my life, I have felt Torah twinkle like an evening star. I have warmed myself in Torah's light like sunbathing at high noon. I have felt the Torah go supernova and threaten to destroy all human life. I have definitely been scorched by Torah. I have seen Torah as a colored orb, sinking away from me. I have had my Torah sunset moments. And I have felt the tug of the dark black hole of Torah, the vortex of Torah into which I can disappear. I can understand a two-sided double-edged Torah, which twists its inner life to allow itself to be read on each side.

In our spiritual journeys, let us be ever mindful of "the other side" and be prepared when we meet it to realize that this, too, is one of the many sides of spiritual life.

JOEL LURIE GRISHAVER[23]

Moving Forward

28 OCTOBER

Who does not increase, decreases.
MISHNAH[24]

I have a colleague who warns me of this constantly. It is his way of pushing me forward, of nurturing me. Then he reminds me of a companion verse which may read like a contradiction but is actually a word of caution: "If you grab at too much, you can't grab at anything." My friend is always afraid that I am taking on too much. I tell him that the work is necessary, that there is an urgency to it. And I quote a third verse to "prove" this: "The Master is knocking at the door."

To some people, the idea of increase or decrease, of grabbing too much or nothing at all, may sound silly. It may play like a form of mental gymnastics or word games. But for me it is really much more. It emerges from the bargain that God made with our people in covenant at Sinai. I seek to do what I am *supposed* to do with my life, what I am driven to do, what I believe I was placed on this earth to do: My *work* (rather than my job), as I like to describe it.

What can you do to discover your life's work? Begin by trying to figure out what your work has to be. Others can guide you in the process, but ultimately you have to be the one who brings it to its conclusion. Accomplishing this may take some measure of introspection and soul-analysis. It may consume hours of contemplative prayer, but it will lead you to discover what God wants of you, what *work* you have to do that no others can do. Once you do, this labor will carry you into Paradise. KO

Angels Who Speak for Us

29 OCTOBER

Rabbi Yehoshua ben Levi said: "An entourage of angels always walks in front of people, with a messenger calling out. And what do they say? 'Make way for the Image of the Holy One!'"

MIDRASH[25]

A common malaise which many of us suffer is feeling that we are insufficient or somehow unworthy. It undermines our spirit and our intent and, unfortunately, leads to distress. Judaism teaches that each person is a world unto him or herself. A Mishnah (Sanhedrin 4:5) expresses this idea by teaching that if we destroy one life it is as if we have destroyed an entire world. What would it take for us to feel our full worth and uniqueness?

Imagine, if we could actually hear God's angels proclaiming our approach with the words, "Here comes an Image of God." Many of us need such a forthright reminder of our relationship to the Divine. When we walk around with a low sense of self, we deny God's presence in our very being. It is as if we have erased the image of God that resides in our souls. Affirming our inestimable worth can help. When you question yourself, you can stand before a mirror and say, "I am created in the Image of God." If you feel shamed or disregarded, you can say, "I am created in the Image of God and no one can take this fact away from me." Today we might not be able to hear God's messengers announcing our arrival. Our lives are so noisy. So let us do this for ourselves.   LF

The Human Quest

30 OCTOBER

God will return to us when we shall be willing to let God in—into our lands and our factories, into our congress and clubs, into our courts and investigating committees, into our homes and theaters.

RABBI ABRAHAM JOSHUA HESCHEL[26]

Religion was not just about how you prayed. It was also about what you learned; what you wore; how you behaved sexually; what you ate; how you cared for your body; if, when, and how you waged war; what you did with articles you found; with whom you traded.

But somewhere along the way, we asked religion to be silent about what people did in their everyday lives. As religion became increasingly relegated to life's leisure moments, for many people it had less of an orienting influence in their lives than a hobby.

While many contemporary Jews are ready to start integrating the religious voice into their daily lives, new thought and bold actions are needed to achieve this.

Letting spirituality and faith speak to us in our work will teach us to move beyond ambition and success, to stop worshipping at the false altars of career and prestige. It will teach us to act on the basis of our better moral impulses and values. It will help us be more creative and socially responsible.

There needs to be a place within us where professional, parent, spouse, friend, child, sibling—and *Jew*—come together and speak as *one*. If God is One, and if we truly know that, then our lives become a conscious imitation of God as its disparate pieces meld together. That consciousness will open us to a real inner joy and satisfaction.

RABBI JEFFREY SALKIN[27]

Children Are Our Future

31 OCTOBER

Each child carries his or her own blessing into the world.
YIDDISH PROVERB[28]

It is hard to deny the secular calendar marking of Halloween this day. Some people just refuse to deal with it, assigning it instead to religious and irreligious ideas that do not comport with Judaism. Others suggest that the Jewish community does not need Halloween, that it is foreign and pagan or at best Christian. As a result, some Jews try to turn Purim into a kind of belated Halloween. Even if this were the right way to go, they still have to wait about four months to celebrate the Jewish "version" of Halloween. Talk about delayed gratification!

Perhaps we should simply acknowledge children's preoccupation with Halloween and use it as an opportunity to nurture them. Even if you do not have children or they do not live with you or they now have children of their own, the obligation remains the same: Reach out your hand to a child and you can touch the future on this *Yom HaYeladim,* on this day of the children.　　　　　　　　　　　　　　　　KO

NOVEMBER

The Memory of Events

1 NOVEMBER

The world exists only on account of the one who disregards one's own existence.

TALMUD[1]

As soon as I turn the page of my calendar to the month of November, I immediately start thinking about Thanksgiving, even though it does not come until close to the end of the month. Local stores start decorating for the holidays. Corn stalks are sold at local farm stands. Fall flowers are everywhere. People even change the dominant colors in their clothing. (I always muse to myself that the whole country is belatedly preparing for Sukkot, since I know that the Pilgrims used Sukkot as their inspiration for Thanksgiving.) In the northeast, the seasonal colors on the trees have peaked and leaves are falling to the ground. In the south, people finally have some respite from the heat. In Israel, rains are beginning to threaten the streets of Jerusalem as mud streams down the Judean mountains. (Our Sukkot prayers for rain seem to have worked.)

At this time of year my mind becomes occupied with details: Where are we celebrating Thanksgiving? What will we eat? Will we have to drive in Thanksgiving weekend traffic? Have the kids made plans of their own? Which of our friends will be alone who we should invite to our house for the holidays?

That was always the way my November began until 1995. Since that time, something else casts a shadow over these items. That year, the first of November coincided with the twelfth of the Hebrew month of Cheshvan. That year, November 1 was a balmy Saturday. After returning from the synagogue, my family spent much of Shabbat afternoon outside. As a result, we did not find out what happened until late in the day, when someone telephoned just after we made *Havdalah*. The timing of the call did not surprise us. It was typical of a family member or friend calling to wish us *shavuah tov,* a good week. But the news he carried this time was not good: While we were preoccupied with prayers and piety, the prime minister of Israel, Yitzhak Rabin, had been assassinated.

Rabin knew that peace was the only viable option for Israel. He offered his life in its name. And we relearned a painful lesson from the Talmud: "The world exists only on account of the one who disregards his own existence." May his memory be a blessing for us all. May we learn the lesson of peace and dedicate our lives to it, as he did.   KO

Our Pursuit of Justice

2 NOVEMBER

Justice, justice you shall pursue.
DEUTERONOMY 16:20

This biblical verse is often quoted to emphasize the Jewish community's commitment to justice. We see the Bible's view of justice in its concern for the widow, the orphan, and the stranger in our midst. We are reminded 37 times in the Torah to "love the stranger." In other words, our tradition teaches us time and again that those at the margins of our society need our concern and care. This is one way we right social and economic injustices and pursue justice.

The Hebrew word *tzedek*, "justice," is the root of another Hebrew word, *tzedakah*. *Tzedakah* is often mistranslated to mean "charity" or "philanthropy." However, "charity" comes from the Greek word *charitas* which means "a loving act," and the word "philanthropy" is derived from the Latin for "the love of man." Both of these concepts—charity and philanthropy—suggest that we must love those whom we help; most of us would have a hard time fulfilling this requirement. The Hebrew word, *tzedakah*, on the other hand, suggests that we give in order to create a more just world. The Jewish value of *tzedakah* recognizes that we cannot love each and every person who needs our help. It does recognize that the world is full of injustices and that we are to extend ourselves in the pursuit of a more just and whole society.   LF

The Seasons of Our Lives

3 NOVEMBER

These are the festivals of God, holy times, that you will announce in its proper time.
LEVITICUS 23:4

A calendar is like the stretching of time across a plain with magnets dropping all along it. The magnets are those special days that attract as we march through our lives. To be without a calendar is to be without a key to the deepest resources of our soul.

Shabbat, for instance, is a day not for work but for God. Imagine the depths we might plumb if one-seventh of our time were dedicated to spiritual awareness, to unselfish acts for God's sake, to arguments not for profit but for the sake of heaven? Passover teaches us the value of sharing relationships in a state of freedom. Next comes the *omer*, when we count each day until Shavuot. At its end is Shavuot, a celebration of receiving Torah at Sinai and also the harvest time when we are commanded to "leave some of your gleaning for the poor and the stranger." What Passover is for family, the High Holy Days are for individuals' spirituality: A time for introspection, remorse, and new beginnings.

In the postbiblical period the rabbis built upon this scheme, adding Purim, for instance, and Simchat Torah. New holidays let us delve even deeper into some inner part of ourselves that has gone unnoticed up to now and allow us thus to enlarge our capacity to be fully human.

So we now have Yom HaShoah (Holocaust Memorial Day), a time to enter history's room of horror beyond belief and recollect beyond all doubt the demonic depths to which even "cultured" people can descend; and Yom HaAtzma'ut (Israel Independence Day), to celebrate the miracle of a place called home where a national anthem trumpets *HaTikvah*, "hope" beyond despair in a land where even deserts come to life.

We are children of history, but our newest holy days that commemorate recent history can make us adults of history too and summon us to additional levels of character.

During the year we commemorate special times, but we should also consider how our ordinary days are spent. If we ignore the full rhythm of the Jewish year, we forfeit the fullness of our own potential and let the days blend indiscriminately together. Only by observing the calendar can we become practiced in those virtues that make life colorful, multifaceted, and glorious beyond words. RABBI LAWRENCE HOFFMAN

The Heart Casts Its Beauty

4 NOVEMBER

*Humans look at the outward appearance
but God looks at the heart.*
I SAMUEL 16:7

Lots of idioms try to approximate the notion above. You've probably heard most of them, such as "Beauty is only skin deep," "Don't judge a book by its cover," or from the rabbinic collection called *Pirke Avot,* "Do not look at the bottle; rather, look at its contents." Parents tell these things to their children as a way of teaching them not to judge others by their physical appearance.

In the quote above, the rabbis are trying to teach us something about human nature, about God, and about our responsibility to emulate God. We humans are preoccupied with physical beauty and this generation of North Americans certainly is focused on the physical. We raise our children with the notion that physical appearance is most important. This preoccupation with physical beauty dominates our way of looking at the world. Look at the magazines that dot the shelves of your local newsstand or bookstore. We elevate "pretty people" and turn them into cultural heroes, seeking their advice, soliciting their opinions.

It's true that the Torah teaches us that human beings are created in the image of God, that the body is God's creation and integrated with the soul rather than just being its storehouse. However, this perspective on the physical is both limited and limiting. What is really important, what makes a difference in the long run, is the essence of each individual, his or her character, and outlook on life, their approach to other humans.

One thing more: When we look to the heart of others, there we may find God looking at our own.   KO

Our Mutual Dependence

5 NOVEMBER

Every people draws sustenance from others, from the heritage of the generations, from the achievements of the human spirit in all eras and all countries. Mutual dependence is a cosmic and eternal law. There is nothing in the world, large or small, from the invisible electron to the most massive bodies in infinite space, which has no bonds with its fellows or with unlike bodies. The whole of existence is an infinite chain of mutual bonds and applies to the world of the spirit as well as to the world of matter.

DAVID BEN-GURION[2]

We live in a world where independence is paramount. Independence connotes strength while dependence often suggests weakness. The popular slogan, "Just Do It," plays on this assumption and implies that to reach our life goals we can do it alone if only we put our minds to it. Despite this advertising catch phrase, those of us committed to living well-integrated lives know that it takes much more than the force of our will and mind to do this. The many dimensions of our lives are not lived in isolation. In fact, we live in relationship to others and our environment. The "Just Do It" attitude suggests that we should ignore the relationships that connect us to each other and vault our way to some spectacular endpoint.

David Ben-Gurion, the first prime minister of the modern state of Israel, insightfully reminds us above that our mutual dependence on one another is a fact of life. As the leader of

Israel at the time of its statehood, he know only too well how much Israel needed the support of the world community to ensure her independence and existence at that precarious moment. Israel could not survive in total isolation. Similarly, our spirits would dry up if we lived apart, unconnected to our past or future. As the world becomes more and more of a "global village," we increasingly realize the interconnectedness of our economy, our environmental policies, and our spiritual lives. Though we may not share common language, culture, or history with others, we do share the experience of being human. Our humanity itself is the starting point. Only when we recognize our mutual dependence will we end the needless violence which tears at our souls. No individual or person or nation can stand alone in the world today.

Commit yourself to enriching the bonds that unite us and dissolving the barriers that give false illusion that independence, and not interdependence, can sustain us.   LF

Battling the Shadow of Death

6 NOVEMBER

The dust returns to the earth where it came from and the spirit returns to God who gave it.
ECCLESIASTES 12:7

Rabbi Joseph B. Soloveitchik, a renowned twentieth-century Orthodox scholar, teaches that for Judaism, the world is the scene of a cosmic battle of life against death. God creates life and loves it. Death is the enemy, the antithesis of God. The Temple, representing perfection and the pure presence of God, is totally devoted to life. Therefore no form of death can enter the Temple. Human beings who come in contact with the dead can enter into the Temple only after they are purified, that is, they are born again to life. Priests are not to have any contact with death. Priests do not touch corpses nor can they be in the immediate presence of the dead. This means that priests do not attend funerals, go to the cemetery, or care for the dead. The only exception is for their closest relations: parents, siblings, wives, children.

Judaism is the religion of human partnership with God to achieve *tikkun olam,* a fixing of the world. Since God is completely on the side of life, Jews must be totally on the side of life. Ideally, every act should advance and nurture life and/or fight and reduce death. In this imperfect world, Jews compromise with death. We live with it, we treat its victims, we show honor to the dead by caring for and burying them. But priests are people totally dedicated to God. They work in the Temple, the place dedicated totally to God. By shunning contact with the dead, priests represent the fundamental Jewish opposition to death, the infinite commitment to work hard so that life wins.

Why then are priests allowed—in fact commanded—to care and mourn for their immediate relatives? Because to insist that they have no contact with their loved ones in death would be inhuman. Prohibiting this care would overrule the deep natural love the priest has for immediate family. Principles—even noble principles like treasuring life—cannot be upheld by dehumanization, by repudiating loved ones.

The priest represents the Jewish ideal of perfection. Some day when the world is perfect, all Jews will be priests to humanity. Jews should advance life; every act and every moment of life should be devoted to the living. But the commitment to life must be built on love, mutual care, and respect for family ties that bind and make us human. If we abandon family or repudiate intimacy—even for the sake of God or to advance life—we serve death, not life.

RABBI IRVING GREENBERG[3]

The Mystery of Miracles

7 NOVEMBER

If there is any miracle in the world, any mystery, it is individuality.

RABBI LEO BAECK[4]

Rabbi Leo Baeck is a hero of the modern Jewish world. He had a chance to leave Europe and come to the United States during World War II, but refused to do so. He felt the obligation to join his people on their long journey into darkness. As a result of this courageous choice of leadership, he was forced to endure Thereisenstat, one of the many Nazi death camps that threatened to annihilate our people. He served as an inspiration to those of our people who were also interred there. Baeck survived. Thus his teaching is more precious than it might ever have been. He taught us many things. All of them were imbued with a profound sense of faith which is all the more affirming when one considers his experiences.

Rabbi Baeck believed in people and he believed in God. Although he experienced the worst of which humans are capable, he also came to know the profundity of faith of individuals that was possible even in the unfathomable depths of despair. This knowledge humbled Baeck immensely. Each person confronted their challenge, as in everyday life, as a remarkable individual. He took what he learned and taught it to others as a witness: Although we are all cast from the same mold of the Divine, we are all unique—including you and me.

KO

The Art of Living

8 NOVEMBER

The greatest art of all is the art of living—and the best preparation for the art of living is the cultivated heart. The cultivated heart is in the human being who knows and appreciates our heritage and our history; who can absorb and understand and translate this understanding into action in the present and also into action for tomorrow.

HENRIETTA SZOLD[5]

According to a well-known expression, we need the so-called "three R's" to succeed in life: reading, writing, and 'rithmetic. These are technical skills that we hope to acquire through formal schooling during childhood. As we mature, we realize that life requires much more and that the cultivation of the heart is a lifelong process. This means extending our focus and vision beyond our own needs and concerns to feel the suffering of others.

Sometimes we become so self-absorbed that we are unable to put our worries in a larger context. Our problems become all-consuming. Not that personal sorrows and heartfelt wounds are not painful or can be easily dismissed. Yet, part of the spiritual journey is to move past our personal wounds and hurts and extend our compassion, love, and kindness to others. While we cannot always lift the pain of others, when our hearts are touched, we can extend to them our care and concern. It does make a difference when people know they are being cared for and held in our hearts. But we need to go one step further. We need to draw on the insights we have gained from our experiences and those of others to shape our present and future to lessen the suffering in our world.

Let us add the "three C's" to the "three R's": compassion, care, concern. These are the foundations of a cultivated heart.

LF

Heavenly Stories

9 NOVEMBER

The heavens are telling the glory of God;
and the firmament proclaims the handiwork of the Divine.
PSALM 19:2

On a good, clear winter night, even when there's the slightest glare from the city lights, every star is as bright as a headlight, and the edge of every cloud is limned by silver moon rays, and even the vast blackness between stars and moon and clouds doesn't seem as coal-black as it does the rest of the year. If you look up now at night, what you see aren't necessarily heavenly bodies but maybe heaven itself, with its endlessness and peacefulness that silence even the most loquacious of us for at least a few moments. In the cold of the night there's a warming of the soul, a softening of the heart, a clinging both to the earth below us and to the skies above us as we sense that maybe there really are demarcations between them and us after all.

"Praise God, sun, and moon," instructs Psalm 148, "Praise God, you highest heavens, and you waters above the heavens." And so we praise, even if it's just silently and without words and without resorting to Psalms. We praise just by looking, just by appreciating, just by acknowledging that there is more above us than we usually have reason to believe there might be, that we can see splendor and majesty just by turning our eyes upward a few degrees more than we usually do, that there is a whole other universe in the Universe.

Doing all this doesn't take much effort. It does take remembering, but that doesn't consume any calories. Remembering to go outside, to look up, to know that there are broader dimensions than what we almost self-immunize ourselves against. Remembering, of course, to put on a jacket or sweater and go away from the glare and, once there, to not do much of anything except be there and elevate your eyesight. Except this time, really *look*. Don't try to find anything specific in the sky: satellites or stars or constellations or planes flying overhead. Whatever you need to see, you will see. And what you see may very well make you shudder with respect that *this* is Creation, and with pleasure that *we* are a part of it. ARTHUR J. MAGIDA

Kindness is Our Highest Duty

10 NOVEMBER

It is a duty to cultivate kindness.
MEDIEVAL TEXT[6]

This idea comes from an interesting medieval text that a father originally wrote for his children. Literally called the "Book of Education" (*Sefer Hachinukh*), it is designed to teach people how to live according to the ways of the Torah. In this volume the author makes his way through every verse of the Torah and determines the individual *mitzvot* that emerge from the text. Then he motivates the reader to follow each mitzvah.

This process of searching the text is an important thing to remember, especially as we recall the dates November 9–10, 1938: *Kristallnacht,* the Night of Broken Glass, when our people's lives were shattered throughout Germany and Austria, when police-initiated rioters looted and destroyed homes, businesses, and synagogues. We must remember but never resign ourselves to the hate that filled the streets along with the shards of broken glass.

Among the many things that the Torah obligates us to do is show kindness to others. This precept seems rather obvious. Who wouldn't suggest—especially in a book on education—that people should be kind to one another? But the author of *Sefer Hachinukh* is offering us something much more subtle. He tells his children—and indirectly us as well—that we must *cultivate* kindness. So how do we go about cultivating kindness, making sure not only that we practice kindness but that others do so, as well? After all, how can we control the actions of others?

The answer is simple. It emerges from one of the first lessons of good teaching. When we express ourselves through an act of kindness, others will observe our example and be motivated to do the same. KO

Disclosure and Our Spirits

11 NOVEMBER

All that is thought should not be said, all that is said should not be written, and all that is written should not be printed.
RABBI MENACHEM MENDL OF KOTZK[7]

How often have you turned on a talk show to find total strangers disclosing the most intimate parts of their lives to thousands of strangers on national television? It has become common in our culture to believe that complete and open communication has few boundaries. There is something perverted in this national pastime of peeping into others' private lives. This attitude harms not only the long-term health of our society but also the integrity of our spiritual selves. Judaism, not unlike other religions, teaches the value of self-control over self-revelation. This discipline in life does not mean that we share our inner lives, conflicts, and troubles with those closest to us. It does mean that we recognize that everything we think, feel, or experience does not have to be expressed.

In the course of one short day we can have many different thoughts and emotions. Often they are inconsistent and can change dramatically from moment to moment. Before we commit our thoughts to words, either verbally or on paper, let us sit with them for a while and discern what benefit disclosure would serve. Only then can we make a wise decision on what to share with others and what to keep to ourselves to maintain our sense of privacy and integrity.

Our relationship with God can provide us a way to express things that we may not choose to share with others.   LF

Divine Gifts

12 November

Three gifts were created in the world: wisdom, strength, and wealth.
MIDRASH[8]

There is no denying that it's better to be rich than to be poor. Or that money may not buy happiness but it can buy things that buy happiness. While much of the world may deride Americans as being overly materialistic, few nations complain when their standards of living rise, and few object to emulating the American way of life. Jeans, rap, and McDonald's remain strong export items around the globe.

Even here at home, while many people criticize our obsession with "things," few are willing to deny their own desires. We may differ as to which objects are worthy of our efforts and sweat, but few are the individuals who are completely indifferent to material reality.

As today's quote implies: Wealth, come by honestly and used reasonably, if shared with others and harnessed to righteous goals, can enhance our lives and our society. While few would deny that wealth can be a great blessing, it can also be a person's undoing. When it becomes an obsession rather than a luxury, when it becomes a goal, when it displaces the abiding sources of happiness and the Abiding Source of meaning, then wealth turns on its owner and becomes a snare and an enemy.

Let our highest goals remain those of Torah, fidelity to God, passionate love of Jews and Judaism, and a resolve to make the world more just and compassionate—and let our wealth serve as a means to achieve those ends. Then and only then can we remain masters of our possessions rather than their slaves. And only then can our possessions move us toward a truer contentment and peace.

RABBI BRADLEY SHAVIT ARTSON

Be Swift to Be Slow

13 NOVEMBER

Be swift to hear but with patience make your reply.
APOCRYPHA[9]

We have to be ready to hear what people are saying to us and we have to be willing to listen to them. Often we are so anxious to reply to someone else that we hardly wait until they are finished speaking before we start talking. Sometimes we even finish their sentences for them. But if we are so busy answering, then we can't really be listening to what they have to say.

It is hard to really listen to others. So much distracts us and we are usually in a hurry, often doing two things at once. We listen to others while we are reading the newspaper or looking at the television. Some of us even type away on the computer while someone is talking to us on the telephone.

Only if you really listen will you be able to hear what people are saying. Pay attention. Once words are spoken, they are difficult to retrieve. Someone might even be saying something that can help you, if you will only listen!   KO

Personal Responsibility

14 NOVEMBER

A person is responsible for one's actions,
whether awake or asleep.
TALMUD[10]

Some of us might think this statement goes too far! How can we be responsible for our actions while we are asleep? This talmudic teaching leaves no room for us to deny our responsibility. In essence, it says, if you accidentally kick your bed partner in the middle of the night, you are responsible for adjusting your position to prevent this from reoccurring. How much more so if we cause harm to someone during the daylight, during our hours of consciousness.

As Jews, we are obliged to own up to our actions no matter how insignificant or minor they may be. This may be one of the most difficult spiritual lessons to learn and integrate into our souls. We look for ways to escape responsibility at every twist and turn. Didn't Adam hide from God after eating of the forbidden tree in the Garden of Eden? Hiding comes naturally; taking responsibility is a learned response. Developing this sensitivity to how our actions impact others and our communities and the larger world is a never-ending, crucial spiritual practice.   LF

Opening Doors

15 NOVEMBER

Today I saw an old woman try to enter a supermarket
The wrong way.
She hadn't mastered the electric doors.
What a world for her, I thought, where doors
Never get touched by hands but only open one way.
BARRY HOLTZ[11]

Doors are magical. They always stand between who we are and who we might become. A closed mind shuts out corridors, rooms, universes for exploration. The door in this poem is even more daunting. This is a glass door that is easily seen through. Through the door is food, sustenance, and the necessities of life. Yet this woman has entered it the wrong way—innocently. She hasn't touched anything. She is simply standing in front of the supermarket as she has done since she was a child, hoping to feed herself and live in the rhythms to which she has become accustomed through years of routine. But this door opens only one way and it opens out toward her, pushing her away from her memories and needs.

We live in a world of rapid change. The world we live in wears the face of progress. We feel stronger, quicker, and more directed than the generation that preceded us. My grandmother always called the television "the radio," and we laughed warmly at her confusion. For her, even the radio was an innovation. But my grandmother and this old woman of the poem knew things that we could never know. They touched their lives with their hands and they were part of a world that survived only by the grace of communities. We all know the right way to go into the supermarket and get what we need. But the question is whether we want to live in a world of electric doors that open only one way. What are we missing by not having the old-fashioned kind of doors that you would hold open for your neighbor?

We are challenged in the modern world to build a sense of etiquette. How will we help each other and become helped ourselves in a world where the right way is programmed by distant hands and where there is less need to help the stranger? How will we teach our children respect for the past when the elderly seem more confused than wise? Can we open our eyes to the wonder of living together so that we might learn what each person has to teach?   RABBI MICHAEL PALEY

Motivating Forces

16 NOVEMBER

If the intention is not pure, the deed is not acceptable.
BACHYA IBN PAKUDA[12]

Often our tradition overlooks the motivation behind the deed. It is enough to act properly. There is even a popular saying that is a response to those who may question individual motivation for attending the synagogue: "Schwartz goes to *shul* to talk to God, but Sussman goes to *shul* to talk to Schwartz." Folk wisdom puts it this way: "Actions speak louder than words." This statement would not satisfy the philosopher-theologian above. He believes that our intentions color our deeds. Thus any intent that is less than noble diminishes the action. Moreover, he argues that improper intention devalues the deed entirely and makes it unacceptable. This principle places quite a burden of responsibility on each of us. We have to consider why we do what we do—everything that we do. Doing so helps us to gain perspective. So before you act, look first to your heart. Your arms and legs will then be willing to follow.   KO

Weaving Connections

17 NOVEMBER

Weave real connections, create real nodes, build real houses.
Live a life you can endure, make love that is loving.
Keep tangling and interweaving and taking more in,
a thicket and bramble wilderness to the outside but to us
interconnected with the rabbit runs and burrows and lairs.
MARGE PIERCY[13]

One way to look at our lives is as a fascinating garden made up of many kinds of soil and an array of seedlings. It begins when we are born and we add to it year in and year out with each new experience and relationship. After a while it becomes clear that one harvest leads to another, since the roots of our lives become intermingled to such an extent it is hard to find where one begins and another ends. Have you ever run into someone whom you have known for a long time and stopped to wonder, "How did we meet?" "How do we know one another?" It is possible that the story of our lives has so many interconnections that the question no longer even makes sense. It is as if we have known each other forever. In many ways our roots have become one. Thus the more we take in, the more richly composted our garden will be.

Yet there are times when we feel despair that we might decide to stop planting. It may seem that the soil of our soul is parched. We cannot seem to find any source of water for our inner garden. Or we cannot bring ourselves to till the soil to keep it freshly oxygenated. So our garden dries up until we once again miss all that it yields and we turn to tend to it again. As Marge Piercy continues in her poem "The Seven Pentacles," "Live as if you like yourself, and it may happen: reach out, keep reaching out, keep bringing in. This is how we are going to live for a long time: Not always, for every gardener knows that after the digging, after the planting, after the season of tending and growth, the harvest comes."   LF

Building Futures

18 NOVEMBER

It is forbidden for a person to enjoy anything of this world without first reciting a blessing.
TALMUD[14]

We didn't get to where we are today without skill, luck, patience, fortitude, great colleagues, and faithful clients. Invariably, we forget to credit the one force that is above and behind everything that we do and everyone with whom we come in contact: God.

In Deuteronomy, Moses told the Israelites that after their forty-year trek through the wilderness they were about to enter "a land where you may eat food without constraint, where you will lack nothing." He continues: "When you have eaten your fill and have built fine houses to live in, and your herds and flocks have multiplied, and your silver and gold have increased, and everything you own has prospered, beware lest your heart grow haughty and you forget the Eternal your God. . . . Remember that it is the Eternal your God Who gives you the power to get wealth, in fulfillment of the covenant God made with your ancestors, as is still the case" (Deuteronomy 8: 11–18).

The wisdom Moses spoke on the eve of his people's entry into Israel still rings true. Its credence and force have a place in every shop and office and boardroom in America. Undeniably, we have prospered in many ways. But the price of this prosperity can be a poverty of the soul. It is time to be as rich internally as we are externally, to know that, as Moses said, it is God Who gives us the power to acquire wealth and that it is God Who gives us sustenance, to Whom we owe obeisance and thanks—and Who we should remember gave us not just this day and its accomplishments, but all of them. RABBI JEFFREY SALKIN[15]

Giving Thanks

19 NOVEMBER

Eat your bread with joy, drink your wine with a merry heart.
ECCLESIASTES 8:7

The Pilgrims didn't realize that they were creating an American institution when they joined with their Native American neighbors at the first Thanksgiving. Little did they know that parades and football games and crowded highways would all grow from their modest dinner. Nevertheless, their celebration emerged out of a desire to express a profound sense of gratitude to God. Armed with an intimate knowledge of the Bible, they recognized that they were not alone. So they took their inspiration from the journey of the Israelites in the desert and their celebration of Sukkot. As with our ancient ancestors, the first Thanksgiving festival followed a bountiful harvest as the celebrants prepared for a long and difficult time ahead. For the Pilgrims, it would be a cold and unforgiving winter. So they paused briefly from their labors to sanctify the moment. They celebrated with a full heart. Today, while sometimes burdened in spirit, we must do the same. In their own way, they helped us understand what the Rabbis had taught many generations before these pioneers found their ways to the American shores: "Rejoicing on a festival is a religious duty."[16]

So this year join together with your neighbors and friends and relatives. Set aside any differences that may have developed over the past year. And however meager it may seem, thank God for all that you have.   KO

Learning to Live

20 NOVEMBER

The art of living lies less in eliminating our troubles than in growing with them.
APOCRYPHA[17]

We may fantasize about living a life free of troubles, just as we might have dreams of winning the lottery. Both are unrealistic. When was the last time your mind was free of all worry? As we mature, we realize that life will always have its share of difficulties and, at times, of crisis. Growing with our troubles means that we can see them from different perspectives and allow ourselves to be in a relationship with them. Some troubles never disappear. What can change is how we see them and how we respond to them. In this way, they become part of the overall landscape of our lives. At times they may be in the foreground, and at other times they may recede to the background.

Our task is to learn how to manage our troubles with grace and ease. We thus learn to prevent them from overwhelming us, depressing our spirit, undermining our efforts, and blocking out all the good in life.   LF

Removing Doubt

21 NOVEMBER

May God deliver us from doubt.
MOSES MAIMONIDES[18]

God's presence in humanity is not limited to one person but resides equally in each person and awaits acknowledgment by that person. The failure of one person to acknowledge God's presence at any moment means that God's presence in the entire world is diminished by exactly the amount of that disbelief. But doubt is inevitable. No one but the Messiah can ever be able to avoid such moments, but such is the task of each of us.

Torah prescribes a way that allows each of the people of Israel to make God's presence palpable. Study and prayer constitute two parts of this way. The third consists of deeds of loving kindness.

We recognize God's presence in the lives and faces of other humans. And we respond to that presence by trying to nurture it in the lives of others. To feed the hungry, clothe the naked, heal the sick, or comfort the bereaved is to emulate God's relationship with humanity and to extend, as it were, the reach of God's love and, therefore, the presence of God. At the same time, by helping to free others from the oppression of their afflictions, we also help them to more successfully maintain God's presence in their lives. As we demonstrate that the way of God—a way of peace and a way of wholeness—has consequences in our lives, our doubt dissipates.

RABBI IRA STONE[19]

Affirming Life

22 NOVEMBER

One person's candle is light for many.
TALMUD[20]

In Dallas, Texas, in 1963, the death of one man changed our entire nation: President John F. Kennedy was assassinated. We were stunned, shocked, bewildered. It took many of us years to recover from it. Most of us remember that day as if it were just yesterday. As Jews, we celebrate life even as we are forced to acknowledge the reality of death. On this day, the anniversary of Kennedy's assassination, we affirm a life fully lived, however short its measure in time.

Many people in our own families may have been taken from us before their time. Grief naturally surfaces when we least expect it. When it does, it has the potential to jeopardize the fragile balance in our lives. And as we mourn those we love, we affirm our belief in God through the words of *Kaddish* even as our anger threatens to undermine our faith in the Holy One of Blessing. Then we must move forward with our lives.

KO

Watching Our Words

23 NOVEMBER

Oppressing someone verbally may be a greater sin than stealing one's money.
TALMUD[21]

Has your wallet been stolen or have your credit cards been misused? Aside from the inconvenience, it is a devastating experience because it is an invasion of a most intimate part of our lives. While the Rabbis realize that stealing is an atrocious invasion, they say that there are even more serious transgressions, such as oppressing someone verbally. Today we call this verbal abuse. How can this be more serious than stealing money?

Language is an important tool we use to express ourselves. We speak with many people over the course of the day. Many of us choose our words wisely and carefully, but others speak without giving consideration to the words they choose or to their tone of voice. When we make a cutting remark or embarrass someone, how often do we discharge our biting words and wish immediately we could take them back? Unfortunately, it is impossible to retract hurtful statements. We can go out of our way to ask for forgiveness if we say something wrong, but we can never fully heal the hurt we have inflicted. When we deprive someone of their composure, it is just as much an invasion and violation of the person's personal integrity as if we had stolen from his or her personal belongings. The next time you feel like lashing out at someone or using sarcasm in a hurtful way, think twice!   LF

A Lasting Message

24 November

*Hear out your fellows, and decide justly between anyone
and a fellow Israelite or a stranger. You shall not
be partial in judgment: hear out low and high alike.
Fear no one for judgment is God's.*

DEUTERONOMY 1:16–17

If you were told you could give one last message to your descendants, what would you tell them? This is the challenge that faced Moses and that will eventually face us all. Moses had forged and guided the Jewish people for forty years in the desert. He knew that he would not be allowed to accompany them; he was destined to die in the desert. So, the entire book of Deuteronomy consists of his farewell message.

It is surprising that at so dramatic a juncture, Moses' opening remarks focus much attention on an issue that applies to a small percentage of the population, the creation of a judicial system. Since the average citizen is neither a judge nor an advocate, and does not usually spend much time in a courtroom, why does Moses make this issue so central?

Perhaps it is because peoples' perception of a society's justice or lack thereof is so heavily influenced by its legal rulings. Indeed, in our country the common perception that numerous criminals are acquitted on the basis of technicalities causes many Americans to feel that the criminal justice system is unjust, even though the percentage of such cases is small.

And so, as the Jews prepared to enter their own Land, Moses reminded them that a just society starts with equal justice before the law. RABBI JOSEPH TELUSHKIN[22]

Spiritual Math

25 NOVEMBER

You shall not add to it nor subtract from it.
DEUTERONOMY 4:2

This is the foundational principle for Jewish law, or so it seems: The Torah was revealed to our people; we need nothing else. But this perspective does not represent the full understanding of the Sinai experience. Sinai does not represent one place or point in time. God's revelation may have formally begun at Sinai (though we experience God with each breath that we have taken since Adam and Eve), but the Divine revelation continues across time. That's why each generation attempts to understand it. Our generation must do the same, each and every one of us. As the dialogue expands, it sweeps across generations and geography. God started speaking to us at Sinai and the dialogue continues unto this day. We just have to keep talking—and listening. Who knows what will emerge from this conversation? KO

Getting Where You Are Going

26 NOVEMBER

To the place that my heart loves, there my feet take me.
COMMENTARY ON THE MISHNAH[23]

Have you ever ended up somewhere unexpectedly? You may ask yourself, "How did I get here?" Sometimes our feet lead us to places and experiences that we did not consciously choose. Most often, we use our rational abilities to analyze situations as they arise and weigh the positive and detrimental aspects and the risks at hand. Through this process, we try to ascertain which course is best for us at any given time. Sometimes we are right; other times we fail. In some cases our mind controls our feet and we may end up in places that we don't want to be. At other times we put our mind on hold, as hard as doing this may be, and allow our heart to be our guides. For in some situations, our heart so yearns to be in a particular place, or with a particular person, that try as we might, we cannot brush aside such deeply felt desires. Then our feet take over and lead us where our heart is aching to be. Allow your feet to point you in the direction of your heart today and soak in the love you seek.   LF

Giving Thanks

27 November

It is good to thank God.
Psalm 92:2a

The English word "Jew" comes from the name of Judah, the fourth son of Leah and Jacob. Judah's name in Hebrew is *Yehudah,* as we read in Genesis (29:35): "She became pregnant again and bore a son, and said, `This time I will give thanks to God.' Therefore, she called his name *Yehudah* ["giving thanks"]." We learn from this that one of the essential qualities of being Jewish is to live in a state of thanks, for as we shall see, it gives us a proper perspective on how to live our lives and engage the world.

The Hebrew word for "thanks," *l'hodot,* includes in it an understanding of acknowledgment. It acknowledges among a number of things that we do not live in a vacuum of existential solitude. It forces us out of that hole that we may be sometimes tempted to step into to. Saying "thank you" is like showering droplets of recognition, appreciation, worth, and acknowledgment on another person. Saying "thank you" forces us to recognize the other. When we say "thank you," we are reminded that we need others.

Giving thanks is also a spiral that feeds itself. Recognizing others means that they not only are seen with our eyes, but are seen in their own eyes as well. On the deepest level, we all want and need to be recognized and acknowledged. We hold each other up when we say "thank you." The life of Judah is filled with moments when he stands up to others or is unafraid to face the truth. In all of these incidents he is able to draw part of his strength from living his life in a state of thanks—being aware of what he has, and not being focused on what he lacks, and at the same times being able to acknowledge those around him. It is from that place that he is able to act beyond himself.

Our tradition says that in the Messianic Age only the sacrifices of Thanksgiving will be offered. May we work to bring that Age closer by living our lives as Jews, by living our lives like our namesake Judah, the one who is thankful.

Rabbi Michael M. Cohen

Painting the Sabbath Vision

28 November

*An artist cannot be continually wielding his or her brush.
The painter must stop at times from the painting to freshen
his or her vision of the object, the meaning
of which the artist wishes to express on canvas.
The Shabbat represents those moments when we pause in
our brushwork to renew our vision of the general plan.
Having done so, we take ourselves to our painting
with clarified vision and renewed energy.*

RABBI MORDECHAI KAPLAN[24]

Artist or not, anyone who lives in the rhythm of Jewish life understands the import of Rabbi Kaplan's words. Shabbat is that unique time that is marked each week in ways that transcend the boundaries of time. We are urged to stop work, to rest, and to reflect on the truly important things in life. The Rabbis go so far as to say that Shabbat is fully beyond time. In it, we move seamlessly between Paradise and the World-to-Come. Any residual memory of Eden is set aside. In its stead, messianic optimism sets the mood for the entire day. There is no other place that we can possibly be.

Just as daily prayer helps to focus me before I reenter my workaday world, Shabbat centers me for the week ahead and helps me gain perspective on the week just passed. For 25 hours (even the number of hours that makes up the day of Shabbat is not usual), the burdens I carry all week long are lifted. Jewish tradition suggests that part of this renewal is a result of the "extra" soul that I am given during Shabbat. So I look forward to it. I cling to it. And at *Havdalah,* when we ritually separate Shabbat from the rest of the week, I am reluctant to let it go. But I do. I must, because I know that it will come again. So I have something special to which I can look forward. KO

The Imitation of Truth

29 NOVEMBER

Everything in the world can be imitated, except truth.
For truth that is imitated is no longer truth.
RABBBI MENACHEM MENDL OF KOTZK[25]

It is a spiritual precept that we must be truthful not only to others but to ourselves as well. The Hebrew word for "truth" is *emet*. It is interesting that this word is made up of the first letter of the Hebrew alphabet, the *aleph;* the middle letter, the *mem;* and the last letter, the *tav.* One way to interpret this combination is to say that truth incorporates within it the beginning, the middle, and the end. One cannot begin to speak truthfully and then change either the middle or the end and still call it truth.

We all indulge in what is commonly called "white lies," lies that we think are not harmful to others but that allow us to extricate ourselves from uncomfortable situations. We tell these white lies when we feel the need to protect someone or ourselves. Let us not deceive ourselves that we are telling the truth at such moments. We are, as the above quote points out, imitating truth. But alas, imitation is not the real thing. In fact, regarding the Hebrew word for truth, *emet,* if we remove the first letter, the *aleph,* we are left with the Hebrew word meaning "death," *meit.* The *aleph* is one of a few letters that symbolizes God's Presence. By removing the *aleph,* we symbolically remove God's Presence. Where there is truth, the Presence of the Holy One is close at hand. When truth is absent, God's Presence retracts and we are left as if dead.

Truth can be painful. It can also be liberating. Let us try to live our lives in an upright and truthful manner and embrace God's spirit in our midst. LF

Living in Two Civilizations

30 NOVEMBER

I see Hanukkah as a time when, as we light the candles, we pause in awe before the Jewish people whose survival through adversity brings light into the darkness of the human soul.

ANNE ROIPHE[26]

The days get shorter. Hanukkah approaches. Once again it is time for us to confront the disturbing question: "Who are we, really?" It is a question that we wish would go away. We want to settle in already. We love being Jews; we love being Americans, moderns, even secularists, to a degree. We don't like being bombarded with "Season's Greetings," but we've made our peace with it. We just want to be. And we want to "be" here among the many blessings, and the enticing lures, of this culture.

Then December comes around. It always does, seemingly by surprise. Suddenly we find ourselves gasping for breath in shopping malls, in public schools, in office buildings, even in front of TVs in our own homes. Many of us are "amphibians" for eleven months of the year. An amphibian, you recall, can live both on land and in water. December is the time of year when we amphibians do best to hit the water. The lighted trees, the greeting cards, the glut of gifts, all of these are part of the land animals' world. They are glitzy and pretty, but they are not "us." In fact we do fine, if not better, without this stuff, for it can make us forget how to swim as Jews.

This is a time to drink deeply from our own spiritual reservoir, and to remember that it supports us throughout the year. We have our own compelling symbols: the sukkah, the seder table, the Purim costumes, the shofar blasts, the eight candles in the Hanukkah menorah, and even the stately white candles we light 52 Friday nights a year.

As we gather with families and friends to light our menorahs this Hanukkah, may we say in earnest the blessing: Blessed are You, for the miracle of our very being, which our ancestors knew "in those days"—and which we ourselves experience, both at "this time of year" and throughout the days of our lives. RABBI LESTER BRONSTEIN

DECEMBER

Last and Best

1 DECEMBER

The ones mentioned last are the most beloved.
JEWISH FOLK SAYING[1]

This folk saying—which in Hebrew is *Akharon akharon chaviv*—is usually translated into English as, "Last but not least." It is probably my favorite expression, so I use it often. Maybe I like it because it makes me feel I am being sensitive in situations that require it. I sometimes freely translate the phrase as "the last is the most lasting." However we choose to translate this phrase, one thing remains clear: There is something special about being last, even though we hated it in elementary school when our friends were choosing teams for kickball in the playground.

During these days that end the secular calendar, we can consider many things that are mentioned last yet have lasting value. We are barraged with requests from organizations for year-end contributions. We weigh these requests against a complicated set of values that might go head-to-head with our tax liability. We may even rush to fill certain retirement accounts or make final quarterly income tax payments so that they can be considered in the current calendar year. Some charitable organizations have benefited from our generosity all year long. Others must wait until this last minute for us to make our decision.

What should we do? Where can our funds, whatever the size, make the most impact? What do we feel is the most important organization in the community, or the one that most needs our support?

As we consider the impact of our contributions, we might realize that funds are not the only way to support an institution, although Jewish tradition requires us to make such contributions, regardless of our financial situation. We must also give of ourselves; loving acts of kindness, or *gemilut chasadim,* as they are called. And the highest among them are *chesed shel emet;* these are *true* acts of kindness (as the Hebrew implies) for they can never be repaid.

Work schedules sometimes slow down at this time of year, so even if it has taken us all year long to find the time to volunteer, this is usually the one act of ours that has the most lasting value, more than that special dress or suit that you may have been eyeing all season. KO

Standing Your Holy Ground

2 DECEMBER

*Take your sandals off your feet, for the place
on which you stand is holy.*
EXODUS 3:5

In the book of Exodus, Moses is living in Midian tending his father-in-law's flock when he hears God say the words above as he stands in front of a bush that is burning but is not being consumed. Overwhelmed by this awesome sight, he listens to God's instructions and removes his sandals to show reverence for the holiness of this unexpected encounter.

Today we do not routinely remove our shoes when we experience a holy moment. What do we do? Unfortunately, there is no outward gesture that proclaims, "Wow, this moment is full of God's Holy Presence!" In this way, we are impoverished. For we *do* need a way to capture sacred moments.

When was the last time a holy moment took place in your life? What did it feel like? How did you embrace it? Perhaps it is too distant to remember. The next time you experience an encounter you would describe as holy, commit yourself to reacting as if you were standing on holy ground and about to remove your shoes. Say a blessing. Slow down. Don't let it pass you by in haste.   LF

Hanukkah Light

3 DECEMBER

It is forbidden to use the Hanukkah light.
MOSES MAIMONIDES[2]

Perhaps you recall this day from your childhood. You get all dressed up for a holiday or a family *simchah* (joyous occasion)—a wedding, for instance, or a birthday party. As you wait for the rest of the family to get ready, your mother or father warns, "Don't go outside. You'll get your clothes dirty."

The fear of dirt runs deep within us, but dirt need not be physical. There are dirty jokes and dirty tricks; people can have foul mouths and filthy minds. We speak even of sin as "moral pollution"—picture Lady Macbeth frantically scrubbing herself free of the "damned spot" that has come from her many crimes.

Spiritually, too, the Torah speaks of purity and pollution. What mud puddles are to brand-new clothes and murder is to moral virtue, ritual impurity is to spiritual sanctity. The problem is that the realm of the spiritual is a lot harder to imagine. But it is real, nonetheless. Just from its exposure to the air, silverware tarnishes. If you leave it long enough, you will forget that there is anything shiny underneath. So, too, the part of ourselves that is spiritual requires periodic shining from the tarnish of daily life.   RABBI LAWRENCE HOFFMAN

Shabbat All Year Long

4 DECEMBER

Shabbat is a taste of what life will be like when the Messiah comes, when the world has to be perfected. According to the Genesis account, this world originally was and is still meant to be a paradise. But only when there is peace, with abundant resources and an untrammeled right to live, will the world be structured to sustain the infinite value of the human being. This is the heart of Judaism.

RABBI IRVING GREENBERG[3]

Shabbat occurs each week—all year long. So what is it about this time of year that makes us think of Shabbat and Rabbi Greenberg's lesson? No matter how much we may want to debate the facts, the commercialism of this season affects all of us. We can try to avoid it or we can use it to reflect on some relevant ideas about messianism and the perfect world taught in Jewish tradition. This is how Rabbi Greenberg continues his lesson: "By an act of will on

Shabbat, we step outside the here and now, and for approximately 25 hours all things are seen through the eyes of love, as if all were perfect. Every seven days we reaffirm our connection to God, to be 'married to the Divine lover.' Is this an escape from reality? No, it's an act of faith to be committed to a life that is growing and seeking perfection, to be so nurtured by *chesed* (the loving act of kindness) and the taste of this Shabbat as to go out and transform the world."   KO

The Gifts We Offer

5 DECEMBER

You shall bring it with your own hands and then lift it as an offering before God.
LEVITICUS 7:30

In the Bible there are numerous kinds of sacrifices which the ancient Israelites made to atone for their sins. Judaism has not been a sacrificial religion since the Second Temple was destroyed by the Romans in 70 C.E. However, we still bring gifts to our communities, and these gifts function in various ways. Some of our offerings play an exculpating role in that we hope they will assuage our guilt for some untoward act or behavior. Other times we give an offering in the hope of annulling illness or some other difficult life moment. Or we may show our gratitude for the riches in our lives.

Which gifts are the ones that we bring personally "with our own hands" before God? So often in today's world we are removed from even our own generosity. We rarely directly give. Instead we write a check and send it to our favorite charity. The question to ask ourselves is how can we truly elevate the offerings we give before the Holy One and to our community and lift them to a new level.   LF

Holy Places

6 DECEMBER

God did not choose the nation for the sake of the place;
God chose the place for the sake of the nation.
APOCRYPHA[4]

The story of the Jewish people is of Jews like us, ejected from their holy spot. They held on tightly to what they had, and if they returned, they usually came back to a frightful mess. But in rebuilding and rededicating the Temple, the Israelites rededicated themselves as well. ("Hanukkah" means "dedication" in Hebrew.) In so doing, they discovered a profound truth: They had survived without the Temple for a while. They had carried the holy place in their hearts, and this act gave them the will to stay "dedicated." The light that burned past all possibility was doubtless this light within.

At this time of year we read another story, that of a young and impetuous Jacob running scared from home. He sleeps and dreams of a ladder leading to the very Source of holiness. Then he awakens to find himself in a barren place of scorpions and rattlesnakes and arid gulches. "God is in this place," he whispers, "and I didn't even know it."

I predict that we will find these stories helpful in the cold, messy months ahead. We need to keep our holy place in our hearts. Perhaps as we embrace one another in song and prayer in whatever makeshift setting we find ourselves, we will realize that the holy spot is not a spot at all, but whatever place we gather in community.   RABBI LESTER BRONSTEIN

Sowing Tears, Reaping Joy

7 DECEMBER

They that sow in tears shall reap in joy.
PSALM 126:5

It seems like we eat a lot more than we should at this time of year. We let our diets and exercise regiment lapse. We're still stuffed from Thanksgiving, and seasonal parties abound. In the midst of this abundance, we have an obligation to thank God, the Source of All. We who have been blessed with much food must be especially sensitive to those who may have little to eat. Like many other verses from the Psalms, the verse above has found its way into the liturgy. The entire psalm from which it is taken is recited on Shabbat and holidays as an introduction to *Birkat HaMazon,* the grace after meals. It was also recited by Prime Minister Menachem Begin during the 1979 White House ceremony at which the Camp David accords were signed. Thus, each time I recite it, images of the ceremony on the White House lawn flash through my mind. It is one of those texts that can never be separated from a particular context for me.

We continue to sow the seeds of peace this time of year as we share meals with others whose faith may be different from ours.

Is this just an optimistic statement? Or is it based on experience? At the end of the *Birkat HaMazon* there is a statement that troubles many of us: "I was young and now I am old but I have never seen the righteous forsaken or their seed begging for bread." This text has always bothered me as well. Sometimes I slip in the word "so" in order to render the text "*so* forsaken that their seed begs for bread." Now I read the text as a challenge, a way for us to join with one another and together repair the world.

May we all one day reap the fruits of our labor in joy. And may it be a blessing for the entire world.   KO

The Meaning of Moderation

8 DECEMBER

The Torah suggests life is a choice of two paths: one of fire and one of ice. If one turns in either direction he will be harmed. What shall he do? Let him walk in the middle.
TALMUD[5]

Walking the path of moderation is challenging and takes constant diligence. How much easier it is to fall to one extreme or another. We could do that without much thought. Indulgence is easy. Moderation, on the other hand, is difficult. Think about the last time you binged on your favorite indulgence. Perhaps it was chocolate cake, ice cream, gambling, liquor, or a shopping spree. We all have our vices, and sometimes they are hard to resist. How can we return to the middle and regain a sense of balance? Doing this is not likely to be simple. The more we wander into the extremes, the more effort is required to regain a sense of moderation. In fact, some of us don't make it back to the middle at all.

Walking the middle path also means that we cannot look for easy escapes. At times it may seem dry and boring, so we think to ourselves, "Why not try a little adventure?" Excitement and variety are necessary for a full life. However, those of us on a spiritual path know the value of keeping a watchful eye open to be aware when we wander into excesses and mindlessness. The middle path is wider than we think. Let us explore its dimensions without wandering over its outer edges. Remember how difficult it can be to return to the middle.   LF

True Power Is Compassion

9 DECEMBER

Let not the wise glory in their wisdom,
nor the powerful in their strength,
nor the rich in their wealth.
JEREMIAH 9:22

I've often marveled at the designation "the Great" in history books tracing the development of Western civilization. Consider for a moment those august individuals who carry that appellation: Alexander the Great, Herod the Great, Charlemagne (which means "Charles the Great"), Catherine the Great, Peter the Great. In truth, the only trait that links these people is their ruthlessness, their despotism, and the fact that they were responsible for the deaths of many, many innocents. "Great" apparently is a term for mass murderers who possess fearsome power.

Moses reveals to us what makes for true greatness when he describes God as "God supreme and Lord supreme, the great, the mighty and the awesome God, who shows no favor and takes no bribes, but upholds the cause of the orphan and the widow and befriends the stranger, providing him with food and clothing" (Deut. 10:17–18). How striking! A claim of greatness that has nothing to do with shows of force or with killing or intimidation. God's greatness, says Moses, is based on moral rectitude, fairness, and compassion for the weakest members of society.

What a role model to hold out to the rest of us! True greatness consists in using our strength, our wealth, our wisdom, and our power to build communities of love, justice, and caring, to reach out to those who cannot fend for themselves, to build bridges with all humanity and with all living things, to care for the earth and all who dwell upon it.

RABBI BRADLEY SHAVIT ARTSON

Love Can Lead Us to the Right Path

10 DECEMBER

Either through love or through hate, a person can stray from the right path.
TALMUD[6]

Common wisdom holds that love leads us to the right path and helps us stay on it, while hate makes us stumble. As might be expected, the Rabbis are not so easily persuaded by this logic. Perhaps they witnessed expressions of hate in the name of love. That's why we pray that the lights of the Hanukkah menorah bring their illumination to the darkest corners of the world. This is particularly important now that the dark hours of the night overwhelm the all too brief hours of daylight. In anticipation of the winter solstice of December 21, we try to brighten our world in many ways. We have to make sure that love, however it is expressed, brings us closer to each other. Likewise, we should be careful that walls built by hate are not erected between us and other people. After all, the primary purpose of love is to bring us closer to each other. We have to make sure that nothing stands in its way.

In its physical expression, which is when we "make love," we are attempting to become as close as is literally possible to someone else: For a brief moment, to become that other in the midst of our passion. The Bible expresses this kind of love as "knowing" the other. Love is expressed in the knowledge of the other or, at least, in the incredible desire to really get to *know* the person. That's why some of the best times are spent talking for hours over a cup of coffee or a glass of wine on the road to love. Too often we make the mistake of confusing sex with love. As a result of our yearning to get closer to another, we think that physical intimacy can transcend the barriers that may exist between us.

Get to know your friends. Love your neighbors. And stay on the right path.   KO

The Steps toward Wisdom

11 DECEMBER

In seeking Wisdom, the first state is silence,
the second listening, the third remembrance,
the fourth practicing, the fifth teaching.
SOLOMON IBN GABIROL

This teaching illustrates that wisdom is not instantly acquired. When we set our minds on learning something new, we need to take many steps until it becomes an integrated part of our being. There are no shortcuts when it comes to developing life-wisdom. The "One-Minute Wisdom" book has yet to be written; and if it did exist, I would find it suspect. While there is no one path to learning profound truths, along the way to doing so we find ourselves in these various modes: silence, listening, remembering, practicing, and teaching. Silence lets us clear our minds of cluttered thinking. Listening lets us distill new information and insights. Remembering provides a way to recall once known but now forgotten wisdom. Practicing draws us into the world, which requires interaction with others. Our wisdom is put to the test when we practice it in real life. And last, teaching others is a way to transmit our learning to others. Can we gently guide them and provide direction for them?

Where are you on this path? When do you find yourself stumbling? When do you excel? This path is well-trodden. We walk it all the days of our lives, whether we know it or not.

LF

Seeing the Face of God

12 DECEMBER

Then I will take My hand away and you will see My back, but My face must not be seen.

EXODUS 33:23

This verse comes at a climatic moment in the relationship between God and Moses. Moses has just weathered the storm of the Golden Calf and has returned to the mountain top to receive a second set of tablets. Moses is feeling strong and even a bit bold. He knows that no one can see the face of God and live, but it is this vision that he wants. He is possibly even willing to die for it, because maybe seeing the face of God is the mission of one's life. And so he asks. And God responds: "Look anywhere or everywhere and you can see My face." Moses is undaunted. "No, I, Moses, want to see Your face." And so the enigmatic response, "You can see My back but My face shall not be seen." Why? How can you see God's back and not God's face? After all, if God has no body, what difference would it make?

When we look at the world, the question is: What do we see? Do we see the world or simply our perception of a piece of that larger reality? When I look at the face of my friend or at a familiar place, I know what they look like; And the fact that it is only my perception is irrelevant. But when I want to see the face of God, I am asking to see the face of the Infinite. And I must remember that I am but a finite being with only relative capacity for seeing. When Moses asks to see the face of God, all he will be able to see is what he thinks God looks like, which in this case is not enough. And so Moses is shown the back of God. The phrase in Hebrew is *panim el panim,* which is often translated "face to face." But it could also be translated as "a face toward a face," meaning two faces looking in the *same* direction. Think of one face wearing the other face as a mask. What would you see? You would see not what you think the other looks like but what the other sees. God cannot show Moses his face for Moses has no capacity to see that. What God can show Moses is what God sees.

In our relationships with other people, we often ask to see their faces but maybe we should ask to see their backs so that we can see the world, maybe only for an instant, the way they see it. Then we can offer them true understanding—a genuine gift. RABBI MICHAEL PALEY

The Powerful Lights of Hanukkah

13 December

"Not by might, nor by power, but by My Spirit," says God.
ZECHARIAH 4:6

Although some people think that Hanukkah is celebrated on different days each year, it is really celebrated on the same eight days every year—the same eight days of joy, light, and celebration. The secular calendar is not always in sync with the Hebrew calendar. The Hebrew calendar is a lunar calendar that also gets corrected by the solar seasons. Thus Hanukkah appears to be somewhat erratic. It occurs sometimes near Thanksgiving, sometimes closer to the end of December, sometimes anytime in between.

Maybe the calendar is hard to follow, but the message of Hanukkah is not. This winter holiday, which often gets lost in the seasonal commercialism that threatens to overwhelm us, is not about the military victory of the Maccabees. Nor is it about a cruse of oil that burned longer than expected. Rather, Hanukkah is about the spirit of God resting on a people and motivating them to do what they never thought possible. Strength of will motivated the Maccabees. Let the Maccabean spirit do the same for you.   KO

A Wise Heart

14 DECEMBER

*Teach us to number our days that we may acquire
a heart of wisdom.*
PSALM 90:12

Why do we have to learn to number our days? And why do so now as we approach the end of the secular year? Don't we realize that each day is precious regardless of when it comes? Actually, no. The hours and the days and the weeks can go by so quickly, one day can so easily roll into the next, that many of us forget to hold each and every one as if it were a precious gift. Certainly some days are more exciting than others. We look forward to special occasions, to opportunities at work, to moments of relaxation. Yet each day, even those that seem the same as yesterday, presents us with new possibilities, new ways to relate and grow.

If we mindlessly go through the motions of any day, we may miss an opportunity. Who knows what will surprise us in the course of 24 hours if we keep our minds alert and our hearts awake and open? By treasuring each day, we place ourselves on the path to acquiring a wise and compassionate heart.   LF

The Miracles of Omission

15 December

A miracle cannot prove what is impossible; it is only useful to confirm what is possible.
Moses Maimonides[7]

Most of us think of miracles—if we think of them at all—as sea-churning, wind-blowing, lightning-flashing, knock-your-socks-off kinds of experiences. So we label the ten plagues and the splitting of the Red Sea as miracles, and even Israel's 1976 rescue at Entebbe of hostages held by terrorists and the birth of a child as miracles. For these indeed are miracles that overwhelm us with the grandeur of their presence and their awesome power.

But they are rare. In the spaces between these miracles, there are the quieter miracles that silently, sometimes imperceptibly, fill our lives. These are the miracles that take time to unfold, that we overlook unless we are alert enough to pause, to gaze, and then to see. Imagine passing that burning bush in the desert so long ago. At a glance, it would appear so ordinary, so insignificant. It is only by pausing, by waiting and seeing that it is not consumed, that the fullness of the miracle would unfold for us. Or imagine entering the Temple in the year 162 B.C.E. on the third day after its liberation by the Maccabees. You look around: People are working, sweeping, singing, washing, scrubbing, by a dim light of one cruse of oil. So where is the miracle? It is only by being present, and aware, throughout the eight days of rededication that we can recognize that we are in the presence of a miracle.

Perhaps, then, quiet miracles happen all around us, all the time, but we just do not slow down to notice. Or perhaps they happen in ways we are unable to perceive, for we are in the end limited by the capacity of our senses and the reach of our technology. Perhaps one of the greatest of miracles is believing that there are miracles at all and that they still happen, even if we never know for sure.

RABBI NINA BETH CARDIN

Encouraging Miracles

16 DECEMBER

A person should not stand in a place of danger and say that a miracle will be wrought for him.
TALMUD[8]

Because it is the Hanukkah season, I am preoccupied with miracles. I think about them all the time. I look for them in everyday life. I try to understand them from a variety of perspectives, asking the same questions over and over again. Did the oil really burn for eight days—and does my belief about this really matter one way or another? How did a small band of poorly trained Israelites band together and defeat the entire Assyrian-Greek army? I believe in miracles. I don't understand them, but I am not prepared to play theological word games with them. I am just not sure that we correctly focus on the miraculous as we consider the events of people's history and our own. It is clear to me that the miracle of the oil is more evident in light of a Judaism that still burns passionately in my soul than in whether or not a bit of oil somehow burned longer than its expected use. Nevertheless, the Maccabees did not wait for a miracle. They brought one on their own and transformed the darkened Temple into a house of light. We can do the same.   KO

Naming Ourselves

17 December

Every person has three names: the one given by one's parents, the one acquired by others, and the one acquired on one's own.

MIDRASH[9]

How many names do you have? Some of us may have childhood nicknames, or names we use only with our spouses or partners, or perhaps a Hebrew name that is very different from our English one. Our first name is given to us by our parents at the time of our birth. Often we are given names of relatives who are no longer living. Their memory can then live through us. Our first name can be a window into our past, our history, our birthright.

Then as we are growing up we may acquire nicknames. These are a statement of our relationships with others and often highlight an aspect of our personality or a quality that others perceive in us. Some of these nicknames may stick with us; others fall into disuse. They are usually statements of endearment, friendship, and intimacy.

There are also attributes assigned to us by others in the context of family, friendship, and work. While these characteristics may capture only a part of our being, they shine through. We may be a worker, a leader, an organizer, a motivator, a loner, a team player, a risk taker. How others think of us points to how we will be remembered; it is a statement of how we walk in the world. It is a statement of our character as seen by others.

Which names have you acquired on your life journey so far? Are they a reflection with which you are content? Which other attributes would you like to acquire as you continue down life's path? What names truly capture your spirit?   LF

New Kings to Rule Over Us

18 DECEMBER

And a new king arose over Egypt who did not know Joseph.
EXODUS 1:8

This seems like a throwaway line. All right, so a new king came and he didn't know Joseph. What's the big deal? It is a little surprising that the new king would not know Joseph, the Jewish boy wonder with his fancy coat of many colors and Freudian dream skills. After all, Joseph had saved Egypt from a terrible famine and had even brought great power to the Pharaohs. But okay, he didn't remember Joseph.

The same question seemed to bother Rashi, the great medieval commentator. How could the Pharaoh not know Joseph? Rashi believes that either the Pharaoh really did know Joseph but feigned ignorance, or it wasn't a new Pharaoh at all but the Pharaoh had just changed. The line is not a throwaway line, however. As soon as we hear that the Pharaoh does not know Joseph, the story of the Israelites in Egypt turns dark. All the good work that generations of Israelites had accomplished is dismissed in a moment, and all of a sudden they are accused of being too numerous, and even a potential threat. Memory in this case has great impact.

We have all been in situations in which we have done much good work and received praise from our peers and superiors. Things are running smoothly and we don't want anything to rock the boat. Then a new boss comes, or we enroll in a new school, or our neighbor moves and a stranger moves in: *"A new king arose who did not know Joseph."* Through no fault of our own, and against our best intentions, the past is forgotten and a new future must be forged. In this story, the Pharaoh has a reason for not remembering Joseph. His goal is to establish himself as the independent sovereign, even as God. He must overcome the past in order to rule the future. He does this at great peril—first to us, but ultimately to himself. It is at this moment that Moses is born. Moses is a seer, one who sees deeply into the world. It is his responsibility, on behalf of the people, to remind the Pharaoh of Joseph. It is the new king who does not know Joseph that sets us on our way, moving from a pleasant stay as strangers in a strange land on the path toward true liberation and freedom.

When our own lives are shaken by a "new king," we can remember that change is inevitable and the direction of our response can be one of hope and redemption.

RABBI MICHAEL PALEY

Healing through Living

19 DECEMBER

God brings the healing before the calamity.
YIDDISH PROVERB[10]

This Yiddish expression is based on a teaching in the Talmud. It arises from a deep-seated faith in God and the eternal optimism of the Jewish people. It also stems from the belief that God is the Author of *all*—good and bad. That's why it is important to find a way to praise God for the good and the bad, as the Rabbis bid us to do, as difficult as it might seem to do sometimes. There are those who may look askance at such a consideration, assigning responsibility for the calamity to God and rejecting the possibility of Divine healing. I believe that God heals, just as I believe that the power to bring on such healing lies deeply embedded in each of our souls. Our challenge is to muster the strength to bring it forward when it is needed.

My mother spins this teaching a little differently. Whenever we are confronted with a major challenge, physical or spiritual, she always says that "things have their own way of working themselves out." This is her way of saying that God will tend to it and that I do not have to worry. But I know that God is my covenantal partner. I may not be able to do the job alone, but neither can God. We have to work things out *together*. When we are puzzled, when we are in deep despair, looking for guidance, inspiration and insight, the answers to our struggles are part of the same Ultimate Reality that caused the pain in the first place. This notion is a part of spiritual logic that evades many of us. But once we begin to understand it, we can find healing and perfect peace. We may be able to find it in the same place that brought us to despair. KO

Standing Up in Hard Situations

20 DECEMBER

In a place where no one is behaving like a person,
each of us must strive to be human.
MISHNAH[11]

We may find ourselves in situations in which no one seems to be doing the right thing. How do we respond? Do we sit quietly and go along with the crowd? Do we leave? Do we speak up and clearly state our view on the subject, though we may be a lone voice? It is never easy to be the only one to voice an unpopular opinion. Nevertheless, it is our responsibility to present another way, another perspective, when confronted by baseness and inhumanity. We can be like Abraham, who debated God about destroying Sodom and Gomorrah to save the city on account of the few righteous souls who lived there. Although Abraham's impassioned argument did not prevail in this particular instance, it is a model for us to imitate.

We are each created in God's image, and our actions must never diminish the holy spark that resides in us, as it does in everything else. At times we do put ourselves on the line. But speak up and allow your image of God to shine forth.   LF

Everlasting Covenant

21 DECEMBER

*You stand this day, all of you, before the Eternal your God
. . . from woodchopper to waterdrawer, to enter into the
covenant of the Eternal your God.*
DEUTERONOMY 29:9–10

God made a covenant with all Jews, regardless of their individual economic status. We see above that Judaism rejects the idea of a hierarchy of professions. The manual laborer has as much dignity as the physician. Work is a necessity for human existence, but not the center of it. As Rabbi Dow Marmur wrote, "It is only those who live to work, rather than work to live, who are snobbish or status-seeking about their jobs."

Hasidism, which began in the eighteenth century as a spiritual revolution against the then-stultifying world of talmudic learning, sanctified the work of common people. In one Hasidic tale a man was rebuked for wearing a tallit and tefillin while repairing his wagon. "Look, he oils the wheels while he prays!" his neighbors taunted. "No," scolded their teacher, "he prays while he oils the wheels. Even in the midst of work, we focus our minds and souls on the higher things. What a holy people we are!" In another Hasidic story, a disciple traveled for miles to visit his teacher, Dov Baer of Mezeritch. He just wanted to see how the sage put on his shoes and tied his shoelaces. To *Hasidim*, everything is potentially usable in this world. No wisdom goes to waste.

Every kind of gainful work can make us better people. We benefit when we keep in mind the words of the second-century sage Ben Azzai: "Treat no one lightly and think nothing is useless, for everyone has a moment and everything has its place" (*Pirke Avot* 4:3). RABBI JEFFREY SALKIN[12]

Finding the Divine Presence

22 DECEMBER

The Divine Presence does not rest upon humans through gloom.
TALMUD[13]

December is a dark month, especially if you live in the northern part of the United States or Canada. It is not that winter is at its worst in December. The bad snows usually wait until February. No, it is just that the nights are long and the days are short and we know that we have now fully arrived into winter. A pervasive gloom seems to dampen our spirits. Some people even develop a seasonal disorder as a result of this. It's especially hard when you begin your work day in the dark and you come home in the dark. It is a little easier when you anchor your day with prayer and seek out community. We especially try to find a light in the midst of all the darkness, knowing full well that the only way to struggle against the darkness is by basking in the light from the Divine.

Sometimes it is we who must bring the light to others. Then we can all shine in God's reflected glory.   KO

The Gift of Judaism

23 DECEMBER

To be a Jew in the twentieth century
Is to be offered a gift. If you refuse,
Wishing to be invisible, you choose
Death of the spirit . . .
Accepting, take full life.
MURIEL RUKESEYER[14]

This poem was written by Muriel Rukeseyer during the early part of the twentieth century, when American Jews were experiencing their newfound ability to melt into the larger American culture. It was the beginning of a new chapter in Jewish history. No longer were Jews *required* to maintain their connection to Judaism, the religion and culture of their forefathers and foremothers. Rather, in America Jewish identity became a choice—a "gift," Rukeseyer calls it, perhaps because it became something we could either accept or dismiss. Of course, the twentieth century also saw the horrors of the Holocaust: European Jews were exterminated, whether or not they actively chose Judaism. As we look back on this century, we see it was a time of both tremendous opportunity and unspeakable tragedy for the Jewish people as a whole.

Now we face the twenty-first century. Do we accept our Jewish identities as a gift? What does this mean for us today? On one level, it means we are to be thankful for the spiritual heritage and wisdom which have been passed down to us. Of course, it is hard to feel gratitude if we are distant from Judaism or if our Jewish past has caused us pain and suffering. Still, Jewish history, culture, and traditions provide us with a path on which to survive the anonymity that plagues our modern world. We can deepen and broaden our understanding of life when we walk on this path and clothe our souls with its many facets. We gain a far-reaching perspective which dispels the invisibility of our otherwise diffused lives. In the twenty-first century, perhaps the "gift" is that we do not go forward unencumbered by history but rather fully aware of all its terrain.   LF

Mighty Impulses

24 December

Who is mighty? One who subdues the evil impulses, as it is said, "One who is slow to anger is better than the mighty, and one who rules one's spirit is better than the one who conquers a city."

MISHNAH[15]

There has been a decline in civility in America. We suffer from road rage; short fuses; foul language in classrooms; cool hip-hop boys wearing their jeans somewhere between their knees and hips and exposing their underpants and more than a few square inches of skin. All this callousness and insensitivity weakens whatever glue still binds our society. It makes us rude, unpleasant people.

To some degree, surliness has also contaminated Jewish life: people berate their rabbis or Hebrew school teachers or administrators, and some prominent national Jewish leaders have even engaged in very public name-calling of each other.

One rabbi I know attributes the current climate of incivility to "an exaggerated sense of entitlement among the upper-middle class." He's absolutely right. But upper-middle class Jews—and every other class, as well—seem to have forgotten some key Jewish teachings about how we should relate to other people: The Bible commands us to "love your neighbor as yourself," and Jewish law prohibits *lashon harah*—saying anything derogatory about someone. Even saying something derogatory that is true is forbidden, and trying to acquit yourself by claiming you said it in jest or that everybody knew about it does not absolve you. The ancient Rabbis went so far as to say that shaming someone was comparable to murder, because blood drains from the face of the person who is shamed just as it does during a homicide.

Reversing the current mood will take hard work. The Rabbis who warned against *lashon harah* knew that lowering our voices is a sign of strength, not weakness; that we all gain by expressing ourselves with force, not venom; that we should always remember that whoever we're talking to has been created in the image of God. And that to desecrate that image is to desecrate God.

Remember as you go through your day that everyone you meet bears the image of God—and that how you treat each person is a test of how you treat the Divine Itself.

ARTHUR J. MAGIDA

The Great Mercy in Us All

25 DECEMBER

There are moments when we feel forsaken. But through God's rachamim, *and the great* rachamim *within us all, we can reach out and bring another in.*

RABBI ELAINE ZECHER

Rachamim, which means "mercy," is one of those Hebrew words whose profound impact is lost in translation. It stems from the word for womb (*rechem*) and captures an image that is uniquely motherly and nurturing. It is a feminine word in the most basic sense.

For many people, this time of year presents an assault on the senses: school vacations; family trips; commercialism; parties. Some people run to exotic, faraway places to find respite. And if we are honest with ourselves, we may even admit that while we feel comfortable in our daily lives all year long, it is this one time of year that we feel alienated and estranged in our communities. In Rabbi Zecher's paraphrase above of Isaiah's words to the Jewish people suffering in exile, she captures the sense of being forsaken that we all feel at various times in our lives. In the very midst of feeling forsaken, our Jewish identity is affirmed. In Isaiah's words, we also find the solution for our estrangement: We can reach out and bring another person in.

So this day, while much of the world is celebrating a different vision of the future in the form of Christmas and we may feel alone, reach out and bring another in. In doing so, you will be brought along as well.   KO

Treat the Elderly Well: They Are Us

26 DECEMBER

The test of a people is how it behaves toward the old.
It is easy to love children. . . . But affection and
care for the old, the incurable, the helpless
are the true gold mines of a culture.
RABBI ABRAHAM JOSHUA HESCHEL[16]

Babies are so engaging that it is hard not to smile when we see a newborn sleeping comfortably or smiling in our direction. Babies signify the future and our hopes for the continuity of our world. The elderly, however, do not often engender the same warmth in us. Some people call old age "the winter of our lives." There is a wonderful Yiddish expression that sees old age a little differently: "To the unlearned, old age is winter. To the learned, it is harvest time."

In our youth-oriented culture, we do not see the old as models of success. Their faces do not tower over us from giant billboards. One reason for this exclusion is our fear of death. When we look into the faces of our parents and grandparents, we are reminded of our own mortality. This is an issue we would like to push aside or deny. Yet we cannot allow our fears to dictate how we treat the elderly.

All societies have to struggle with how they treat the elderly. Do we abandon or embrace those who have lived and contributed to our world and are now in the declining years of their lives? With age comes maturity and wisdom. As we read in Leviticus 19:32, "You shall rise before the aged and show deference to the old." We do not abandon those who are old and turn our attention only to the young. We know that age has nothing to do with the holiness of each person. As we treat another, may we be treated as well.   LF

Innocence

27 DECEMBER

Will You sweep away the innocent with the guilty?
GENESIS 18:23

When Abraham is faced with the imminent destruction of Sodom and Gomorrah, he insists that a passion for righteousness binds God no less than it does humanity. The primary implication of Abraham's passion is that the innocent deserve consideration, even if the punishment of the guilty is mitigated, or even revoked.

As the Midrash observes, "If You desire the world to endure, there can be no absolute strict judgment, while if You desire absolute strict judgment, the world cannot endure." Small wonder then that Abraham, who is credited with bringing humanity in touch with the marvel of God's unity and God's love, is an advocate on behalf of the guilty. It is the only way to protect the innocent. Even in the midst of a hateful population, Abraham's attention and energy are fixed on those who did care, those who did perform deeds of righteousness, even in a benighted age. For their sake, he argues on behalf of all their kinfolk, whether worthy or not.

So central is that trait that the Talmud established it as the ultimate test of Jewish lineage: "Whoever is merciful to other people is without a doubt a child of our father Abraham; whoever is unmerciful to other people cannot be a child of Abraham our father."

To be Jewish is to show mercy, even to the undeserving. We act not like those who oppressed and brutalized our ancestors, but rather like our father Abraham, sustaining an entire community because of the innocent in its midst.

RABBI BRADLEY SHAVIT ARTSON

The Purpose of the Commandments

28 DECEMBER

The commandments were given to refine human beings.
MIDRASH[17]

Some people reject the idea of any kind of commandment. They consider themselves in control of their own destiny and do not want anyone to direct them to do anything. They look upon themselves as autonomous, self-directed individuals who require guidance from no one else and not even from God. For most North Americans, the basic idea of a commandment runs contrary to the fundamental principles inherent in a democratic form of government. Instead of arguing with such people, I simply suggest that they exercise their autonomy by voluntarily taking on the commandments and thereby entering into a relationship with God. Such an approach allows everyone to benefit from the potential for holiness inherent in the *mitzvot*.

But commandments are hard to see, and people want to be able to see things, to touch them. This is the way most of us interface with our world. So these commandments are given concrete form through ritual, which are those actions that make up our daily routine and provide mooring for our storm-tossed lives. Their main function is to help us bridge the gap between ourselves and God. They are a human response to the commandments. Through their implementation, each of us can become a better individual and help make the world better also.   KO

How Do We Define Richness?

29 DECEMBER

Who is rich? One who is happy with their portion.
MISHNAH[18]

We all have dreams of becoming rich. Just witness the response to lotteries everywhere in the country. Thousands of people drive long distances to stand in line for a chance to become instantly wealthy without having to work for it. But it is too easy to confuse material wealth with being rich. The Rabbis redefine richness in an altogether different way. For them, it has nothing to do with our bank accounts or the size of our houses. It has everything to do with our inner spiritual state. When we are content with who we are with, with our strengths and our deficiencies, with where we have been and where we are today, *then* we are rich.

Certainly, we can strive to improve ourselves and better our lives materially. Yet at some point we must also make peace with who we are deep down and what we can—and cannot—realistically strive to become. Happiness is more than the slogan, "Don't worry. Be happy." Happiness will follow when we are truly at one with ourselves and project this sense of wholeness and well-being to others.   LF

On the Passing of Time

30 DECEMBER

Our duty is, with renewed vigor, to enter the twenty-first century wisely, having plumbed the meaning of our own experience . . . and then to produce our own ethical will, a testament to what we seek to preserve and what we believe wants change, a testament we can then pass on to the new generations that follow ours.
ALBERT VORSPAN AND RABBI DAVID SAPERSTEIN[19]

Franz Rosensweig, the Jewish philosopher and teacher, called us "the eternal people." He meant that we exist outside of history. We Jews, he said, are still around because we do not operate on the same fleeting plane as other peoples. For Rosenzweig, so-called "Jewish history" was merely a time line of our encounters with the short-lived politics of the world around us. We, meanwhile, remained unchanged. Our real history consists of the Exodus from Egypt, receiving the Torah at Mount Sinai, being exiled from our land, and ultimate redemption. Everything else was temporal, and thus not Jewish. Rosenzweig warned that once we chose to reenter history, we would run the risk of becoming perishable like any other nation. Thus he was not a Zionist.

Most of us would call this "eternal people" idea a romantic pining for a world that never was. We would prefer to identify every Jewish triumph and catastrophe with a larger human politics. We would characterize Judaism as a response to history rather than a dodging from it. And we would be right.

But not entirely right. Rosenzweig's romanticism carries with it an important lesson, one that he himself was not necessarily trying to make. The lesson is this: We Jews have seen so much history that we can now put single events into perspective in a way that few peoples can. We know that what seems today to be an earthshaking occurrence may ultimately be seen as a mere blip in time. We also know that great historians, chroniclers, and media reporters have missed subtle events that eventually changed everything and everyone. We measure the meaning of short-range history in terms of the cosmic events in our religious mythos: Exodus, Sinai, Land, Exile, Redemption.

So while others tear their hair out about the passing of another decade, we don't get so excited. From our point of view, the lightning-fast changes in our world are part of the gigantic, excruciatingly slow process of "redemption" which is far from over. We have seen political "messiahs" come and go. Not every quick dream comes true. New regimes don't always improve upon the old. We always hope, but not without peering around the corner first.

Meanwhile we Jews have indeed chosen to reenter history rather than continue to wait for history to inflict its wrath upon us. We are active now, via the State of Israel and our individual involvement in politics the world over. If we insist upon participating merely as members of the great human family, then we run the risk of contributing as much to the ongoing problem as any other well-meaning human has done. But if we enter history as Jews—as a people with a near-eternal memory and with a mind toward bringing our redemption that our Torah teaches us is "not in the heavens" but well within our grasp—then we just might be giving a sense of eternity to humanity, which desperately needs to see beyond the flipping of pages in a fresh new date book. Every act that we do—from simple personal encounters to major business deals to political policy to sanctifying time itself—could be done with the distinct recollection that we were slaves in Egypt and that one day we set out on the millennial quest for a world in which no one need be enslaved again.

If we are looking for a New Year's resolution, perhaps this would be a good place to begin.   RABBI LESTER BRONSTEIN

The Final Consolation

31 DECEMBER

God is with me. I do not fear.
PSALM 118:6

This text, which is among my favorites, concludes the familiar *Adon Olam* hymn. Since it is used to bring the Shabbat morning service to a close in most synagogues, many people are already out of their seats, maybe folding their *tallitot* and wishing their neighbors *Shabbat Shalom,* when these words are sung. After a long morning of worship, the words that might fortify us for the week ahead are lost in a rush to leave the sanctuary. As the words that conclude this installment of our dialogue with God, they serve as a *nechemta,* as a final word of consolation and uplift. This is a common technique of the Rabbis. We are never to be left in despair. Rather, we should always be left inspired and uplifted. It reminds me of the way that the book of Ecclesiastes ends. After a volume full of a variety of statements, the editors wanted to make sure that the reader understands the author's primary lesson: The only path is the one that leads to the Divine.

In the original psalm from which the words above—"God is with Me. I do not fear"—are taken, the text continues, "What can a human do to me?" Indeed, as the secular New Year approaches, I know that God is with me in whatever I do. Therefore I shall fear nothing and no one.   KO

ENDNOTES

JANUARY

1. The *Shehecheyanu* prayer.
2. Adapted from Harold Schulweis, *In God's Mirror: Reflections and Essays*. Hoboken, N.J.: KTAV Publishing Co., 1990.
3. Babylonian Talmud, *Shabbat* 151b.
4. Babylonian Talmud, *Taanit* 8b.
5. *Avot de Rabbi Nathan* 23.
6. Babylonian Talmud, *Rosh Hashanah* 4b.
7. Babylonian Talmud, *Niddah* 31b.
8. *Genesis Rabbah* 44:1.
9. Adapted from Irving Greenberg, *Sacred Times*. New York: National Jewish Center for Learning and Leadership, 1992.
10. Babylonian Talmud, *Eruvin* 13b.
11. Babylonian Talmud, *Eruvin* 18b.
12. Babylonian Talmud, *Yevamot* 14b.
13. Babylonian Talmud, *Nedarim* 41a.
14. Jerusalem Talmud, *Kiddushin* 4:12.
15. Abraham Joshua Heschel, *Man's Quest for God*. New York: Charles Scribner's Sons, 1954.
16. *Song of Songs Rabbah* 6:17.
17. Adapted from Irving Greenberg, *Visions and Voices*. New York: National Jewish Center for Learning and Leadership, 1994.
18. Babylonian Talmud, *Berakhot* 19b.
19. Babylonian Talmud, *Berakhot* 58a.

FEBRUARY

1. Babylonian Talmud, *Taanit* 20a.
2. *Likutei Maharan* 1:123d.

3. Babylonian Talmud, *Berakhot* 28b.

4. *Pirke Avot* 4:3.

5. Joseph B. Soleveitchik, *The Lonely Man of Faith*. Wheaton, Ill.: Doubleday, 1965.

6. *Sefer HaChinukh* 2:5.

7. Babylonian Talmud, *Eruvin* 100b.

8. *Genesis Rabbah* 13:2.

9. Mishnah *Peah* 1:1.

10. Adapted from *Wisdom of the Ages*. New York: National Jewish Center for Learning and Leadership, 1993.

11. *Pirke Avot* 2:9.

12. Babylonian Talmud, *Berakhot* 17a.

13. Zohar ii, 47a.

14. Babylonian Talmud, *Makkot* 10b.

15. *Pirke Avot* 4:20.

16. Babylonian Talmud, *Berakhot* 17a.

17. From the *Ahavah Rabbah* prayer.

18. Neil Gillman, "Sabbath Week" column, *The Jewish Week*, 208, no. 39 (January 26, 1996): 48.

19. *Genesis Rabbah* 53:7.

MARCH

1. *Pirke Avot* 3:21.

2. *Mivchar Hapeninim* #338.

3. *Siach Sarfei Kodesh*.

4. Adaped from *Vision & Voices*, New York: National Jewish Center for Learning and Leadership, 1994.

5. Babylonian Talmud, *Bava Metzia* 49a.

6. Jerusalem Talmud, *Haggigah* 1:76.

7. *Ethics,* iii. Def 13, Explanation.

8. *Shirat Yisrael*.

9. Jerusalem Talmud, *Peah* 8:8.

10. Jerusalem Talmud, *Chagigah* 1:8.

11. Adapted from *Vision & Voices,* New York: National Jewish Center for Learning and Leadership, 1994.

12. Jerusalem Talmud, *Kiddushin* 4:12.

13. Aryeh Kaplan, *Jewish Meditation*. New York: Schocken Books, 1985.

14. Leo Baeck, *The Foundation of Judaism and Ethics*. New York: Macmillan Press, 1929.

15. Elie Wiesel, *Somewhere a Master: Further Hasidic Portraits and Legends*. New York: Summit Books, 1982.

16. *Midrash Tehillim* 136:10.
17. *Pirke De Rebbe Eliezer* 25.
18. Babylonian Talmud, *Sotah* 11b.
19. Adapted from Lori Lefkowitz, "Attending to Details: A Pesach Meditation on God, Grandmothers and Gratitude," *Sh'ma: A Journal for Jewish Responsibility,* 27 (April 18, 1997).
20. *Midrash Tehillim* 16:11.
21. *Seder Eliyahu Rabba* 26.
22. *Pirke Avot* 3:17.
22. B. Halper, ed., *Shirat Israel*. Leipzeig, 1924, p.132.

APRIL

1. Midrash to Proverbs 22:6.
2. Record Group 23, Henrietta Szold Readings and Quotations. Hadassah Archives, New York.
3. *Tanchuma, Noach* 1.
4. Mishneh Torah, *Yad, Deot* 1.7.
5. Menachem Hacohen, *Haggadah Ha'am*. New York: Adama Press, 1987.
6. Translation adapted by Rami M. Shapiro.
7. Commentary to Deuteronomy 7:15.
8. *Pesikta de Rav Kahana* 107a.
9. Adapted from *Vision & Voices*. New York: National Jewish Center for Learning and Leadership, 1994.
10. Babylonian Talmud, *Nedarim* 41a.
11. *Pirke Avot* 2:1.
12. Kaufmann Kohler, *Jewish Theology*. New York: The Macmillan Co., 1918.
13. *Or Adonai*.
14. *Genesis Rabbah* 68:4.
15. Adapted from *Vision & Voices*. New York: National Jewish Center for Learning and Leadership, 1994.
16. *Likutey Shoshanah* 109b.
17. David Wolpe, *Healer of Shattered Hearts: A Jewish View of God*. New York: Penguin, 1991.
18. Babylonian Talmud, *Pesachim* 54b.
19. *Four Centuries of Jewish Women's Spirituality,* edited by Ellen M. Umansky and Dianne Ashton. Boston: Beacon Press, 1992.
20. Harlan J. Wechsler, *What Is So Bad About Guilt? Learning to Live with It Since We Can't Live Without It*. New York: Simon and Schuster, 1990.
21. Babylonian Talmud, *Menachot* 99a.
22. *Exodus Rabbah* 31:3.

23. Adapted from *Orim: A Jewish Journal at Yale.* 2, no. 1 (Autumn 1986): 127–128.

24. Diary, April 3, 1915.

25. Grace Aguilar, *Vale of Cedars.* New York: Appleton, 1850.

26. Adapted from Dov Peretz Elkins, *Prescriptions for a Long and Happy Life: Age-Old Wisdom for the New Age.* Princeton, N.J.: Growth Associates, 1993.

MAY

1. Babylonian Talmud, *Bava Batra* 8a.

2. *Mekhilta* to Exodus 14:31.

3. This selection is based on a story in Yaffa Eliach, *Hasidic Tales of the Holocaust.* London and New York: Oxford University Press, 1982.

4. Babylonian Talmud, *Zevachim* 116a.

5. Mark Twain, "Stirring Times in Austria," *Harper's Monthly Magazine,* 96, no. 64 (March 1898).

6. Translation adapted by Rami M. Shapiro.

7. Hannah Senesh, *Her Life and Diary.* New York: Schocken Books, 1973.

8. Adapted from Bernard S. Raskas, *Jewish Spirituality and Faith.* Hoboken, N.J.: KTAV Publishing Co., 1989.

9. Janusz Korczak, *The Ghetto Diary.* New York: Schocken Books, 1978.

10. Albert Einstein, *The World as I See It.* Seacacus, N.J.: Citadel Press, 1993.

11. Bernard S. Raskas, *Jewish Spirituality and Faith.* Hoboken, N.J.: KTAV Publishing Co., 1989.

12. Babylonian Talmud, *Berakhot* 22a.

13. Mikha Yosef Berdyczewsky, *"On Sanctity,"* 1899.

14. *Kol Kitvei Tchernichowsky.* Vilna: Hotsa'at Vaad Ha-Yovel, 1929–1932.

15. Abraham Joshua Heschel, *Man is Not Alone.* New York: Noonday Press, 1951.

16. Etty Hillesum, *An Interrupted Life.* New York: Pantheon Books, 1983.

17. Babylonian Talmud, *Berakhot* 7a.

18. Adapted from *Wisdom of the Ages.* New York: National Jewish Center for Learning and Leadership, 1993.

19. Adapted from *Vision & Voices.* New York: National Jewish Center for Learning and Leadership, 1994.

20. *Al Parashat Derakhim* 3:30.

21. Address to Vassar College students, Poughkeepsie, New York, 1915.

22. *Pirke Avot* 3:22.

23. Bernard S. Raskas, *Jewish Spirituality and Faith.* Hoboken, N.J.: KTAV Publishing Co., 1989.

24. Babylonian Talmud, *Megillah* 6b.

25. Nina Beth Cardin, "The First Generation of Women's Rabbinate," in *Conservative Judaism*, 48, no. 1 (Fall 1995): 15–20.
26. *Hilkhot Teshuvah* 3:4.
27. *T'shuvah*, 2, no. 1 (November 1993): 1.
28. *Ben Hamelekh HaNazir, sof sh'ar* 18.
29. Babylonian Talmud, *Eruvin* 13b.
30. From the daily *Amidah,* the central prayer in the worship service.
31. *T'shuvah,* 1, no. 1 (September 1992): 1.
32. *Genesis Rabbah* 49:1.

JUNE

1. Babylonian Talmud, *Shabbat* 10b.
2. Babylonian Talmud, *Ketubot* 109b.
3. Babylonian Talmud, *Niddah* 30b.
4. *Ahavah Rabbah* prayer, from the morning service.
5. Nina Beth Cardin, *A Tapestry in Time*. West Orange, N.J: Behrman House, Inc., 1999.
6. Babylonian Talmud, *Berakhot* 13a.
7. *Kedushat Levi, Parashat Chukat.*
8. *Pirke Avot* 4:1.
9. Babylonian Talmud, *Ta'anit* 7a.
10. Anne Frank, *The Diary of a Young Girl*. New York: Bantam Books, 1993.
11. Ibid.
12. Babylonian Talmud, *Rosh Hashanah* 16b.
13. *Pirke Avot* 3:9.
14. Harold Schulweis, *In God's Mirror: Reflections and Essays*. Hoboken, N.J.: KTAV Publishing Co., 1990.
15. Babylonian Talmud, *Shabbat* 88b.
16. Samson Raphael Hirsch, *Horeb: A Philosophy of Jewish Law and Observances*. London: Soncino Press, 1962.
17. *Pirke Avot* 2:14.
18. *Pirke Avot* 5:11.
19. *Bereshit Rabbah* 8:5.
20. Psalm 85:12.
21. *Pirke Avot* 3:14.
22. Adapted from *Wisdom of the Ages*. New York: National Jewish Center for Learning and Leadership, 1993.
23. Babylonian Talmud, *Eruvin* 54a.
24. *Sichot HaRav* 288.
25. *Pirke Avot* 1:17.
26. *Sefat Emet,* 135b.
27. Adapted from *Vision & Voices,* New York: National Jewish Center for Learning and Leadership, 1994.

JULY

1. *Guide for the Perplexed* 1:31.
2. Marvin Lowenthal, trans., *The Memoirs of Glückel of Hameln*. New York: Schocken Books, 1977.
3. Used as the introduction to the *Havdalah* ceremony.
4. Adapted from Harold Schulweis, *In God's Mirror: Reflections and Essays*. Hoboken, N.J.: KTAV Publishing Co., 1990.
5. Moses Montefiore. *Liberal Judaism*. New York: Macmillan, 1907.
6. Ellen M. Umansky and Dianne Aston, eds., *Four Centuries of Jewish Women's Spirituality*. Boston: Beacon Press, 1992.
7. *Pesikta de Rab Kahana*, 29.
8. Etty Hillesum, *An Interrupted Life*. New York: Pantheon Books, 1983.
9. Translation adapted by Rami M. Shapiro.
10. *Sichot HaRav* 6a.
11. Translation adapted by Rami M. Shapiro.
12. Babylonian Talmud, *Taanit* 7a.
13. Samson Raphael Hirsch, *Judaism Eternal*. London: Soncino Press, 1956.
14. Leo Baeck, *The Essence of Judaism*. New York: Schocken Books, 1978.
15. Babylonian Talmud, *Eruvin* 54a.
16. Babylonian Talmud, *Sukkah* 49b.
17. *Mishle Binyamin*.
18. Lawrence Kushner, *God Was in This Place and I, i Did Not Know: Finding Self, Spirituality and Ultimate Meaning*. Woodstock, Vt.: Jewish Lights Publishing, 1991.
19. Martin Buber, *The Way of Man*. Seacacus, N.J.: Citadel Press, 1995.
20. *Torat Hayim—Living Torah,* vol. 1, no. 15 (January 12, 1997).
21. *Ben Sira* 6:14.
22. *Learn Torah with . . . Parashat Shoftim,* vol. 2, no. 48 (August 17, 1996).

AUGUST

1. *Tanchuma*, Pekudei 3.
2. *Pesikta de Rab Kahana* 12:25.
3. Leviticus 19:15.
4. Babylonian Talmud, *Shevuot* 30a.
5. Babylonian Talmud, *Nedarim* 32a.
6. Ben Sira 7:6.
7. Commentary to Job 5:21.
8. *Pirke Avot* 4:2.
9. *Pesikta de Rav Kahana* 12:25.
10. Adapted from *Sacred Time*. New York: National Jewish Center for Learning and Leadership, 1993.

11. Samson Raphael Hirsch, *The Nineteen Letters of Judaism*. New York: Feldheim Publishers, 1960.
12. Adapted from Joseph B. Soleveitchik, *The Lonely Man of Faith*. Wheaton, Ill.: Doubleday, 1965.
13. Adapted from *Sacred Time*. New York: National Jewish Center for Learning and Leadership, 1992.
14. Midrash HaGadol, Genesis 41:1.
15. Babylonian Talmud, *Berakhot* 17a.
16. Babylonian Talmud, *Berakhot* 34b.
17. *Sifre* No. 33 to Deuteronomy 6:6.
18. *Zohar,* i 85b.
19. Lawrence Kushner, *Honey from the Rock: An Easy Introduction to Jewish Mysticism*. Woodstock, Vt.: Jewish Lights Publishing, 1990.
20. Babylonian Talmud, *Yoma* 86b.
21. *Avot de Rabbi Natan* 31b.
22. *Torat Hayim—Living Torah,* vol. 1 (March 17, 1997).
23. Marcia Falk, *The Book of Blessings*. San Francisco: HarperSanFrancisco, 1996.
24. *Learn Torah With . . . Parashat Miketz,* vol. 2, no. 10 (December 23, 1995).
25. Babylonian Talmud, *Shabbat* 64b.

SEPTEMBER

1. *Pirke Avot* 2:4.
2. Babylonian Talmud, *Sotah* 14a.
3. Babylonian Talmud, *Kiddushin* 49b.
4. *Pirke Avot* 2:4.
5. *Learn Torah With . . . Parashat Bo,* vol. 2, no. 15 (January 27, 1996).
6. *Bet Aharon.*
7. *Mekhilta* 19:5.
8. Martin Buber, *Tales of the Hasidim*. New York: Schocken Books, 1975.
9. Babylonian Talmud, *Rosh Hashanah* 26b.
10. Rosh Hashanah liturgy.
11. Adin Steinsaltz, *The Strife of the Spirit*. Northvale, N.J.: Jason Aronson, Inc., 1988.
12. Lawerence S. Kushner, *Eyes Remade for Wonder: A Lawrence Kushner Reader*. Woodstock, Vt.: Jewish Lights Publishing, 1998.
13. From the *siddur.*
14. Abraham Joshua Heschel, *Who Is Man?* Stanford, Calif.: Stanford University Press, 1965.
15. *Guide for the Perplexed,* 3.49.
16. *Orim: A Jewish Journal at Yale,* vol. 3, no.1 (Autumn 1987): 126.

17. *Pirke Avot* 2:3.

18. Henry Slonimsky, *Essays.* Cincinnati: Hebrew Union College Press, 1967.

19. *Mishneh Torah,* Hilkhot Teshuvah 2:2.

20. Martin Buber, *Tales of the Hasidim.* New York: Schocken Books, 1975.

21. Excerpted from a *D'var Torah* delivered Rosh Hashanah 1989.

22. Lawerence Kushner, *Eyes Remade for Wonder: A Lawrence Kushner Reader.* Woodstock, Vt.: Jewish Lights Publishing, 1998.

23. Record Group 23, Henrietta Szold Readings and Quotations. Hadassah Archives, New York.

24. *The Jewish Press,* May 24, 1996.

25. Prayer said upon going to sleep at night.

26. Maurice Samuel, *The Professor and the Fossil: Some Observations on Arnold Toynbee's* A Study of History. New York: Knopf Books, 1956.

27. *Torat Hayim-Living Torah,* vol. 1.

28. *Numbers Rabbah* 19:27.

29. Ben Sira 3:9.

OCTOBER

1. Jerusalem Talmud, *Berakhot* 9:1.

2. Adapted from *Sacred Times.* New York: National Jewish Center for Learning and Leadership, 1992.

3. Sacrifices of Cain and Abel, 6.

4. Babylonian Talmud, *Bava Kamma* 38a.

5. Kushner in Lawrence A. Hoffman, ed., *My People's Prayer Book: Traditional Prayers, Modern Commentaries—Vol. 2, The Amidah.* Woodstock, Vt.: Jewish Lights Publishing, 1998.

6. Babylonian Talmud, *Berakhot* 64a.

7. Samuel Raphael Hirsch, *God's Protective Covering.*

8. Adin Steinsaltz, *The Strife of the Spirit.* Northvale, N.J.: Jason Aronson Publishers, 1996.

9. Yiddish proverb.

10. Babylonian Talmud, *Ta'anit* 11a–b.

11. Babylonian Talmud, *Berakhot* 57b.

12. Marvin Lowenthal, trans., *The Memoirs of Glückel of Hameln.* New York: Schocken Books, 1977.

13. Babylonian Talmud, *Sukkah* 46a–b.

14. Record Group 23, Henrietta Szold Readings and Quotations. Hadassah Archives, New York.

15. *Ecclesiastes Rabbah* 13.

16. *Orot HaKodesh.*

17. Allegorical Interpretations, 1.2.

18. *Genesis Rabbah* 34:10.

19. Adapted from Ira Stone, *Seeking the Path to Life: Theological Meditations on God and the Nature of People, Love, Life and Death*. Woodstock, Vt.: Jewish Lights Publishing, 1992.

20. *Shekel HaKodesh* 12c.

21. Zohar ii, 11b.

22. Zohar ii, 84a.

23. Adapted from *Learn Torah With . . . Parashat Yitro*, vol. 2, no. 17 (February 10, 1996).

24. *Pirke Avot* 1:13.

25. Deuteronomy Rabbah, *Re'eh*.

26. Abraham Joshua Heschel, *Man's Quest for Freedom*. New York: Charles Scribner's Sons, 1954.

27. Adapted from Jeffrey Salkin, *Being God's Partner: How to Find the Hidden Link Between Spirituality and Your Work*. Woodstock, Vt.: Jewish Lights Publishing, 1994.

28. Yiddish proverb.

NOVEMBER

1. Babylonian Talmud, *Hullin* 89a.

2. *Atlantic Monthly,* vol. 208, no. 5 (November 1961):85–87.

3. Adapted from *Sacred Times*. New York: National Jewish Center for Learning and Leadership, 1992.

4. Leo Baeck, *The Foundation of Judaism and Ethics*. New York: Macmillan Press, 1929.

5. Record Group 23, Henrietta Szold Readings and Quotations. Hadassah Archives, New York.

6. *Sefer Hachinukh* #601.

7. *Emet V'Emunah*. Jerusalem: S. Weinfeld, 1940.

8. *Genesis Rabbah* 22:6.

9. Ben Sira 5:11.

10. Babylonian Talmud, *Bava Kamma* 3b.

11. Excerpt from Barry Holtz, "*Yahrzeit* Poem," *Response Magazine* (Summer 1974).

12. Bachya Ibn Pakuda, *Duties of the Heart*. Jerusalem: Feldheim Publishers, 1970.

13. Marge Piercy, "The Seven Pentacles," in *Circles of Water*. New York: Knopf, 1982.

14. Babylonian Talmud, *Berakhot* 35a.

15. Adapted from Jeffrey Salkin, *Being God's Partner: How to Find the Hidden Link Between Spirituality and Your Work*. Woodstock, Vt.: Jewish Lights Publishing, 1994.

16. Babylonian Talmud, *Pesachim* 68b.

17. Book of Barukh.

18. *Iggeret Teman*.

19. Adapted from Ira Stone, *Seeking the Path to Life: Theological Meditations on God and the Nature of People, Love, Life and Death*. Woodstock, Vt.: Jewish Lights Publishing, 1992.
20. Babylonian Talmud, *Shabbat*.
21. Babylonian Talmud, *Bava Metzia* 58b.
22. Adapted from *Sacred Times*. New York: National Jewish Center for Learning and Leadership, 1992.
23. *Avot de Rabbi Natan* 12:10.
24. Mordecai Kaplan, *The Meaning of God in Modern Jewish Religion*. New York: Jewish Reconstructionist Foundation, 1962.
25. Martin Buber, *Tales of the Hasidim*. New York: Schocken Books, 1975.
26. Anne Roiphe, "Taking Down the Christmas Tree," *Tikkun,* vol. 4, no. 6.

DECEMBER

1. Jewish folk saying.
2. *Mishneh Torah, Hilkhot Hanukkah* 4:6.
3. Irving Greenberg, *The Jewish Way*. New York: Touchstone, 1988.
4. II Maccabees 5:19.
5. Jerusalem Talmud, *Hagigah* 2:1.
6. Babylonian Talmud, *Sanhedrin* 105b.
7. *Guide for the Perplexed* 3:24.
8. Babylonian Talmud, *Shabbat* 32a.
9. *Tanchuma, Vayakel.*
10. Yiddish proverb, based on Babylonian Talmud, *Megillah* 31b.
11. *Pirke Avot* 2:6.
12. Adapted from Jeffrey Salkin, *Being God's Partner: How to Find the Hidden Link Between Spirituality and Your Work*. Woodstock, Vt.: Jewish Lights Publishing, 1994.
13. Babylonian Talmud, *Shabbat* 31a.
14. Muriel Rukeseyer, "Letter to the Front" in *Jewish Women in America,* ed. Paula E. Hyman and Deborah Dash Moore, eds. New York: Routledge, 1977.
15. *Pirke Avot* 4:1.
16. Abraham Joshua Heschel, *The Insecurity of Freedom*. New York: Schocken Books, 1972.
17. *Leviticus Rabbah* 13:3.
18. *Pirke Avot* 4:1.
19. Albert Vorspan and David Saperstein, *Tough Choices: Jewish Perspectives on Social Justice*. New York: Union of American Hebrew Congregations, 1992.

GLOSSARY OF TERMS

Afikomen: The piece of matzah that has been hidden and then found during a seder, the Passover celebratory meal. It is then shared among the seder participants. Usually, a reward is given to the finder of the *afikomen*.

Al chet: For these sins, confessional on Yom Kippur.

Bal tashchit: The commandment not to be wasteful.

Beit Midrash: Study house.

Beshert: Yiddish word which literally means "fated." Commonly used to refer to one's intended soul mate or life partner.

Binah: Insight and understanding, intelligence; the third *sefirah* in the Kabbalistic understanding of the world.

Birkat hamazon: Grace after meals.

Chametz: Foods that contain leaven, which is prohibited during Passover.

Chesed: Act of kindness.

Chesed shel emet: The highest form of loving acts of kindness. It refers to taking care of ritual arrangements for those who have died.

Cheshbon hanefesh: An accounting of the soul; introspection.

Da'at: Knowledge; in the Kabbalah, it results from a harmonizing between the *sefirot* of *chokhmah* and *binah*.

Derekh Eretz: Behaving civilly.

Emet: Truth.

Emunah: Faith, faithfulness.

Gemilut chasadim: Loving deeds of kindness, such as visiting the sick, feeding the hungry, comforting mourners.

HaMakom: The Place; a name for God.

Havdalah: The ritual (using wine, candle, and spices) marking the end of Shabbat and the beginning of the rest of the week. It acknowledges the distinction between sacred and profane time.

Hefker: Ownerlessness; anarchy.

Kavannah: Intention; refers to the inspired motivation behind prayer.

Kevittel: A short note containing a short petition for God's blessings.

Kristallnacht: Literally, "the night of broken or shattered glass." Refers to the Nazi attacks on Jews on November 9–10, 1938. The name developed because the windows of Jewish stores and homes were broken throughout Germany, ostensibly a retaliation for the assassination by a Jew of Ernst Vom Rath, third secretary of the German embassy in Paris. Kristallnacht marked a turning point in the Nazis' treatment of German and Austrian Jews.

L'chayim: For life, used as a common toast.

Lashon hara: Slanderous talk, gossip.

Megillah: Literally, "a scroll." Refers to the books of the Bible kept on single rolled scrolls; the term is generally used to refer to the scroll of Esther, which is read during Purim.

Mezuzah: Literally "doorposts." It refers to the both the parchment on which portions of the Torah are written and the case in which it is placed. The *mezuzah* is placed on the right-hand side of a doorpost.

Midrash: Refers to the nonlegal sections of the Talmud and the rabbinic books containing biblical interpretations; sometimes referred to as "legend."

Minyan: Quorum of ten for a prayer service.

Mishnah: Legal codification of Oral Law, compiled by Rabbi Judah the Prince in the early third century.

Mitzvah: Plural, *mitzvot*. Refers to 613 commandments traditionally acknowledged to have been given by God. Colloquially used to refer to a good deed, especially when pronounced as *mitzveh*.

Musar: Ethical guidance and advice encouraging strict behavior regarding the Halakhah or Law. It developed into a full-scale literature beginning in the nineteenth century.

Nechemta: Final word of consolation and uplift, a literary convention of the Rabbis.

Omer: See *Sefirat HaOmer*.

Piyyut: Plural, *piyyutim*. Medieval liturgical poems written for special occasions and festivals.

Rachamim: Mercy.

Rebbe: The charismatic spiritual leader of Hasidic sects.

Rosh Chodesh: The first day(s) of the new moon.

Schlepped: Yiddish expression, carried in a burdensome manner.

Seder: Hebrew word for "order." Refers to the Passover meal, which celebrates the holiday and retells the Exodus through reading of the Haggadah.

Sefirat haomer: The counting of the Omer is the period of time between Passover and Shavuot. During this time, certain observances of mourning are maintained such as refraining from cutting hair and from getting married. It is also a time when we spiritually prepare ourselves for the giving of the Torah, which takes place on Shavuot.

Shema: Often called the watchword of the Jewish faith, this prayer is the closest thing to a Jewish creed. It proclaims the unity of one God.

Sukkah: The temporary hut that we construct during the holiday of Sukkot.

Tanakh: Refers to the Hebrew Bible. Developed from the initial letters of *Torah, Nevi'im,* and *Ketuvim*—Pentateuch, Prophets, and Hagiographa.

Tefillah: Prayer.

Tekiah: The blast of the shofar; also, a particular shofar sound.

Teshuvah: Repentance, a return to the ways of God. Although we are supposed to do *teshuvah* all year long, it is the focus of the High Holiday period and the month that precedes it.

Tikkun Olam: Mystical notion of repairing the world.

Tisha b'Av: An observance on the ninth of Av that primarily marks the destruction of both Temples, as well as other mournful periods of Jewish history.

Tokhechah: Rebuke, traditionally articulated by the Prophets on behalf of God.

Tzaddik: Righteous person, often refers to a hisidic rabbi or miracle worker.

Tzedakah: Righteous giving through charity; the word is derived from the root for "justice."

Tzedek: Justice.

Yahrzeit: From the Yiddish, the anniversary of one's death. It is commemorated by lighting a 24-hour candle and saying the Mourner's Kaddish.

Yetzer hara: The evil inclination, that part of our psyche that drives us for food, shelter, sex, and so on. It is not wholly negative, since it also drives us to procreate. Sometimes it is translated as the libido. The *yetzer hara* and the *yetzer tov,* the good inclination, together make up the full human being.

Yetzer tov: The good inclination. Keeps the *Yetzer HaRah* in check. Sometimes translated as conscience or superego.

Yom HaAtzma'ut: Israel Independence Day.

Yom HaShoah: Day of commemorating the Holocaust. It is observed one week prior to *Yom HaZikaron*.

Yom HaZikaron: Day of remembrance for Israel's fallen soldiers, observed for the 24-hour period just prior to *Yom HaAtzma'ut*.

Yom Yerushalayim: A relatively new holiday that celebrates Jerusalem's reunification at the conclusion of the Six Day War in 1967. It is celebrated on the 28th day of Iyar, which typically falls in May.

Zion: Another name for Jerusalem.

OUR TEACHERS: AUTHORS OF QUOTED TEXTS

Texts are the touchstone of Jewish spirituality. The authors of individual texts become our teachers as we study their writings.

Abraham ben Samuel ha-Levi Hasdai: Early thirteenth-century translator and Hebrew poet in Barcelona.

Isaac Abravanel or (Abrabanel): (1437–1509) The last of the great Jewish statesmen in Spain, he moved to Italy after the expulsion of the Jews. His encyclopedic knowledge extended to Christian literature. Although he wrote a commentary on Maimonides' *Guide for the Perplexed,* he eventually argued that Judaism cannot be reduced to a creed, since every line in the Torah is to be given unconditional credence.

Grace Aguilar: (1816–1847) English author of Portuguese Marrano descent, who wrote novels addressed primarily to Jewish women.

Ahad HaAm: (1856–1927) Literally, "one of the people," the pen name of Asher Ginzberg. He thought that science had refuted religion and substituted a high-level appreciation for humanity and the notion of nationhood for God and revelation. Considered to be the foremost proponent of Cultural Zionism, he believed that the Jewish people has an unusual genius for high culture centered on ethics and that the Jewish state would be the spiritual center of Judaism.

Baal Shem Tov: (1700–1760) Literally, "master of the good name, "also called the *Besht.* The name Baal Shem Tov was used by the founder of Hasidism, Israel Ben Eliezer, a charismatic leader who became known through the oral tradition of his students who handed down tales of his travels and good works.

Leo Baeck: (1873–1956) A liberal theologian, he won recognition after the publication of the *Essence of Judaism.* He had a unique nonphilosophic approach to human piety and believed that ethics without religion reduced to mere moralism. The only modern Jewish theologian who endured and survived Nazi death camps, he contended that evil was the misuse of human freedom.

David Ben-Gurion: (1886–1973) Played a decisive role in the establishment of the State of Israel and was its first prime minister and minister of defense.

Mikha Yosef Berdyczewsky: (1865–1921) Critic of the Diaspora, he felt that it was detrimental to the true Jewish spirit. Influenced by Nietzche in his call for radical human change, he also stressed the value of physical development and military strength. He believed that universalism, not particularism, was the cause of what he called "the Diaspora mentality," and he felt that Judaism as a religion should be dissolved so nationalism could grow.

Baruch Bokser: (1945–1990) Rabbi, professor of rabbinics and ancient Jewish history at The Jewish Theological Seminary of America in New York. Among his many publications is *The Origin of the Seder.*

Martin Buber: (1878–1965) A religious existentialist influenced by Hasidic thought, most remembered for his dialogic I-and-Thou approach to relationships with God and between people.

Simcha Bunem of Przysucha: (1765–1827) Hasidic rebbe in Poland who was known for his intellectual rigor and disbelief in miracle workers.

Nina Beth Cardin: Contemporary rabbi, writer, and editor. She also lectures on a variety of Jewish issues, with special emphasis on women's contemporary spiritual matters.

Marcus Ehrenpreis: (1869–1951) Rabbi in Sweden and Galicia, author of *The Soul of the East,* 1928.

Albert Einstein: (1879–1955) Physicist and Nobel prize winner; discoverer of the Theory of Relativity.

Elimelekh of Lizensk: (1717–1787) Founder of the Polish and Hungarian branches of Hasidim.

Mendl Epstein: Contemporary rabbi and writer. Author of two books about Jewish law and women.

Marcia Falk: Contemporary American-Jewish poet, translator, and feminist linguist, who has created blessings using innovative form and language to introduce feminist concepts into Jewish prayers.

Rabbi Louis Finkelstein: (1895–1991) Scholar and administrator who was chancellor of The Jewish Theological Seminary of America. Was influential in blending traditional elements with Conservative Judaism.

Anne Frank: (1929–1945) Teenage author of a diary composed while she and her family were hiding from Nazis in Amsterdam. Died in Bergen-Belsen in 1945.

Laura Geller: Contemporary rabbi of Temple Emanuel in Beverly Hills, California. One of the first women ordained as rabbi by Hebrew Union College–Jewish Institute of Religion, she has contributed to Jewish liturgy and ritual that have a feminist perspective.

Glückel of Hamln: Eighteenth-century German-Jewish woman whose diaries shed light on the economic status and business dealings of the Jews in that period.

Irving (Yitz) Greenberg: Contemporary rabbi; president of Jewish Life Partnership/Kol Israel Haverim; founder and president emeritus of CLAL: The National Center for Learning and Leadership; author and speaker.

Menachem Hacohen: A former member of the Israeli Parliament.

Theodor Herzl: (1860–1904) Founder of modern political Zionism. His solution to anti-Semitism was the creation of a Jewish state, which he describes in his book *The Jewish State*. He presided over five Zionist Congresses. He is well known for his famous phrase of optimism, "If you will it, it is no dream."

Abraham Joshua Heschel: (1907–1972) Philosopher who attempted to illumine the relationship between God and people; this relationship provides the foundation for religion. Heschel articulated a contemporary theology that is the result of insights garnered from traditional sources which shed light on contemporary problems and conflicts. He argued that religion has faded in the modern world because we have not attempted to recover the dimension of reality in which a divine encounter might take place.

Etty Hillesum: (1914–1943) A young Dutch woman who chronicled in her journal the experience of living in Amsterdam during the years 1941–1943 under Nazi occupation. In 1943 she was deported to Auschwitz, where she died.

Samson Raphael Hirsch: (1808–1888) Probably the foremost spokesperson for Orthodox Judaism in the nineteenth century in Germany. Best known for his philosophy, which melded traditional Torah study with secular education. Also an ardent opponent of Reform Judaism.

Barry Holtz: Professor of Jewish Education at The Jewish Theological Seminary of America and program consultant for the Mandel Foundation.

Hasdai ibn Crescas: (ca. 1340–1410) As chief rabbi of the Aragonian Jewish communities, he was one of the most influential leaders of Spanish Jewry and worked hard toward its reconstruction following the terrible persecution of 1391. His magnum opus, *The Light of the Lord,* is a collection of dogmas listed in order of their importance.

Abraham ibn Ezra: (1092–1167) Famous Spanish Jewish grammarian and biblical exegete. His Bible commentaries were based on linguistic and factual examinations of the text.

Moses ibn Ezra: (ca. 1055–ca. 1135) Spanish Hebrew poet and philosopher.

Solomon ibn Gabriol: (ca. 1020–1057) Poet and philosopher who lived in Spain. His writings reflect mystical tendencies and scientific knowledge, especially of astronomy. His major philosophical work, *Mekor Chaim,* is devoted primarily to the issues of matter and form and is written in the style of a dialogue between student and teacher.

Bachya Ibn Pakuda: (mid-eleventh century) A moral philosopher who lived in Muslim Spain. His major work, *Duties of the Heart,* was written in the year 1000 and was a major influence in pietistic literature.

Aryeh Kaplan: Contemporary rabbi and author whose translations and teaching have made mystical Jewish teachings accessible to English-speaking beginners for the first time.

Mordecai Kaplan: (1881–1983) Philosopher; founder of Reconstructionism. He defined Judaism as an evolving religious civilization. Also founded the Young Israel movement (of young Orthodox Jews who wanted more than their synagogues were offering them) and developed the idea of the bat mitzvah and the concept of a synagogue center.

David Kimchi: (1160–1235) Also known as Radak; Franco-Spanish commentator on the Bible. He provided students with logical, grammatical explanations of difficult words and passages.

Kaufmann Kohler: (1893–1926) Rabbi and radical thinker who influenced the early direction of the Reform movement through his radical program adopted at the Pittsburgh conference of the Central Conference of American Rabbis.

Abraham Isaac Kook: (1865–1935) Religious thinker and first Ashkenazic Chief Rabbi of Palestine. His work became an important bridge between the Orthodox and secular pioneers during the early years of building the State of Israel.

Janusz Korczak: (1879–1942) Polish author, and progressive educator, who headed Jewish orphanages in Warsaw from 1911 until his death in Treblinka.

Rebbe of Koznitz: (1733–1814) Israel ben Shabbtei Hapstein Kozienice, Polish hasidic rebbe and preacher who was well schooled in both talmudic and Kabbalistic teachings.

Rabbi Levi Yitzchak of Berdichev: (1740–1810) Hasidic rebbe who consolidated the Hasidic movement in Central Poland and Luthuania, he was one of the most famous rebbes in the third generation of Hasidic leadership.

Moses Maimonides: (1135–1204) Moses ben Maimon, also called the Rambam, perhaps one of the greatest thinkers in all of Jewish history. Trained as a physician, Maimonides was also a commentator and philosopher. Under the influence of Aristotelian thought as articulated by Arabic philosophers of the Middle Ages, he was best known for his *Guide for the Perplexed* and his *Mishneh Torah,* an accessible compilation of Jewish law.

Benjamin Mandelstamm: (1806–1886) Hebrew author who was a staunch supporter of the Haskalah (Enlightenment). He encouraged the Russian government to forbid the printing of the Talmud and to close down religious schooling in order to compel secular education on Jewish children.

Menachem Mendl of Kotzk: (1787–1859) Hasidic leader known for his furious zeal and harsh practices.

Moses Montefiore: (1784–1865) English Jewish philanthropist and community worker, related by marriage to the Rothschild family. Amassed a fortune as a stockbroker and investment banker. He used his position and his finances to struggle for Jewish emancipation in England and contributed funds for economic development, schools, and orphanages in Palestine. During his lifetime he was the principal spokesman for world Jewry.

Nachman of Breslov: (1772–1810) The great-grandson of the Baal Shem Tov and the founder of the Breslover Hasidim. One distinctive Breslov practice is *hitbod-*

idut, which means "being in solitude." In addition to reciting daily prayers, Breslover Hasidim try to spend an hour alone each day in meditation. Nachman is still considered to be the leader of the Breslover Hasidim, since his followers believe that no other leader can follow as his successor.

Philo of Alexandria: (ca. 20 B.C.E.–50 C.E.) Jewish philosopher who was part of the Jewish aristocracy in Alexandria, Egypt. Philo wrote in Greek and is best known for his biblical allegorical interpretations of the Bible.

Marge Piercy: An American Jewish poet and novelist, whose work is influenced by her political activism, her feminism, and her Judaism.

Ann Roiphe: Contemporary author and journalist.

Franz Rosenzweig: (1886–1929) Philosopher and theologian who is best known for his book *Star of Redemption.* An exponent of existentialism, he rejected traditional philosophical methods and bases his belief in God in personal, not objective, experience.

Muriel Rukeseyer: (1913–1980) Award-winning poet and political activist who stressed the interconnectedness of people and events.

Israel Salanter: (1810–1883) Israel Ben Ze'ev Wolf, founder of the Musar movement, which stressed ethical teachings.

Maurice Samuel: (1895–1972) American author and translator of Yiddish literature; ardent Zionist who advocated the adoption of the Balfour Declaration, which called for giving land for a Jewish state.

David Saperstein: Contemporary rabbi; director of Religious Action Center of Reform Judaism in Washington, D.C.

Harold Schulweis: Contemporary rabbi of Valley Beth Shalom in Encino, California. Author of many articles and books, including *For Those Who Can't Believe.*

Hannah Senesh: (1921–1944) A gifted poet born in Budapest. In 1943 she joined parachutists from Palestine who jumped into Nazi-occupied Europe on rescue missions. At age 23 she was captured and executed.

Shlomo of Karlin: (1638–1792) Lithuanian Hasidic rebbe who became the head of the Karlin Hasidim in 1792.

Rachel Simon: British Jewish woman of the late nineteenth century whose insightful diary and personal papers reveal a great deal about the Jewish community in which she lived.

Henry Slominsky: (1884–1970) Philosopher and professor at Hebrew Union College–Jewish Institute of Religion.

Joseph B. Soloveitchik: (1903–1993) Foremost proponent of modern Orthodoxy, the fusion of classical halakhic Judaism and American culture. For many years he was the leading spirit of Yeshiva University and the Rabbincal Council of America.

Baruch Spinoza: (1632–1677) Dutch philosopher who questioned many of Judaism's core teachings. Excommunicated in 1656 for his heretical views. Today, Spinoza is often considered to be the father of modern philosophy.

Israel Spira: Rebbe of Blushov. Before emigration to the United States, he was known as the Rebbe of Pruchnik, where he had been the rabbi until 1932. He was one of the first survivors to arrive in the United States after World War II. Many of his stories about surviving the Holocaust are compiled in *Hasidic Tales of the Holocaust.*

Adin Steinsaltz: Contemporary Israeli talmudist who has prepared a modern Hebrew and English translation of the Talmud.

Henrietta Szold: (1860–1945) Ardent Zionist philanthropist and founder of Hadassah. In 1918 she was responsible for the dispatch of the American Zionist Medical Units to Palestine; in 1927 she was the first woman to become a member of the Zionist Executive. After the Nazi rise to power she became the active leader of Youth Aliyah to bring young people from Europe to Palestine.

Mark Twain: (1835–1910) Pseudonym of Samuel Clemens, American writer and humorist, whose work is characterized by broad humor and biting satire.

Albert Vorspan: Former vice-president of Union of American Hebrew Congregations, and director of its Commission on Social Action.

Lillian Wald: (1867–1940) Social worker who established the Henry Street Settlement on New York's Lower East Side.

Elie Wiesel: Writer, primarily of fiction, who is the pivotal figure in intellectual culture related to the Holocaust.

Elaine Zecher: Rabbi at Temple Israel in Boston.

Sheldon Zimmerman: President of Hebrew Union College–Jewish Institute of Religion.

SOURCES OF
QUOTED TEXTS

While the texts we have shared in these pages provide the reader with a great deal of insight and inspiration, it is important to realize that most of them come from larger works. These are described below.

Apocrypha: Religious writings, dating from the second century B.C.E. to the first century C.E., which are not included in the Hebrew Bible although they are in the Christian Bible.

Avot de Rabbi Natan: Small tractate that provides an expansion to the tractate of the Mishnah called *Pirke Avot* (Ethics of the Fathers). Ascribed to Rabbi Nathan the Babylonian.

Ben Sira: (ca. 170 B.C.E.) A Jerusalem sage who belonged to the class of learned scribes. He was the author of *Wisdom of Ben Sira,* also called *Ecclesiasticus,* which was translated into Greek by his grandson in 132 B.C.E. and incorporated in the Apocrypha. The book contains wise axioms and is similar in form to the biblical book of Proverbs.

Ecclesiastes: The fourth of the five scrolls in the Hagiographa section of the Bible. The author (called Kohelet in Hebrew and traditionally identified as King Solomon) seeks to discern the purpose of human life, with all its trials, but finds no spiritual support in faith or intellect. The book's motto is "Vanity of vanities, all is vanity." The author does insist, however, that God's laws must be kept, even if doing so results in tragedy.

Exodus Rabbah: Midrashim on Exodus. The first part of this was edited no earlier than the tenth century C.E. and the second half is thought to have been compiled earlier.

Ezekiel: The third of the major prophets, Ezekiel witnessed the destruction of Jerusalem and Judea and went into exile to Babylonia. His prophecies have great poetic beauty and mystic power. The most famous chapter (chapter 37) describes his vision of a valley of dry bones that are resurrected, symbolizing the rebirth of Israel.

Genesis Rabbah: Midrashim on Genesis edited in Palestine in about 425 C.E.

Haggadah: Literally, "the telling (of the story)." A book that contains the story of the Exodus from Egypt told in a ritualized form for use during the Passover seder.

Isaiah: (740–701 B.C.E.) Prophet in Jerusalem who protested against moral laxity. His famous vision described a time when "nation shall not lift up sword against nation, neither shall men learn war anymore" (Isaiah 2:4). He is the first of the three major prophets.

Jeremiah: (7th–6th centuries B.C.E.) Prophet belonging to the priestly family of Anathoth near Jerusalem, he witnessed the destruction of Jerusalem. His prophecies foretell the doom of his people as punishment for their sins. Jeremiah is the second of the major prophets.

Jerusalem Talmud: Compilations of the laws and discussion of the early rabbis in Israel, mainly in the Academy of Tiberias. Much smaller in length than the Babylonian Talmud and considered less authoritative; its final form was completed sometime at the beginning of the fifth century C.E.

Lamentations: Third of the five scrolls in the Hagiographa section of the Bible. It contains five chapters of elegies and mourning over the destruction by the Babylonians of Judea, Jerusalem, and the Temple. According to rabbinic tradition, the author was Jeremiah. Lamentations is read in the synagogue on the fast of Tisha B'av, which commemorates the destruction of the Temple.

Mekhilta: Oldest rabbinic commentary on the Book of Exodus, dated no earlier than the fifth century in Palestine.

Micah: (8th century B.C.E.) Prophet in Judea who spoke for the people against oppression of the ruling classes. He was the first to threaten erring Judeans with exile to Babylon. His book is among the twelve books of the so-called minor prophets.

Midrash Tehillim: Midrashim on Psalms that contain material dated as early as the third century and as late as the thirteenth century.

Midrash to Proverbs: Midrashim on Proverbs edited most likely in Babylonia in approximately the mid-fifth century.

Mishnah: Legal codification, expounding the Bible and constituting the core of Oral Law, compiled and edited by Rabbi Judah the Prince in the early part of the third century.

Pirke Avot: The volume of the Mishnah that contains teachings on interpersonal, societal, and spiritual concerns. Also called the *Ethics of the Fathers*.

Pirke De Rebbe Eliezer: *Midrashim* which date from the eighth century C.E.

Proverbs: A biblical book. The second in the Hagiographa, it is a collection of moral sayings.

Psalms: First book in the Hagiographa section of the Bible, it consists of 150 psalms traditionally ascribed to King David, who is often called the Psalmist.

Seder Eliahu Rabbah: Also called *Aggadat Bereshit,* a collection of homiletic *midrashim.*

Sefer Hachinukh: A book which educators place in the category of *mitzvah* education, it follows the weekly Torah reading and the *mitzvot* that emerge from each. It was written in thirteenth-century Spain by a father to his son.

Shulchan Arukh: Authoritative law code written by Joseph Caro, a sixteenth-century Spanish legal codifier. It is still recognized by traditional Jews throughout the world.

Song of Songs: First of the five scrolls incorporated in the biblical Hagiographa, it consists of a collection of poems about sexual love and courtship. The composition of the book has been attributed to King Solomon.

Songs of Songs Rabbah: *Midrashim* on the Song of Songs, edited in the fifth century in Palestine.

Zechariah: Prophet (6th century B.C.E.), whose prophecies are concerned with contemporary events and foretell the ingathering of the exiles and the expansion of Jerusalem. His book is one of the twelve books of the minor prophets.

Zohar: Mystical biblical commentary on sections of the Five Books of Moses and parts of the Hagiographa (Song of Songs, Ruth, Lamentations). It dwells on the mystery of creation and gives symbolic explanations of the stories and events in the Bible.

CONTRIBUTORS

Rabbi Judith Z. Abrams is the founder and director of Maqom: A Place for the Spiritually Searching, a school for adult Talmud study on the Internet. She is the author of books on the Talmud.

Rabbi Bradley Shavit Artson is the Dean of the Ziegler School of Rabbinic Studies at the University of Judaism. He served as rabbi of Congregation Eilat in Mission Viejo, CA, and is the author of *It's a Mitzvah! Jewish Living Step-by-Step.*

Rabbi Tsvi Blanchard is a senior teaching fellow at CLAL–National Jewish Center for Learning and Leadership.

Rabbi Lester Bronstein is the spiritual leader of Temple Beth Am Shalom in White Plains, New York, and a member of the *tzedakah* singing group Beged Kefet.

Rabbi Nina Beth Cardin has taught at The Jewish Theological Seminary of America and is former associate director of the National Center for Jewish Healing. She is the former editor of *Sh'ma* and is the author of *Tears of Sorrow, Seeds of Hope: A Jewish Spiritual Companion for Infertility and Pregnancy Loss* (Jewish Lights).

Rabbi Michael M. Cohen is spiritual leader of Israel Congregation in Manchester, Vermont, and lectures at Green Mountain College in nearby Poultney. He also serves on the faculty of the Arava Institute for Environmental Studies on Kibbutz Ketura in Israel.

Rabbi William Cutter is professor of education and modern Hebrew literature at Hebrew Union College–Jewish Institute of Religion. He is also a chaplain at UCLA Medical Center.

Rabbi Amy Eilberg is the co-founder of the National Center for Jewish Healing and has spent many years in Jewish hospice work in the Jewish community. She is a pastoral counselor in private practice in Palo Alto.

Rabbi Dov Peretz Elkins is the spiritual leader of The Jewish Center in Princeton, New Jersey, and is the author of many books.

Rabbi Edward Feinstein serves as a rabbi at Valley Beth Shalom in Encino, California, and is former director of Camp Ramah in Ojai, California.

Rabbi Mordecai Finley is co-rabbi of Makor Ohr Shalom in Los Angeles and is founding rabbi of Ohr HaTorah, also in Los Angeles.

Rabbi Nancy Flam is co-founder of the National Center for Jewish Healing and former director of Ruah Ami, Bay Area Jewish Healing Center in San Francisco.

Rabbi Elyse Frishman is the spiritual leader of Congregation B'nai Jeshurun in Franklin Lakes, New Jersey, and co-editor of the new Reform prayerbook project for the Central Conference of American Rabbis.

Rabbi David Gelfand is the spiritual leader of The Jewish Center of the Hamptons in East Hampton, New York.

Rabbi Neil Gillman is Professor of Jewish Philosophy at The Jewish Theological Seminary of America in New York. He is the author of *The Way Into Encountering God in Judaism* and *The Death of Death: Resurrection and Immortality in Jewish Thought* (Jewish Lights), and *Sacred Fragments: Recovering Theology for the Modern Jew,* winner of the National Jewish Book Award.

Rabbi James Stone Goodman is the spiritual leader of Temple Neve Shalom in St. Louis.

Rabbi Leonard Gordon is the spiritual leader of the Germantown Jewish Centre in Greater Philadelphia and is chairperson of the Board of Directors of the National Havurah Committee.

Rabbi Irving (Yitz) Greenberg is the president of Chaverim Kol Yisrael: Jewish Life Network, and is president emeritus and co-founder of CLAL–National Jewish Center for Learning and Leadership. He is the author of *The Jewish Way*.

Joel Lurie Grishaver is the creative chairperson of Torah Aura Productions and is the author of many books, including *The Binding of Isaac*. He received the Covenant Foundation award in 1998 for outstanding Jewish educators.

Rabbi Lawrence A. Hoffman is professor of liturgy at Hebrew Union College–Jewish Institute of Religion in New York and is principal investigator for Synagogue 2000. He is editor of the *My People's Prayer Book: Traditional Prayers, Modern Commentaries* series (Jewish Lights).

Rabbi Abie Ingber is the executive director of the Hillel Foundation at the University of Cincinnati and lectures at Hebrew Union College–Jewish Institute of Religion, Cincinnati.

Rabbi Elana Kanter serves as assistant rabbi at Temple Beth El in Birmingham, Alabama, and was the recipient of the Covenant Award for outstanding Jewish educators in 1998.

Rabbi Irwin Kula is president of CLAL–National Jewish Center for Learning and Leadership, and is spiritual leader of Aitz Hayim Center for Jewish Living in Chicago.

Rabbi Lawrence Kushner is spiritual leader of Congregation Beth El in Sudbury, Massachusetts, and lectures at Hebrew Union College–Jewish Institute of Religion, New York. He is the author of many books, including *Invisible Lines of Connection: Sacred Stories of the Ordinary* (Jewish Lights).

Dr. Lori Lefkovitz directs KOLOT, The Center for Jewish Women's and Gender Studies of the Reconstructionist Rabbinical College in greater Philadelphia.

Rabbi Adina Lewittes is the assistant dean of the rabbinical school of The Jewish Theological Seminary of America and is spiritual leader of Kol HaNeshamah in Englewood, New Jersey.

Arthur J. Magida is former senior editor for the *Baltimore Jewish Times*. He is the author of *Prophet of Rage* and *Land of the Poison Wind*, and co-editor of the two-volume *How to Be a Perfect Stranger: A Guide to Etiquette in Other People's Religious Ceremonies* (Jewish Lights).

Rabbi Vivian Mayer is the spiritual leader of Congregation B'nai Israel in Danbury, Connecticut.

Rabbi Michael Paley is executive director, Synagogue and Community Outreach Commission, UJA-Federation, New York.

Rabbi James Ponet is the director of the Joseph Slifka Center for Jewish Life at Yale University.

Rabbi Bernard S. Raskas is rabbi emeritus of Temple of Aaron Congregation in St. Paul–Minneapolis.

Rabbi Rachel T. Sabath is a senior fellow at CLAL–National Jewish Center for Learning and Leadership, and is co-author of *Preparing the Heart for the High Holy Days* and *Striving toward Virtue*.

Rabbi Jeffrey K. Salkin serves Community Synagogue in Port Washington, New York, and is author of *Putting God on the Guest List: How to Reclaim the Spiritual Meaning of Your Child's Bar or Bat Mitzvah, For Kids—Putting God on Your Guest List: How to Claim the Spiritual Meaning of Your Bar or Bat Mitzvah,* and *Being God's Partner: How to Find the Hidden Link Between Spirituality and Your Work* (all Jewish Lights).

Rabbi Sandy Eisenberg Sasso is co-rabbi of Congregation Beth-El Zedeck in Indianapolis and is the author of many children's books.

Rabbi Amy R. Scheinerman has served synagogues in Maryland, North Carolina, and Virginia.

Rabbi Harold Schulweis is the spiritual leader of Valley Beth Shalom in Encino, California, and is author of many books, including *For Those Who Can't Believe*.

Rabbi Rami Shapiro is spiritual leader of Congregation Beth Or in Miami. He founded the Rasheit Instititute for Jewish Spirituality, the Jewish Futures Fund, Lighthouse Books, and the Virtual Yeshiva.

Rabbi Mychal B. Springer is the director of chaplaincy at Beth Israel Hospital in New York City.

Rabbi Ira Stone is spiritual leader of Temple Beth Zion-Beth Israel in Philadelphia and is the author of *Seeking the Path to Life: Theological Meditations on God and the Nature of People, Love, Life and Death* (Jewish Lights).

Rabbi Joseph Telushkin serves as the spiritual leader of the Synagogue for the Performing Arts in Los Angeles. He was previously director of education at the Brandeis–Bardin Institute in Southern California and is the author of many books, including *Jewish Literacy*.

Rabbi Harlan J. Wechsler is the founding rabbi of Congregation Or Zarua in New York and is author of *What's So Bad About Guilt?* and *For Those Who Doubt*.

Sharon L. Wechter is a consultant in Jewish education and was formerly acquisitions editor for UAHC Press as well as associate chaplain at Williams College. She is director of the Bureau of Jewish Education in Bridgeport, Connecticut.

Rabbi David Wolpe is the spiritual leader of Sinai Temple in Los Angeles and is author of many books, including *What Jews Believe*.

THEME INDEX

Purpose: January 3, 30; February 3; April 27; May 11, 24, 27; July 27; October 8

Relationship with the Earth: February 12; March 16; June 17

Relationship with God: January 25; February 6, 7, 9, 18, 25, 27; April 3, 7; May 2, 4, 7, 21; June 27; July 6, 25, 28; August 22, 30; September 7, 16, 27; November 21; December 28

Relationships with Others: March 23; April 1; May 29; June 8; July 5; August 5, 25, 27; September 2, 24, 27; October 12, 24; November 14, 17; December 9, 25

Resilience: January 14; May 1, 12, 28; July 11; August 16; November 30; December 13

Revelation: March 18; April 7; June 16; November 25

Righteousness: January 11, 24, 31; September 28

Ritual: February 10; April 4, 10, 21; July 1

Self-knowledge/ Self-perception: January 1, 19; March 9, 14, 31; April 5, 11; July 5, 14; August 1; September 11; November 16

Shabbat: January 27; March 1; May 22; July 20, 22; September 24; November 28; December 24

Silence: March 4, 30; May 19; August 23

Slowing Down: January 27; March 1; July 20; August 21; November 15

Speech: March 4, 7; April 14; May 13; June 4, 7; November 11, 23; December 24

Spiritual Journey: January 2, 9, 22; February 26; April 24; May 25; July 27; August 24; September 23; October 3, 13, 17, 27; November 20; December 23

PERMISSIONS

We gratefully acknowledge permission from the following sources to reprint material or adapt from the original: Behrman House for excerpts from *A Tapestry in Time* by Rabbi Nina Beth Cardin © 1999; CLAL–The National Jewish Center for Learning and Leadership to reprint selections from *Sacred Times* © 1992, *Wisdom of the Ages* © 1993, *Visions and Voices* © 1994, and *Sh'ma: A Journal of Jewish Responsibility,* vol. 27, © 1997 (Rabbi Tsvi Blanchard, Rabbi Nina Beth Cardin, Rabbi Irving Greenberg, Rabbi Irwin Kula, Dr. Lori Lefkovitz, Rabbi Adina Lewittes, Rabbi Joseph Telushkin); Growth Associates Publishers, 212 Stuart Rd. E., Princeton, N.J. 08540, for excerpts from *Prescriptions for a Long and Happy Life: Age-Old Wisdom for the New Age* by Rabbi Dov Peretz Elkins © 1993 (Princeton, N.J.: Growth Associates, 1993); Jewish Lights Publishing for selections from *Being God's Partner: How to Find the Hidden Link Between Spirituality and Your Work* by Jeffrey K. Salkin © 1994, *Eyes Remade for Wonder: A Lawrence Kushner Reader* by Lawrence Kushner © 1998, *Honey from the Rock: An Introduction to Jewish Mysticism* by Lawrence Kushner © 1977 and 2000, and *Seeking the Path to Life: Theological Meditations on God and the Nature of People, Love, Life and Death* by Ira F. Stone © 1992; *The Jewish Week* for selections from its weekly "Sabbath Week" and "Musings" columns (Neil Gillman, Lawrence A. Hoffman, David Wolpe); KTAV Publishing House, Inc. for excerpts from *Jewish Spirituality and Faith* © 1989 (Bernard Raskas) and *In God's Mirror* © 1990 (Harold Schulweis); *What Is So Bad About Guilt? Learning to Live With It Since We Can't Live Without It* by Harland J. Wechsler, © 1990 by Harlan J. Wechsler, Ph.D., reprinted with permission of Simon & Schuster; Slifka Center for Jewish Life at Yale University for selections from *Orim: A Jewish Journal at Yale* published by Yale Hillel (William Cutter, James Ponet); Torah Aura Productions for selections from *Learn Torah With . . .* and *Teshuvah* (James Stone Goodman); Union of American Hebrew Congregations for selections from *Torat Hayyim: Living Torah* (Rabbi Elyse Frishman, Sharon Wechter).

Spiritual Inspiration for Family Life

TOUGH QUESTIONS JEWS ASK *For ages 12 & up*
**A Young Adult's Guide to
Building a Jewish Life**
by *Rabbi Edward Feinstein*
6 x 9, 160 pp, PB, 978-1-58023-139-8 **$14.99**

THE KIDS' FUN BOOK OF JEWISH TIME
by *Emily Sper*
9 x 7½, 24 pp, Full-color illus., HC, 978-1-58023-311-8 **$16.99**

**FOR KIDS—PUTTING GOD ON
YOUR GUEST LIST, 2ND ED.
How to Claim the Spiritual Meaning of
Your Bar or Bat Mitzvah**
by *Rabbi Jeffrey K. Salkin*
6 x 9, 144 pp, PB, 978-1-58023-308-8 **$15.99**

For ages 9 & up   **THE BOOK OF MIRACLES
A Young Person's Guide
to Jewish Spiritual Awareness**
by *Rabbi Lawrence Kushner*
6 x 9, 96 pp, HC, Two-color illustrations. 978-1-879045-78-1 **$16.95**

**WHEN A GRANDPARENT DIES
A Kid's Own Remembering Workbook for
Dealing with Shiva and the Year Beyond**
by *Nechama Liss-Levinson, PhD*
8 x 10, 48 pp, HC, Two-color text. 978-1-879045-44-6 **$15.95**
For ages 7–13

Spiritual Inspiration

THESE ARE THE WORDS
A Vocabulary of Jewish Spiritual Life
by *Arthur Green*
6 x 9, 304 pp, PB, 978-1-58023-107-7 **$18.95**

THE ENNEGRAM AND
KABBALAH, 2ND ED.
Reading Your Soul
by *Rabbi Howard A. Addison*
6 x 9, 192 pp, PB, 978-1-58023-229-6 **$16.99**

GOD'S TO-DO LIST
103 Ways to Be an Angel
and Do God's Work on Earth
by *Dr. Ron Wolfson*
6 x 9, 144 pp, PB, 978-1-58023-301-9 **$15.99**

SACRED INTENTIONS
Daily Inspiration to Strengthen the Spirit,
Based on Jewish Wisdom
by *Rabbi Kerry M. Olitzky* and
Rabbi Lori Forman
4½ x 6½, 448 pp, PB, 978-1-58023-061-2 **$15.95**

RESTFUL REFLECTIONS
Nighttime Inspiration to Calm the Soul,
Based on Jewish Wisdom
by *Rabbi Kerry M. Olitzky* and *Rabbi Lori Forman*
4½ x 6½, 448 pp, PB, 978-1-58023-091-9 **$15.95**

Books by Lawrence Kushner

EYES REMADE FOR WONDER
The Way of Jewish Mysticism and Sacred Living
A Lawrence Kushner Reader
6 x 9, 240 pp, PB, 978-1-58023-042-1 **$18.95**

INVISIBLE LINES OF CONNECTION
Sacred Stories of the Ordinary
5½ x 8½, 160 pp, PB, 978-1-879045-98-9 **$15.95**

HONEY FROM THE ROCK
An Introduction to Jewish Mysticism
6 x 9, 176 pp, PB, 978-1-58023-073-5 **$16.95**

THE BOOK OF WORDS
Talking Spiritual Life, Living Spiritual Talk
6 x 9, 160 pp, PB, Two-color text. 978-1-58023-020-9 **$16.95**

THE BOOK OF LETTERS
A Mystical Hebrew Alphabet
In calligraphy by the author
6 x 9, 80 pp, HC, Two-color text. 978-1-879045-00-2 **$24.95**

GOD WAS IN THIS PLACE & I, i DID NOT KNOW
Finding Self, Spirituality & Ultimate Meaning
6 x 9, 192 pp, PB, 978-1-879045-33-0 **$16.95**

THE RIVER OF LIGHT
Jewish Mystical Awareness
6 x 9, 192 pp, PB, 978-1-58023-096-4 **$16.95**

Add Greater Meaning to Your Life

Healing/Recovery/Wellness

TWELVE JEWISH STEPS TO RECOVERY
A Personal Guide to Turning from
Alcoholism & Other Addictions ...
Drugs, Food, Gambling, Sex ...
by *Rabbi Kerry M. Olitzky* & *Stuart A. Copans, M.D.*
Preface by *Abraham J. Twerski, M.D.*
6 x 9, 144 pp. Quality PB, ISBN 1-879045-09-5 **$15.99**

RENEWED EACH DAY
Daily Twelve Step Recovery Meditations
Based on the Bible
Edited by *Rabbi Kerry M. Olitzky* & *Aaron Z.*
Vol. 1: Genesis & Exodus
6 x 9, 224 pp. Quality PB, ISBN 1-879045-12-5 **$14.95**
Vol. 2: Leviticus, Numbers & Deuteronomy
6 x 9, 280 pp. Quality PB, ISBN 1-879045-13-3 **$18.99**

RECOVERY FROM CODEPENDENCE
A Jewish Twelve Steps Guide to Healing
Your Soul
by *Rabbi Kerry M. Olitzky*
6 x 9, 160 pp. Quality PB, ISBN 1-879045-32-X **$13.95**

100 BLESSINGS EVERY DAY
Daily Twelve Step Recovery Affirmations,
Exercises for Personal Growth & Renewal
Reflecting Seasons of the Jewish Year
by *Rabbi Kerry M. Olitzky*
4½ x 6½, 432 pp. Quality PB, ISBN 1-879045-30-3 **$16.99**

Spirituality

DOES THE SOUL SURVIVE?
A Jewish Journey to Belief in Afterlife, Past Lives & Living with Purpose
by *Rabbi Elie Kaplan Spitz*
6 x 9, 288 pp. Quality PB, ISBN 1-58023-165-9 **$16.99**
HC, ISBN 1-58023-094-6 **$21.95**

SIX JEWISH SPIRITUAL PATHS
A Rationalist Looks at Spirituality
by *Rabbi Rifat Sonsino*
6 x 9, 208 pp. Quality PB, ISBN 1-58023-167-5 **$16.95**
HC, ISBN 1-58023-095-4 **$21.95**

MOONBEAMS
A Hadassah Rosh Hodesh Guide
Edited by *Carol Diament, Ph.D.*
8½ x 11, 240 pp. Quality PB Original, ISBN 1-58023-099-7 **$20.00**

THE WOMEN'S TORAH COMMENTARY
New Insights from Women Rabbis on the 54 Weekly Torah Portions
Edited by *Rabbi Elyse Goldstein*
6 x 9, 496 pp. HC, ISBN 1-58023-076-8 **$34.95**

THE WOMEN'S HAFTARAH COMMENTARY
New Insights from Women Rabbis on the 54 Weekly Haftarah Portions, the 5 Megillot & Special Shabbatot
Edited by *Rabbi Elyse Goldstein*
6 x 9, 560 pp. HC, ISBN 1-58023-133-0 **$39.99**

Add Greater Meaning to Your Life

THE SACRED ART OF LOVINGKINDNESS
Preparing to Practice
by *Rabbi Rami Shapiro*; Foreword by *Marcia Ford*
5½ x 8½, 176 pp, PB, 978-1-59473-151-8 **$16.99**
(A SkyLight Paths Book)

DISCOVERING JEWISH MEDITATION
Instruction & Guidance for Learning an
Ancient Spiritual Practice
by *Nan Fink Gefen*
6 x 9, 208 pp, PB, 978-1-58023-067-4 **$16.95**

I AM JEWISH
Personal Reflections Inspired by the Last
Words of Daniel Pearl
Edited by *Judea* and *Ruth Pearl*
6 x 9, 304 pp, Deluxe PB w/flaps, 978-1-58023-259-3 **$18.99**

THE WAY INTO *TIKKUN OLAM*
(REPAIRING THE WORLD)
by *Rabbi Elliot N. Dorff, PhD*
6 x 9, 320 pp, HC, 978-1-58023-269-2 **$24.99**; 6 x 9, 304 pp, PB,
978-1-58023-328-6 **$18.99**

ISRAEL—A SPIRITUAL TRAVEL GUIDE,
2ND ED.
A Companion for the Modern Jewish Pilgrim
by *Rabbi Lawrence A. Hoffman*
4¾ x 10, 256 pp, illus., PB, 978-1-58023-261-6 **$18.99**